C000193710

LORDS
of the ISLES

LORDS of the ISLES

FROM
VIKING
WARLORDS
TO
CLAN CHIEFS

TIMOTHY
VENNING

AMBERLEY

First published 2015

Amberley Publishing
The Hill, Stroud
Gloucestershire, GL5 4EP

www.amberley-books.com

Copyright © Timothy Venning 2015

The right of Timothy Venning to be identified as the Author
of this work has been asserted in accordance with the
Copyrights, Designs and Patents Act 1988.

All rights reserved. No part of this book may be reprinted
or reproduced or utilised in any form or by any electronic,
mechanical or other means, now known or hereafter invented,
including photocopying and recording, or in any information
storage or retrieval system, without the permission in writing
from the Publishers.

British Library Cataloguing in Publication Data.
A catalogue record for this book is available from the British Library.

ISBN 978 1 4456 4485 1 (paperback)
ISBN 978 1 4456 4505 6 (ebook)

Typeset in 10.5pt on 13.5pt Sabon.
Typesetting and Origination by Amberley Publishing.
Printed in the UK.

Contents

Acknowledgements

My sincere thanks go to the following: Carolyn MacDonell, especially for photographs and MacDonell information, and Ranald MacDonell, chief of Glengarry, for the same; Maggie MacDonald, clan archivist of MacDonalds on Skye, for clan history and genealogy advice, and Norman MacDonald of the MacDonald Family History Society, Edinburgh, for the same; and all those whose photographs were used via the www.geograph.org.uk website.

Introduction

The romantic-sounding title of 'Lord of the Isles' is still borne today by the heir to the British crown, as inherited from the Stuart kings of Scotland. James IV confiscated it from the last of the MacDonald family to hold it in 1494, along with the semi-feudal lordship their ancestors had established in the twelfth century which claimed suzerainty over the Inner and Outer Hebrides and the nearer portion of the north-western mainland of Scotland. As such the lordship was central to the political and cultural structures of this region, geographically remote from the kingdom's Lowlands power base. At the time of Somerled 'the Mighty' (d. 1164), their founding dynast, the new lordship which he created had not been part of the kingdom of Scotland, or 'Alba', but a nebulous territory sandwiched between that (a merger of the Gaelic kingdom of Argyll and the probably Brittonic kingdom of the Picts) and the Scandinavian settlements in the Outer Hebrides and the Orkney Islands. All these lands seem originally to have been Gaelic in settlement, with mainland Caithness (adjacent to Orkney) as one of the early provincial sub-states that made up the early kingdom of the Picts as remembered by medieval writers. But this was changed by the flood of Scandinavian settlement from around 750, presumably caused by a mixture of restless explorers and landless adventurers seeking new and more fertile lands at a time of population increase in mountainous Norway. As shown by recent DNA studies confirming the evidence of saga, archaeology and place names, the existing population in the Hebrides and Orkneys suffered what amounted to 'ethnic cleansing'. Most lines of male descent in the region are traceable from the Norse, and any political control of the islands by the kings of Dalriada in Argyll (or of the mainland by the kings of the Picts in Moray and Fortrenn/Fife) ended.

In time, new lordships coalesced around charismatic and expansionist warlords, whose power rested on the ability to attract followers by military success and acquisition of land and loot to distribute. The most prominent and long-lasting of these lordships was the jarldom of Orkney, established by Norse relatives of the dukes of Normandy, which lasted from around 870 to the fifteenth century, but there were many others that failed to last as long due to a mixture of dynastic failure, bad luck, lack of resources or stability and conquest by predatory neighbours. The kingdom of the Isle of Man was the most successful of these 'second-tier' states, smaller than Orkney but usually aided by its physical distance from the latter (and from Norway), which impeded conquest. While Orkney attracted a fluid 'mini-empire' of vassals in the northern and central Hebrides, Man tended to control the south and to make claims on Galloway; but Man was also at risk from a more powerful neighbour, in this case the Scandinavian kingdom of Dublin. Dublin in turn was fought over by rival warlords, one family descended from the leaders of the Scandinavian attack on the Anglo-Saxons in 865–71. This was the stark world of the 'Viking' sagas, peopled by a mixture of bold, generous heroes and bloodthirsty psychopaths – and some men with aspects of both, among them ex-king Erik 'Bloodaxe' of Norway and jarls of Orkney with such evocative names as Thorfinn 'Skull-Splitter'. One of these jarls, Sigurd I, even suffered what must be one of the most bizarre violent deaths on record, as he attached the severed head of a Caithness warlord he had killed to his saddle as a trophy but was fatally gashed by his victim's tusk-like teeth when his horse stumbled and jolted him against the object. Two jarls, brothers, in turn died at the hands of their serial killer wife, Erik's daughter, who then married the third brother, who pre-empted her next planned homicide. A later princess of Orkney tried to kill a half-brother with a poison-dipped shirt, but caught the wrong victim; her mother assisted her and she later claimed other victims before her foes burnt her in her house. Other prominent Scandinavian womenfolk in this violent 'settler' society, where wits mattered as well as brawn, included the remarkable Aud 'the Deep-Minded', heiress daughter of Hebridean settler chief Ketil 'Flatnose', who married the king of Dublin and ended up immigrating successfully to Iceland with her grandchildren and a collection of portable wealth. Lordships rose and fell dependant on the skills of their holders and the power of their predatory neighbours, with no one dynasty securing Man until the arrival of Godred 'Crovan' ('White Hands') in 1079, after which his descendants ruled almost continually until annexation by Scotland in 1265. This violent northern world of temporary dynasts and swift reversals of fortune was far from the milieu of the legalistic 'feudal' civilisation emerging in contemporary mainland

Europe and spreading to England after 1066, though it was closer to the ancestral traditions of the Anglo-Saxons (as seen in the saga *Beowulf*). It was also the world in which a third successful new lordship was created by Somerled in the central Hebrides and Argyll after around 1130. But in his case a claim can be made for a partially Gaelic origin for both his lordship and his alignment (and even his name?), and the question of the Gaelic or Norse origin of the new lordship is still a 'live issue'.

Nevertheless, the kings of Norway, from whose lands many of the Scandinavians had emigrated, claimed all their kin's lands in what is now Scotland as their own vassal lands. The question of whether important colonists (on islands or the mainland) had been acting as vassals of the kings of Norway at the time – or had been forced to submit to them later – was obscured by claims (accurate or propaganda?) in non-contemporary literary epics. Control was sporadically enforced in person by the more far-voyaging kings of Norway or by their nominees from unifying founder Harald 'Finehair' onwards, and their rule of all lands in north-western Scotland that could be traversed by warship was accepted in a treaty by King Edgar in 1098. The major arteries of travel and trade were then the sea, and such links in the mixed Scandinavian-Gaelic world of the early medieval Western Isles were then closer with Norway than with the distant and preoccupied Scots realm. The attentions of the Scots kings, increasingly Anglo-Norman in culture and political orientation, were focussed on England and the nearer Continent. The major lords of the nearer Highlands – mostly Gaelic in descent and outlook – were of dubious loyalty to the dynasty of Malcolm III's half-English sons in any case, and these men and their successors did not at first bother with the far north. (By contrast King Macbeth, whom Malcolm killed in 1057, had been a ruler of Moray.) Sporadic revolts broke out connected to branches of the Scots royal family who had been excluded from the throne (such as the enigmatic 'MacHeths', Somerled's allies). But as the Norse crown declined in power and 'reach' and the Scots kings, baulked of expansion southwards, reasserted their power in the Highlands, the balance of power shifted from Norway to Scotland and successive kings, such as Alexander II and III, intervened aggressively in the western Highlands and then the nearer Hebrides. The local lords began their long and precarious 'balancing act' between maintaining a degree of ancestral autonomy and appeasing their better-resourced royal neighbours without attracting either invasion or local revolt – initially balancing the kings of Scots against the kings of Norway. Whichever local 'great power' warlord turned up with a fleet was likeliest to secure (temporary) allegiance, but neither national leader could stay in the area long and so submission was dubious.

Haakon 'the Good' was the last King of Norway to traverse the Hebrides with his fleet in 1263, ending with a naval demonstration of his power in the Firth of Clyde and a muddled clash with the Scots army (not really a proper invasion) on the beach at Largs. After his death control of the region was formally ceded to Scotland in 1266, although Orkney remained a Norse vassal until it was pledged to Scotland as surety for an unpaid dowry in 1469 and never redeemed; Man also passed to Scotland in 1265 but was claimed and eventually secured by the expansionist kingdom of England to the south. The latter's attempt to conquer all Scotland after 1296 diverted the Scots kingdom's attention south again and secured the dynasts of the north-west a breathing space – and also caused the collapse of one of the two contending branches of Somerled's lordship, by now known as the lordship of the Isles. (The 'kingship of the Isles' was in fact an older but less defined Gaelic term, linked to individual strongmen and not one dynasty.) The MacDougalls of mainland Argyll backed the cause of Comyn (and Edward of England) against Robert Bruce in 1306, so his triumph led to their eviction from their lands and the elevation of their pro-Bruce rivals, the MacDonalds of the Hebridean littoral and adjacent islands. In due course the weakened Scots kingship, barely 'first among equals' against its strongest supporters, appointed the MacDonald lords as its effective viceroys over the region in return for their loyalty – with a Stuart marital alliance to the family giving its descendants the lordship to the exclusion of genealogically senior kin. When the kings of Scots grew more threatening, some MacDonalds allied to the kings of England in retaliation and in 1462 even tried to divide Scotland with them. The emergence of the centralised 'Renaissance' monarchy saw the lordship being broken up by military force and its vassal dynasts, the chiefs of the local 'clans', transferred to direct subordination to the Scots kings. As before, this was only sporadically enforced; local wars continued within a framework of defined custom, and what was now seen as a culturally alien and politically defiant Gaelic world became distrusted by and gradually subdued by the powers in Edinburgh. But this was not complete by the time of centraliser James VI's succession to England in 1603. The crises of the 'British Revolution' in the mid-seventeenth century and then the second loss of power by the Stuarts in 1688 gave new chances for notable military contributions, if not ultimately success, to the lords of the north-west and their clansmen. Charles I, Charles II, James VII and II and the two excluded Stuart claimants in 1715–46 all relied heavily on Highland military manpower, and the latter seemed at times to come close to success, if providing in the end more of a romantic 'last stand' against the centralising machine at Westminster.

The achievements and appealing story of a politico-cultural world far removed from the usual central British historical 'narrative' are still relevant today in an era of hoped-for devolution, and in this sweeping study are traced from the early Scandinavian settlements through to the disaster of 1746. This is the 'history of the margins' in the eyes of southern England – but of a region once the centre of a very different world.

Rulers of Orkney and 'the Isles' to 1066

The early 'Viking' Hebrides and Orkney, mid- to late ninth century: Ragnald/Rognvald and other leaders

A gradual process of conquest from around the late eighth century AD is probable as the 'Vikings' (the name usually given to these new arrivals, probably meaning 'men of the fjords', i.e. coastal Norway) were recorded as sacking the Northumbrian island monastery of Lindisfarne in 793 and Iona, the centre of Christianity in the Inner Hebrides founded by pioneering missionary St Columbcille (Columba) in 563, in 795. They returned to the latter again in 802, 806 (when the abbot fled to Kells in Ireland with his most precious relics) and 825 (when a monk called Blathmac was martyred for refusing to disclose the hiding place of valuables), so they were evidently active in the region then. Whether there was a neat, 'linear' development from initial exploration for suitable farming land (plus opportunistic attacks on the locals for plunder and slaves) to settlement is uncertain; the process of Scandinavian settlement was probably haphazard and down to individual initiative by small groups of émigrés. The place names of the region, previously Pictish or Brittonic, were certainly largely changed to Scandinavian ones; the incomers' language prevailed, so they were culturally and probably numerically dominant. Whether the previous inhabitants had been a 'normal' part of mainland British culture (apart from the comparative poverty and political atomisation caused by geography and the poor soil) is still unclear, and some historians maintain that the unusual building of the defensive 'broch' towers in the Roman period implies a different culture to that of the Caledonians in the Highlands. But in any case, this was now overrun by a Scandinavianised culture looking towards Norway, plus a (predominantly male?) influx of Scandinavians.

The principal headland and the islands north of it, called 'Orca' by the Greco-Roman geographer Ptolemy around AD 120 (so the name must be Brittonic), became 'Orkney' – 'ey' being the Norse for 'island'. Notably the Hebrides became known as the 'Sudreys', 'Southern Islands', and the lands south of Caithness were now 'Sutherland' – thus being defined by their orientation as seen from the Scandinavian settlements on the Orkneys. As of the ninth and tenth centuries they became ruled by the Orkney-based jarldom of that region, not by any mainland lordship. Some settlements were erected on 'Pictish' sites and so there may have been continuity as opposed to complete 'ethnic cleansing' – the debate over this is similar to that concerning Germanic settlement by the Anglo-Saxons in previously Romano-Celtic England. Does the existence of a supposed 'Mormaership of Caithness' in the thirteenth-century Scots 'creation myths' of the mainland Pictish kingdom imply a local Pictish sub-kingdom, or was this wishful thinking? The recently discovered DNA patterns show a clear break between the early inhabitants and the Scandinavian settlers, with a majority of modern inhabitants – at least in the male line – descended from the latter but some Pictish descent in the female line. This suggests the truth of the later literary picture in Scandinavian (mostly Icelandic) sagas of the incoming Vikings killing the menfolk and marrying their women by force.

The people of the region became known as the 'Gall-Gaedhil', that is the 'Foreign Gael' – meaning Gaelic Scandinavians and so a fusion of the two peoples and cultures. As far as politico-military leadership of the region is concerned, the dearth of evidence for the ninth century suggests an atomised society with at best local leadership by vigorous and successful warriors. It is doubtful if there was any regional coalescence into one polity – even a brief, personal dominion by one warlord for his lifetime – until the emergence of the jarldom of Orkney, as the sagas do not record any such men (though if they left no descendants keen to keep up their memories they could easily have been forgotten). Those successful ninth-century warlords who are recorded in sagas or in the writings of their victims seem to have ruled in the southern Hebrides, orientated towards the Isle of Man or the Viking settlements in eastern Ireland, rather than in the north.

The jarldom was established over the Viking settlers in the Orkneys, Shetlands and Hebrides in the 870s by a dynasty closely connected to the dukes of Normandy – Ragnald/Rognvald, Jarl of More in Norway, supposedly granted the territory by his brother-in-law King Harald 'Finehair' (d. 934?), was the father of Hrolf/Rollo, the first duke. His ancestry is disputed, with the Norse sagas and the *Orkneyinga saga* giving him different ancestors, but his father Eystein 'the Noisy's father

Ivarr was probably ruler of 'Uppland' (the region north of modern-day Oslo) in the early ninth century. Ivarr's father was a jarl called Halfdan, who may have been the semi-mythical 'Halfdan the Old' who was also ancestor of the Norwegian royal house. According to saga, Rognvald received the islands as thanks for his leadership of an expedition sent by King Harald, long-reigning unifier of Norway, to deal with dangerous Norwegian exiles on the Orkneys and Shetlands who were plotting to overthrow him, a campaign in which Rognvald's son Ivarr had been killed. This probably followed Harald's unification of Norway, which led to the enemies of the new ruler (hereditary lord of Vestfold) being expelled to the western seaways. But the date of this process is unclear, though the sagas make it clear that it occurred when Harald, who died around 934 after a reign of around fifty years, was a young man. Was the expedition involving Rognvald the royal expedition by King Harald around the mid-late 870s, or a separate one – either on the king's behalf, or a private venture which was 'tidied up' in later stories as being by royal command? The likelihood is that there was a necessary interest from the new kingdom of Norway in the lands ruled by its expatriates in the islands off Scotland – partly as a matter of 'colonial' desire by King Harald to conquer them for his prestige, but also to keep an eye on potential competitors as indicated in the *Orkneyinga saga*. The region could provide manpower for expeditions to overthrow him by his exiled rivals. Capable and independent-minded warriors who had lost out in power struggles in Norway are recorded as fleeing there; they could utilise local manpower to challenge Harald, so he needed a 'trusty' to control or neutralise them. Unlike the settlements of the Norse in Ireland, the region was within his reach by means of naval expeditions but the King of Norway could only afford to go there occasionally. The main traditional story, preserved or embellished in the *Orkneyinga saga*, has it that King Harald's expedition to the region to suppress his exiled rivals followed his defeat of them within Norway at the crucial Battle of Hafrsfjord – the event seen by subsequent historians as marking the first unification of Norway – the date of which, within the later ninth century, is uncertain; it was estimated at 875 in the 1950s but could have taken place as late as the 880s.

The idea of an expedition by King Harald in person also occurs in a thirteenth-century Icelandic account of the island's settlement, the *Landnámabók*, which was written centuries later but reflected the family traditions of men who had fought for or against Harald then settled in Iceland around 870–900. It has Harald putting down his dangerous rivals in the Hebrides after unifying Norway, but a further outbreak then occurring in the (southern?) Hebrides after he went home. This was suppressed on his behalf by his local ally from the time of his first expedition, an expatriate Norse noble called Ketil 'Flatnose' (son of Bjorn 'Rough-Foot') whom Harald appointed as his local viceroy. This was presumably the lordship of the 'Sudreys', i.e. the present Inner and Outer Hebrides, as a separate lordship from Orkney to the north; it may have included the Isle of Man. The Icelandic *Eyrbyggja saga* (late thirteenth or early fourteenth century) has Ketil as Harald's lieutenant on the expedition, holding the region for him after he went home. An alternative Icelandic story, in the *Laxdaela saga* (1230s–60s?), has Ketil as one of the exiled troublemakers driven out of Norway by Harald, who assumed power after Harald's departure at the end of his expedition to the Hebrides. According to this version, Ketil Bjornssen was a lord in Romsdal in Norway, married to Ingvild, the daughter of Ketil 'Wether', and father of Bjorn and Helgi (sons) and Aud and Thorunn (daughters). He left Norway rather than submit to Harald, and refused to accompany his sons to Iceland as it was a 'land of fishermen' and there were more rich pickings in the Hebrides. Harald had to recognise Ketil as his local viceroy there as it was too difficult to tackle him. The latter source apparently derives from one of Ketil's own descendants in Iceland, albeit three centuries later, so could be more accurate; the claims that Ketil was always loyal to Harald may be propaganda designed to stress the links of his family to Norway and the loyalty of the area's best-known lord to the country's kings. Possibly late eleventh-century and early twelfth-century Norwegian kings (e.g. Magnus 'Bareleg') encouraged this interpretation to win local loyalty from the chieftains of the Hebrides. For that matter, the notion of an expedition by Harald in person was useful to King Magnus as it showed him as emulating his greatest ancestor in his own expedition to Orkney, the Hebrides, Man and Wales in 1098–99 – though that is not to say that Harald's expedition never took place.

But the uncertain dating of Ketil makes it unclear whether he was Harald's willing or unwilling instrument. The establishment of Harald's power in the region clearly occurred after around 875, and Ketil's daughter Aud's son Thorstein 'the Red' is credibly reported as being an active warlord as Sigurd of Orkney's ally in the 870s–80s. There is also the possible identification of Ketil with Caitill 'the Fair', commander of the Gall-Gaedhil, who was defeated in Munster in Ireland in 857 by the Scandinavian king of Dublin 'Amlaith' (i.e. Olaf?), his co-ruler Ivarr and his Irish allies; but the nearly identical names may be a coincidence. Were Caitill and Ketil the same man? Should Ketil be placed in the 850s–60s rather than as a contemporary of Harald? And did he really fight for an Irish Viking overlord of the Hebrides (e.g. 'Amlaith') in the 850s, rather than fighting for Harald in the 870s? In any case, his lordship of the southern Hebrides was ephemeral, and unlike Rognvald and Sigurd of Orkney he did not create a locally based dynasty. Most of his sons immigrated to Iceland, and one of them, Bjorn, created further trouble for King Harald in Norway – according to the sagas in an attempt to reclaim the lands of which Ketil had been deprived by Harald. Possibly Ketil established his lordship as an ally of the king of Dublin around 850, and only transferred his allegiance to Harald later (*c.* 875?) to ward off an attack by him from Norway.

Ketil's daughter Aud 'the Deep-Minded' was married off to Olaf 'the White', king of the Gall-Gaedhil in Dublin in the 850s and the 860s. Olaf was probably the same man as 'Amlaith', son of the 'king of Lochlainn' (i.e. Norway), who Irish records say took over Dublin in 853, but this is not certain and some scholars believe that there were two men. Amlaith was apparently sent by his father Guthfrith, possibly ruler of Vestfold in Norway, to Ireland to take charge of the demoralised Norsemen there after they had lost control of Dublin to the newly arrived (851) 'Dark Foreigners', i.e. the Danes. His success was linked to the losses that the Danes in Ireland sustained in a failed attack on Gwynedd in Wales in 856, in which their commander Orm/Gorm was killed by King Rhodri 'Mawr' ('the Great'). Most of Amlaith's campaigns were in southern Ireland, where he fought his Scandinavian rival Caitill 'the Fair' in Munster in 857 and then aided Cearbhall, the Irish king of Osraige/Ossory (a sub-kingdom of Munster), in his efforts to break away from the kingdom of Munster and secure a 'transfer' to the overlordship of neighbouring Midhe in a campaign in 859. This war, in which the joint army of Amlaith and Cearbhall invaded Midhe and may have marched as far as Armagh, culminated in a rulers' conference in Westmeath where the transfer was granted by 'High King' Mael Sechnaill (r. 846–62). Cearbhall's ex-overlord Mael Gualae, the king of Munster who was thus humiliated by the Viking–Osraige coalition, ended up captured by the Scandinavians of Dublin and sacrificed to the god Odin. Amlaith married the daughter of the next Irish 'High King', Aed Findliath (reigned 862–79), of the northern, Cenel Eóghain branch of the 'Uí Néill' dynasty, who usually alternated the 'High Kingship' with Mael Sechnaill's southern, Midhe branch. If Amlaith was Olaf 'the White' (which historians such as Gwyn Jones doubt), then this either (most likely) preceded or (less likely) followed his marriage to Aud, daughter of Ketil – Olaf's son by Aud, Thorstein, must have been born by around 860. Amlaith had an adult son, Carlus, killed in a battle in Ireland in 867, who was somewhat older than any son he could have had by Aud; the alliance of Amlaith and Aed

Findliath was already in existence by the early 860s, before the latter
became High King in 862.

Amlaith also left Dublin for a time for 'Lochlainn' around 855–56,
and returned with two new co-rulers whom the Irish sources call his
'brothers', Ivarr and Auisle – which poses a problem as if this Ivarr was
really the ruler known in the sources as 'the Boneless' (see below) then
he was the son of Ragnar 'Lothbrok' ('Leather Breeches'), not of any
King of Norway or a Guthfrith. Nor is there any mention in English
or Norse sources of an 'Olaf' as a son of Ragnar and brother of Ivarr,
Halfdan and Ubbe Ragnarrson. Possibly the men were 'blood-brothers'
or brothers-in-law? Amlaith also invaded mainland Scotland in 865–66
to defeat and force tribute out of the King of Scots, Constantine son
of Kenneth MacAlpin, who reigned from 862 to 877; and in 870–71
he successfully besieged Dumbarton Rock, 'capital' of the British
kingdom of Strathclyde/Alt Claith. The rocky fortress was too strong to
be stormed, but the Scandinavians starved it out until the well ran dry
and forced the garrison to surrender, taking off a large amount of loot
and slaves. King Artgal was also captured, and became a Scandinavian
vassal. Amlaith then married either the daughter of King Constantine
of the Picts and Scots, or else the 'daughter of Cinaed', which would
probably be the daughter of Kenneth MacAlpin and thus Constantine's
sister (though there was another contemporary King Cinaed in Brega
in central Ireland). If Amlaith was Olaf 'the White', this marriage and
alliance would represent an extension of his lordship from Dublin into
central Scotland, via control of the southern Hebridean seaways – and
enforcing vassalage on the kingdom of Scots would give him the ability
to take his men safely overland from the Clyde to the Forth to raid and
trade in the eastern seas and link up with the post-867 Viking kingdom
of York. Ketil, as a major local chieftain, would have been a logical
ally and a suitable son-in-law. In this case, Ketil would seem to have
been active and powerful in the 860s, before Harald 'Finehair' emerged
as King of Norway. If Amlaith was not Olaf, then he and Ketil would
have been rivals. According to the Icelandic *Laxdaela saga*, Ketil died
at around the same time as his grandson Thorstein, shortly before his
daughter Aud went to Iceland (*c.* 885).

Olaf and Aud were the parents of Thorstein 'the Red', who was born
around 850–55 as he was active and militarily experienced in the 870s
and had a son, Olaf, who accompanied Aud to Iceland after Thorstein
was killed. Olaf 'the White' is recorded in Icelandic sources as the son
of a Norwegian jarl, Guthfrith, whom Irish sources call the 'king of
Lochlainn' (Norway), which would seem to mean that Olaf was the
elusive 'Amlaith'. But the Icelandic *Landnámabók* calls him the son of

an expatriate in Ireland called Ingvald Helgasson – who is recorded, implausibly given the usual timescale, as a great-grandson of Ragnar 'Lothbrok', who was in fact active around 860 (see below). Ingvald's father, Helga's husband, was Frodi. The kingdom of Dublin was shared (voluntarily or not) by Olaf after around 870 with Olaf's rival, Ivarr 'the Boneless', one of the sons of the infamous pirate leader Ragnar 'Lothbrok' (allegedly killed in a pit of snakes in Northumbria around 860) and co-leader of the 'Great Army's invasion of England in 865–66. As seen above, an Ivarr – possibly the same man – had also ruled with Olaf or 'Amlaith' in Dublin in the mid- to late 850s and is confusingly called Amlaith's brother. But it is not certain that Olaf was the same man as this King 'Amlaith' of the 850s. Ivarr 'the Boneless' was definitely not in Ireland in 865–70, though, as the *Anglo-Saxon Chronicle* has him campaigning in England with his brothers Halfdan and Ubbe Ragnarrson. They landed in East Anglia in 865–66 and extorted horses and supplies from the locals, conquered York and the kingdom of 'Deira' in 867, were besieged in Nottingham by the armies of Wessex and Mercia during an invasion of the latter in 868, conquered East Anglia and killed its king, St Edmund, in 869 and were fought to a standstill by kings Aethelred and Alfred in Wessex in 870–71. The nature of Ivarr's unusual sobriquet is uncertain; possibly it was due to his excessive weight, or else to some wasting disease (brittle bone disease?) with which the Irish and Norse were unfamiliar. Certainly Ivarr, co-ruler of conquered York with his brother Halfdan from 867, was back in Ireland as co-ruler of Dublin with Olaf from around 871; the sources are muddled as to whether Olaf ruled with or was expelled by him. According to the Irish sources 'Amlaith' had already spent considerable military effort in local wars in Ireland, sacking the important monasteries of Lismore in 867 and Armagh in 869, but may have been short of men by around 871 and had to come to terms with the better-resourced and aggressive Ivarr on the latter's return from England with warriors who had defeated a series of Anglo-Saxon kingdoms and were ready for another war.

According to Irish sources, Olaf returned to Norway around 871 to aid his father (Guthfrith?) in the wars of king Harald's youth; Icelandic sources state that he was killed in battle in the British Isles – by King Constantine in Scotland or in a raid on England – sometime in the 870s. Ivarr took over sole control of Dublin, but died in 873; his brother Halfdan later ruled Dublin as well as York, expelling Eystein, the son of King 'Amlaith', who may thus have been the son of Olaf 'the White' by an uncertain marriage. If not, Eystein was the son of Olaf's predecessor, 'Amlaith'. Halfdan was then evicted from Dublin by Irish 'High King' Aed Findliath, 'Amlaiths ex-ally, who installed Ivarr's son Bardar

('Barith' in Gaelic sources) as king of Dublin and was killed in battle against the Gall-Gaedhil on Strangford Lough in 877. This brought temporary peace to Ireland, leaving a stalemate with the Scandinavians in control of Dublin as junior allies of the Irish Uí Néill rulers of Midhe but not dominating the inland kingdoms as had seemed possible in the 840s–50s. Aud and Thorstein, by 871 possibly already expelled from Dublin by Olaf in order to make way for the succession to Dublin of his son by an earlier marriage (i.e. Eystein), joined Aud's father Ketil in the Hebrides in the mid-870s. They ended up creating a new lordship on mainland Scotland, centred on Caithness and Sutherland. Thorstein is written of in the *Laxdaela saga* as lord of half of Scotland, which implies extensive conquests; he was the main local ally of Sigurd of Orkney in a joint invasion of Caithness. His daughter by an Irish princess named Thora (a Scandinavian name), granddaughter of Olaf/Amlaith's ally King Cearbhall of Ossory in Munster, was Grua/Gruoch (a Scots name), whom his mother Aud married off to an allied 'mormaer' of Caithness called Duncan soon after his death. (The fact that he had a daughter of marriageable age by around 880–95 indicates that he must have been at least in his early thirties then.) After he was killed in battle in the late 880s – probably by local Scots chieftains, as the *Laxdaela saga* blames it on Scots treachery – Aud, then in Orkney, heard that her father Ketil was dead too. She secretly fitted out a ship to sail to Iceland, and sailed there with her son Olaf, marrying off another daughter in the Faroes en route. The *Laxdaela saga* noted that there were very few men, let alone women, who came out of such a turbulent experience with so much wealth and so many followers. She joined her brothers Bjorn 'the Easterner' (so called as he settled to the east of most of the arrivals in Iceland) and Helgi in western Iceland as a prominent settler; the parsimonious Helgi would not let her bring all her large party to live at his farmstead, so she joined Bjorn instead and settled at Hramm on 'Broadfirth'. Most of her surviving children lived with her and are recorded in the Icelandic sagas as founding families. She died around 920, traditionally after her son Olaf's wedding feast at Hramm.

Ragnald's family in control

Around the mid- to late 870s, Ragnald or Rognvald established control over the local Viking settlements in the 'Nordreys' (as the Orkneys were called to distinguish them from the 'Sudreys', the Southern Islands, south of Skye), probably on behalf of Harald of Norway – or else of Olaf 'the White' of Dublin, who also needed to keep a wary eye on the region. The established thirteenth-century literary sources make Harald of Norway his patron and overlord, but this may reflect contemporary Norwegian desires to stress the control their kings' ancestors had over the Hebrides and Orkney and to show that their national unifier, Harald 'Finehair', controlled the region and was accepted as overlord by its nobles. By around 1200 the notion of a Norse king in Dublin, such as Olaf, as overlord of the Hebrides was of no political importance and could be ignored – but Norwegian rule of the Hebrides was still a 'live issue'. On Ragnald's return to Norway to take over his family's lands around 875–80, his brother Sigurd took over Orkney as jarl and embarked on a conquest of northern Scotland in alliance with Olaf's son Thorstein 'the Red'. The Pictish kingdom had been united with that of Dalriada by Kenneth MacAlpin in the 840s, but was currently concentrating on the threat posed by the Scandinavians in Dublin and York. These two Viking lordships were currently using the lowland corridor from Forth to Clyde as a transit route between the east and west coasts, and as such were threatening to take over the crumbling British state of Strathclyde/Alt Claith, whose 'capital', Dumbarton Rock, fell to Scandinavian attackers (possibly Thorstein's father Olaf 'the White', or else an unrelated 'Amlaith') in 870–71. In reply, the new kingdom of 'Scotland' under Kenneth's sons (Constantine, d. 877, and Aed 'Wingfoot', d. 878) and nephew (Giric, d. 889) was seeking to help and annex Strathclyde itself, and had no men or time to spare for north of the Great Glen – so the opportunistic jarls of Orkney moved in. If Thorstein's father Olaf had been the warlord who defeated Scots king Constantine in 865–66, he may even have felt he had a hereditary claim on the region and called on the descendants of his father's vassals to help him.

Caithness and Sutherland (the 'Southern Lands' of the jarldom) were added to the realm of Orkney, which probably held sway as far south as the Moray Firth. After Thorstein's death and Aud's departure to Iceland, Sigurd ruled as sole warlord. But Sigurd then died in the bizarre fashion described earlier, succumbing to blood poisoning around 892 when his leg was gashed by the teeth of the severed head of a Scots mormaer, Gillebride, killed in a recent clash with him, as it hung from his saddle. According to the *Orkneyinga saga*, the two warlords had agreed to meet for combat between forty men from each army to resolve their differences, but Sigurd treacherously brought not one but two riders on each horse, and then had the extra men dismount to help while the original forty charged the Scots on horseback. Sigurd was buried at 'Ekkjalsbakka', possibly in Strath Oykel near the Dornoch Firth (near his southern frontier). Sigurd's son Guthorm died within a year, around 893–94, and the jarldom passed to Ragnald's sons Hallad and Einar, who were sent by Ragnald from Norway when he heard that the jarldom was vacant. Ragnald himself was supposed to have been treacherously murdered later in Norway, around 900, by King Harald's sons Halfdan 'Longleg' and Gudrod; Harald then exiled Halfdan and gave a daughter as compensation to Ragnald's other son, Thorir, who remained in Norway. Einar, Ragnald's youngest son – born of a 'thrall', a slave, and disregarded by his father, who gave him only one ship to establish his inheritance – overcame his disadvantages and after arriving in Shetland from Norway gradually extended his power, killing those who resisted. He eventually ruled Orkney and Shetland alone. Tall and one-eyed according to the saga tradition, he was called 'Turf Einar' due to his introduction of that plant as a fuel to the islands, and took sole power when his incompetent brother was forced to abdicate. He proved a successful ruler, killing the pirate chiefs Thorir 'Treebeard' and Kalf 'the Scurvy'. Having killed Harald of Norway's exiled son Halfdan, who now invaded Orkney, in battle at sea in retaliation for his father Ragnald's death, he sacrificed him to Odin in the legendary manner of the 'blood-eagle'. He was forced to accept King Harald as his overlord when the latter invaded and drove him to flee Orkney to Caithness, and paid the king compensation for the slaying of Halfdan. Einar died in his bed around 920, after a long reign.

Einar's sons Arnkel and Erlend then divided the jarldom, a solution to disputed rights followed by the sons of Sigurd 'the Stout' (Einar, Brusi and Somerled) in 1014. The former two then had to admit the deposed King of Norway, Harald's son Erik 'Bloodaxe', as their overlord in around 937 and join in his southern expeditions. According to the later Norse sagas, e.g. the *Heimskringla* and the saga of Olaf Tryggvason, Erik took over control of Orkney soon after his expulsion from Norway by his younger brother Haakon and Jarl Sigurd, which was sometime in the mid-930s – a few years after the death of his father, Harald 'Finehair'. The *Orkneyinga saga*, however, dates this takeover to the time that Erik was already fighting Olaf Sihtricson over York, i.e. the mid-940s. It also claims that Erik was promised rule of the recently conquered (927) Scandinavian state of York by King Athelstan of England, probably in the wake of the latter's defeat of a major Scots/ Irish/Scandinavian coalition at Brunanburh in 937; Athelstan was thus using Erik and his Norsemen as a counterweight to Olaf Guthfrithson, current king of Dublin and claimant to York. The Orkneymen would thus have been a valuable asset to Erik's army if he took over Orkney around 937, but Athelstan died before he could install Erik in York (autumn 939) and the latter was occupied by Olaf Guthfrithson instead. Erik consoled himself with raiding around the English and Welsh coasts, while Olaf went on to secure the Scandinavian-settled eastern Midlands (the 'Danelaw') and thus hold a large but precarious realm across two British islands. Later on Olaf died in a raid on English-held Bernicia in 941 and was replaced by his cousin Olaf Sihtricson. Athelstan's brother King Edmund of England regained York in 944–46, and on his death in a brawl in 946 Erik was able to occupy York for two brief periods of rule in the later 940s and early 950s, possibly invited in by the autonomist Archbishop Wulfstan of York. He was overthrown by partisans of Olaf Sihtricson on the first occasion, returned to power by another invasion, and was finally expelled by Edmund's brother, King Eadred of England, in 954. His vassals Arnkel and Erlend of Orkney (and his own brother Ragnald, according to late sources) were killed with him at Stainmore in the Pennines after he lost control of York for the second time, to King Eadred in 954, and was ambushed by senior Northumbrian thegns while heading back to his ships in the Solway Firth. The late eleventh-century local clerical historian Simeon of Durham and the early thirteenth-century writer Roger of Wendover both name 'Earl Maccus' as Erik's betrayer, and the latter also blames Oswulf, the 'high reeve' of Bamburgh, who became the next ruler of York/Northumbria as 'earl' under King Eadred (presumably as a reward). The two slain jarls of Orkney were succeeded by Einar's youngest son, Thorfinn 'Hausakljudfr' ('Skull-Splitter'), evidently a ferocious Viking of the old school, who married the daughter of the Mormaer of Caithness and maternal granddaughter of Thorstein 'the Red'. By this marriage his descendants had claims on Caithness, both via the native Gaelic line and via Thorstein's family. Thorfinn had to admit the overlordship of Erik's widow (Gunnhilde) and sons who had managed to escape from the debacle at York, but they left for Norway in a year or so in order to link up with the King of Denmark, Harald 'Bluetooth' (possibly Gunnhilde's brother), in a war with Erik's brother Haakon (before Haakon died *c.* 962). Before they left, the Norwegians arranged for Thorfinn's younger son Arnfinn to marry Erik's daughter Ragnhild.

Thorfinn was succeeded in turn by his sons around 977. The eldest two, Arnfinn and Havard, were both murdered by their Norwegian wife Princess Ragnhild, Erik's bloodthirsty daughter. She was first married to Arnfinn but arranged his murder at Murkle in Caithness (*c.* 980) and married his older brother Havard. Known as 'the Harvest-Happy' from the good harvests in his reign, Havard was undermined by his unscrupulous wife; according to the *Orkneyinga saga* she was already encouraging an ambitious nephew of his, Einar 'Oily-Tongue', to do away with him and marry her at her wedding feast to Havard. Einar duly rebelled and killed Havard at Stromness, but faced such a backlash from the disgusted nobles that Ragnhild pretended she had nothing to do with his plot and abandoned him, encouraging a cousin of his (another Einar) to murder him. She then married the third son of Thorfinn, Liot. But when she attempted to make him her third victim, he struck first. Liot had to accept his youngest brother, Skuli, who had left Orkney for the King of Scots' court, as Scots-sponsored Earl of Caithness on the mainland, but kept him from asserting his claim to Orkney itself. He later killed Skuli in battle, defeating his invasion. He now claimed control of Caithness and Ross too, coming into conflict with the kings of Scots, but fell fighting Mormaer Maelbrigde of Moray (the principal block to his southward advance) at the Battle of Skidmore around 985.

Sigurd and Thorfinn and their families from the 990s to Stamford Bridge

Liot was succeeded around 985 by his surviving brother, Hlodvir, who re-established a link with Caithness by a more indirect means than his predecessors, marrying his sister to a local official as his 'steward' there. However, the latter was killed by two Gaelic lords who were in turn killed by Hlodvir's son and successor Sigurd (acceded c. 989). Sigurd, 'the Stout', was the most ambitious of the dynasty so far in transnational politics and took advantage of the descent of Norway, once overlord of his uncles, into civil war in the later 980s after the death of King Harald 'Greycloak'. Sigurd regained control of Caithness by defeating Mormaer Findlaech of Moray, father of the later Scots king Macbeth, at Skidmore and installed his nominee Gilli as ruler of the Hebrides. He was forced to convert to Christianity by the warlord Olaf Tryggvason, the new King of Norway, in 995 at the point of a sword as Olaf called in at Orkney with his fleet and summoned Sigurd to meet him on board ship at south Ronaldsway. But Sigurd abandoned his religion and his new patron as soon as possible, and after Olaf's disappearance and probable drowning in battle in the Baltic Sea in 1000, Sigurd allied himself to King Malcolm II of Scots (r. 1002–34) instead. He married the king's (younger?) daughter, subsequently identified as Donada, probable widow of his foe Mormaer Findlaech of Moray. The rulers of Moray had an uneasy position as a junior line of the royal house of Scots and as such potential challengers to its current dynasty, the family of Kenneth MacAlpin; their ancestor Ruadhri was supposed to have moved north from Argyll in the eighth century. (This genealogy is thirteenth century in its surviving form, so some historians claim its reliability is doubtful.) By the time of Malcolm II's reign the Moray/Scots relationship was also complicated by Moray's new connections to some of Kenneth's family, Malcolm's rivals – for instance, the granddaughter of King Kenneth

III, Gruoch, who married firstly Mormaer Gillacomgain of Moray (k. 1032) and later his killer, Malcolm II's probable grandson King Macbeth McFindlaech (k. 1057). Malcolm II had killed Kenneth III and his heir, and broke with custom in not allowing rival lines of the royal house to alternate the succession as he was to name his (elder?) daughter's son by Thane Crinan of Atholl, Duncan, as his heir. Keeping the succession in one line of the royal family was unprecedented and invited rebellion by those excluded, and this challenge to the tradition of 'tanistry' (rotation of the throne by naming a brother or cousin, not son, as heir) was at the root of the overthrow of Duncan by his cousin Macbeth of Moray in battle near Elgin in 1040.

Sigurd, involved in Ireland in traditionally wide-ranging Viking fashion, was killed at Clontarf near Dublin on Good Friday (23 April) 1014 while fighting as part of an Irish–Viking coalition against 'High King' Brian Boru. The latter – an Irish equivalent of King Alfred in England – was at last reversing the tide of Scandinavian attack in Ireland, having risen from a junior sub-king of Munster to rule firstly Munster (976) and from 1002 all of Ireland as the first 'High King' from outside the Uí Néill dynasty. He had also retaken Limerick, centre of Viking power in western Ireland, from the Scandinavians. Brian was at risk of being regarded as a usurper by the offended Uí Néill kings in Midhe – who had held the High Kingship for six hundred years – having forced their 'High King' Mael Sechnaill II to abdicate in his favour, as well as by Munster's traditional rival Leinster and by the embattled Viking dynasts of Dublin. Sigurd was apparently lured into the war to help the Dublin Scandinavians and Brian's enemies in Leinster by Brian's ex-wife, the vengeful Queen Gormflaith, a Leinster princess and former consort to Olaf 'Cuaran' (the late king of Dublin), who sent her son king Sihtric 'Silkenbeard' of Dublin to Orkney to win Sigurd over. (Sigurd's mother Edna was Irish, daughter of an obscure local king.) According to the Icelandic *Njáls saga* Sihtric was invited to join Sigurd and his brother-in-law, Jarl Gilli of the Sudreys, at their high table in Sigurd's hall for the Christmas feast of 1013 and invited Sigurd to join in the war, promising him the kingship of all Ireland if Brian was killed. Sigurd's nobles thought the war none of their business, but Sigurd agreed to intervene and to bring his fleet to Dublin (blockaded by Brian in autumn 1013) by Easter Day 1014 – unaware that Sihtric was also to promise the High Kingship to another putative ally, the Man warlord Brodar. Sigurd clearly saw himself as a new Olaf 'the White', ruling in both Ireland and the Hebrides, but Irish resistance was now stronger and the forces of Brian's Munster and its allies (including Brian's predecessor as High King, Mael Sechnaill of the Uí Néill dynasty) outnumbered the Viking–Leinster coalition by around 7,000 to 6,000. According to the main Irish account of the battle, the *Cogad Gáedel re Gallaib* (*War of the Gaels and the Foreigners*), Sigurd and his fleet arrived in Dublin Bay with Brodar's Manxmen in the early hours of Good Friday, and the Dubliners and Leinstermen (under King Mael Morda of Leinster, Gormflaith's brother and Sihtric's uncle) marched out to join them on the shore. Sihtric stayed in charge of the garrison of Dublin. The Orkneymen and Manxmen held the first line of their army, with the Dubliners behind them and the Leinstermen in the rearguard; the Vikings would have been the better armed, with heavy mail coats and battleaxes. But Brian and his son Murchad, with or without Mael Sechnaill's help, won the day at Clontarf after a fight lasting until the evening high tide, and Brodar's wing of the enemy force was the first to collapse. The Vikings and Leinstermen were defeated, Mael Morda was killed, and as the Vikings fled to their ships they found that the tide was higher than expected and was carrying some vessels out to sea. The battle ended with a clash in the sea as the losing side waded out to board their vessels and the Irishmen chased them. Sigurd was killed, but Murchad (heir to Brian's kingdom) and his nephew Toirrdelbach fell too; the octogenarian 'High King' Brian was also slain, away from the battlefield (in his tent in an opportunistic attack by the retreating Scandinavian Manx captain Brodar). Other losses in the battle included several local Irish kings in Brian's army, including Tadhg Mór Ua Cellaigh (O'Kelly) of Uí Maine in Connacht. The kingdom of Dublin was preserved for Sihtric while the Uí Néill regained the 'High Kingship' of Ireland; Brian's family held onto Munster. Traditionally Sigurd fought under a magical 'raven banner' woven for him by his mother, which would droop when defeat was imminent; similar flags are linked to the earlier pirate chieftain Ragnar 'Lothbrok' and his sons, and to the later King of Norway Harald 'Hardradi'. All three flags appeared at major Viking defeats – Ragnar's at 'Cynwit' (Countisbury?) in Devon against King Alfred's West Saxons in 878, Sigurd's at Clontarf and Harald's at Stamford Bridge in 1066.

Sigurd was succeeded jointly by his three adult sons – Somerled (d. *c.* 1018), Einar and Brusi. The youngest son, Thorfinn, was around five in 1014 and was living at his grandfather Malcolm II's court; he was given Caithness and Sutherland by Malcolm, and was given Orkney territory by his older brothers once he was adult enough to rule. He succeeded to their lands as they died, first claiming Somerled's territory, which the harsh and grasping Einar had seized on the ruler's death and had refused to give to Thorfinn as the latter had already been given a portion of the jarldom (the mainland part) by King Malcolm. The more generous Brusi forced Einar to hand over this land to Thorfinn (*c.* 1018). After the discomfited Einar planned to murder Thorfinn the latter was 'tipped off' by one of his lords, Thorkell 'the Fosterer' (from Hrossey/Rousay), whom the *Orkneyinga saga* portrays as the honest and fearless spokesman of the nobles in Einar's realm who endeavoured to mitigate their lord's incessant demands and was eventually forced to flee to save himself from Einar's wrath. Eventually the three jarls – Einar, Brusi and Thorfinn – were officially reconciled, along with Thorkell, and agreed to exchange visits to each other. But Thorkell now killed the treacherous Einar in his hall on finding that the jarl was laying an ambush for Thorfinn at their imminent meeting, and Thorfinn took Einar's lands (autumn 1020). Thorkell served as Thorfinn's local host, mentor and leading commander. When the new King (St) Olaf of Norway claimed suzerainty over Orkney around 1022, he gave a third each to Thorfinn, who had been to his court to see him and gain his goodwill against Einar earlier, and Brusi and kept the other third for himself. Having induced and intimidated the visiting Brusi to accept him as overlord and let the kings of Norway hold all the rights that they had held under Harald 'Finehair', he presented the same terms to Thorfinn when the latter arrived at his court, so he had to give way too. But this period of Norwegian dominance ended when Olaf was overthrown and expelled from Norway by Cnut of England and Denmark (1028). Thorfinn then inherited Brusi's lands too on his half-brother's death (*c.* 1031), but later reluctantly had to share rule with his nephew Ragnald, Brusi's son, in 1038 when the new King Magnus of Norway, Olaf's son, demanded it. He also saw off an attack by the mysterious 'Karl Hundason' ('Churl, son of the Dog', probably an insulting nickname), the 'King of Scots' according to the *Orkneyinga saga*, in which Karl sends his new nominee Earl Margad(?) to take over Caithness from Thorfinn, the latter driving the invader out so that Karl can attack Thorfinn by sea. Thorfinn routed him at the Battle of Deerness. Thorfinn then defeated a second Scots attack at Tarbat Ness. This garbled story clearly reflects an attempt by one of Malcolm II's grandsons, kings Duncan (r. 1034–40) or Macbeth (r. 1040–57), to reconquer Caithness; which one was 'Karl' is unclear but it was more likely to be Duncan as Macbeth was probably Thorfinn's half-brother and ally. Macbeth, ruler of the mormaership of Moray in 1034–57, was to kill Duncan in battle near Elgin in 1040 and may have been encouraged to revolt by Thorfinn's defeat of his cousin and rival if this was pre-1040. In any case, the result was confirmation of Orkney naval control of the seas south to the Moray Firth.

The bickering between Thorfinn and Ragnald saw Ragnald, who had fought for Magnus's father St Olaf at Stiklestadr against King Cnut in

1030 and shared Magnus's subsequent exile at the court of Yaroslav 'the Wise' in Russia in the 1030s, return with Magnus to Norway when the latter was recalled to head a revolt in 1035. The *Orkneyinga saga* has Ragnald as one of the men sent to Russia by a faction of disgruntled Norwegian nobles to ask for Magnus's return to head a revolt against Cnut's wife Aelfgifu and son Sweyn, Ragnald being chosen as he was known to Magnus as a loyalist of his late father. The suspicious Yaroslav made the deputation all swear that they were telling the truth, no doubt fearing a trick by Cnut, who had murdered assorted rivals to the English and Scandinavian thrones. Once Sweyn and his mother had been evicted and Magnus was King of Norway, Ragnald then received Magnus's backing to take over his late father Brusi's lands in Orkney and went there with his authority. Thorfinn had to accept this division of lands to avoid an attack from Norway. The two rulers cooperated on summer raids around the coasts of England and Ireland for a few years, dated by the *Orkneyinga saga* to the reign of King Harthacnut of England (1040–42), but fell out. Ragnald tried to drive Thorfinn out in the early to mid-1040s but was defeated in a naval battle in the Pentland Firth; he fled to Norway to get Magnus's aid, and returned with a small force. He attacked Thorfinn on Orkney, and the latter fled but returned to surprise and evict Ragnald, who was holding court at Kirkwall. The loser sought aid from Magnus again, but this time only received one ship; Magnus clearly did not see his victory as likely but felt honour-bound to give him some help. (An alternative version has it that Ragnald only attacked Thorfinn by surprise once, as below.) Unable to fight an open battle, Ragnald drove Thorfinn out in a surprise winter attack on his hall on mainland Orkney, which was set afire, causing him to flee from the flames by breaking down a rear wall and running out into the darkness carrying his wife. Thorfinn then fled to Caithness, leaving Ragnald in control on the mainland. But Ragnald was killed around Yule/Christmas 1046 when Thorfinn returned and caught him on Papa Stronsay with a few men collecting malt to brew ale for the feast. He burnt Ragnald's house down in turn, and according to the *Orkneyinga saga* allowed the non-combatants to leave the building but blocked the way to the jarl's warriors. Ragnald sneaked out dressed as a priest and made a run for it, but was caught hiding among the rocks on the beach as his dog started barking. Ragnald was killed and this time Thorfinn remained unchallenged, as King Magnus concentrated on fighting Cnut's nephew Sweyn Estrithson over Denmark and died in 1047; his uncle and successor Harald 'Hardradi' ('Hard [i.e. stern] Ruler'), a former Byzantine officer in the Scandinavian Varangian Guard, continued the war.

Thorfinn, probably also lord as far south as the Isle of Man, was a factor in the turbulent world of mid-eleventh-century Scottish politics and apparently fought against his cousin Duncan in the 1030s – assuming Duncan to be his foe in the sagas, 'Karl Hundason'. It is not certain if he was an ally of his half-brother Macbeth, whom he was possibly to accompany on pilgrimage to Rome in 1050. He travelled via Germany, meeting Emperor Henry III. His nickname 'Raven Feeder' testified not to his love of birds but to the glut of bodies which his battles provided for the ravens. But he was also a capable administrator, and he established the islands' first bishopric, held by Thorolf (along with a major church), at his headquarters at the Brough of Birsay. Thorfinn apparently died at Birsay, aged around sixty according to the *Orkneyinga saga*, which would put his death at 1064–65.

Despite his power, it is not even agreed by all sources exactly at what date Thorfinn died. The *Orkneyinga saga* says that it was late in the reign of King Harald 'Hardradi', Magnus's successor, who arrived in Orkney in summer 1066 with a large fleet to reassert Norwegian control after the end of his long war with Sweyn Estrithson, Cnut's nephew, for Denmark in 1064. Formerly a Viking mercenary in the Varangian Guard in the Byzantine/Eastern Roman Empire in the 1030s after being driven out of Norway by Cnut's men, this venerable and highly experienced commander had fought the Arabs in Sicily and then battled Sweyn Estrithson over Denmark for seventeen years. The saga composed of his adventures recorded or created a whole series of unlikely exploits, including being thrown in a prison pit in Constantinople and forced to kill a 'dragon' (snake?) sent to dispose of him. More certainly, the death of the emperor he had served in Sicily, Michael IV 'the Paphlagonian', in 1041 and the overthrow of his nephew Michael V in a revolution in 1042 led to Harald losing favour and voyaging back up the Black Sea and River Dnieper to Kiev in Russia. He thence returned with his Russian wife to his Norwegian homeland, where his 'help' may not have been altogether welcome to his nephew Magnus, whom he succeeded in 1047. The archetypal opportunistic, restless and loot-hungry Viking, he was known as 'Hard Ruler' from his stern but fair legal judgements. He also had a personal link to the Orkney kin – the late Jarl Ragnald, Thorfinn's nephew, had saved his life after his first battle at Stiklestadr in 1030 and smuggled him out to safety in Russia. It was thus natural for him to emulate kings Harald 'Finehair' and Olaf Tryggvason in voyaging south-west to take over Orkney. Thorfinn's sons Paul and Erlend, the sons of Harald's previous wife's sister, were forced to accompany Harald on his invasion of England in 1066, in which Harald sought to restore the exiled Earl of Northumbria, Tostig Godwinson, and claim at least the kingship of York (possibly England too). As Tostig could tell him, the Norman Duke William was also claiming England and his invasion threat kept the English army on the south coast in summer 1066, enabling the Norsemen to land unopposed in Yorkshire. The Norwegians defeated the new earl, Morcar (grandson of Earl Leofric of Mercia and Lady Godiva), and his brother Earl Edwin of Mercia at Gate Fulford in September 1066 and occupied York. But Tostig's elder brother Harold II Godwinson, the new King of England, arrived hastily from London days later, on 25 September, and a great battle was fought with him at Stamford Bridge. The saga of the kings of Norway presents the English as catching the Norwegians and Orkneymen relaxing unawares on the banks of the River Derwent, awaiting the arrival of some promised local hostages, when the English army were spotted instead with their mail coats glinting in the sun as they advanced, showing that they were not civilians. The invaders had to run across the bridge to the safer far bank to put on their mail coats while a lone warrior held the bridge behind them to keep the English back; he was eventually stabbed from below by an Englishman climbing under the bridge. King Harold offered Tostig his earldom back if he defected (he refused) and offered Harald 'Hardradi' seven feet of English earth to lie in 'as he is taller than other men'. King Harald and Tostig both fell in the battle, which was a total English victory; the two jarls of Orkney were among the few survivors who fled home by sea and who could only man around a dozen out of several hundred waiting ships. Harald's son Olaf remained on Orkney with his cousins Paul and Erlend for winter 1066/67 before sailing home in the spring to join his brother Magnus 'Barefoot' (so called because he fled the battlefield at Stamford Bridge without his shoes) as king.

Main source of details to *c*. 1200: the *Orkneyinga saga*, with the 'caveat' that this is heroic literature, probably of oral origin, with (elaborated?) stories rather than written annals.

2

Orkney Between Norway and Scotland, 1066 to 1471

The Battle of Stamford Bridge probably seriously reduced the manpower of Orkney as well as that of their overlord Norway, which remained ineffective for nearly thirty years under King Harald's sons, Magnus 'Barefoot' and Olaf 'Peace-King'. But Paul and Erlend were not the sort of men to take advantage of this as their ancestors had done; nothing was done to rebuild the dynasty's power over the northern seas and no exploits of theirs are recorded. They were feeble enough for Malcolm III of Scotland to divorce their mother(?) Ingibiorg Finnsdottir (niece of Thorfinn's lieutenant Kalv Arnesson) in the late 1060s without fear of reprisal, whether or not this was consensual or forced by Malcolm to make way for his next wife. The latter was the famed (St) Margaret, heiress after her unmarried brother Edgar 'the Atheling' to the defunct Anglo-Saxon kingship of England and foe of the new Norman king, William I. From now on Malcolm was more concerned with England than with the once fearsome jarls of Orkney, invading England in Edgar's cause in 1068 and 1069 and being invaded in turn by William and forced to become his vassal in 1072. The two jarls' probable half-brother Duncan, Malcolm's eldest son, was taken off as an English hostage and probably did not return until the 'Conqueror' (not his contemporary nickname) died in 1087.

In 1093, when Malcolm was killed attacking Alnwick Castle, it was his brother Donald 'Ban' and his surviving sons by Margaret who had most success in the succession struggle, the latter with Norman help. Paul and Erlend took no advantage of the attempt of Duncan to secure the Scots throne in 1094, or to save him from being killed by Donald 'Ban'. Scotland duly fell to English king William II's nominee, Malcolm and Margaret's son Edgar, in 1097; with no Orkney support, Duncan's son William lost out and had to live on his estates in Cumbria. The ineffective brothers were helpless against Norway too. They were required to attend on, and were then deposed by, the son of Olaf 'Peace-King', Magnus 'Bareleg' of Norway (r. 1093–1103), so called due to his wearing the local Scots kilt instead of breeches on his Hebridean voyage in 1098. Magnus installed his eight-year-old son Sigurd, later King of Norway and a noted Crusader, as his deputy ruler in Orkney. The restless and ambitious son of Jarl Paul, Haakon, had been exiled to Norway earlier due to his disputes with Erlend's sons and had lived both there and in Sweden, taking service with the latter's Christianising King Inge. He now achieved his revenge as, having encouraged King Magnus to invade Orkney and emulate Harald 'Finehair' in 1098, he became the boy Sigurd's regent. The Orkney forces also joined Magnus for his successful Irish Sea expedition in 1098–99, when he ravaged as far as the island of Anglesey in Wales and a lucky bowshot from his fleet killed the Anglo-Norman Earl Hugh of Chester, who was waiting with his men on the shore to oppose their landing. Magnus later campaigned in Ireland, where he was to die in battle in 1103, and deported Paul and Erlend to Norway where they soon died; Erlend's son Erling died on one of Magnus's Irish Sea expeditions, in or after 1098.

When Sigurd succeeded his father to Norway and returned home in 1103, Haakon became governor and (in 1105) Earl of Orkney. Around 1108, his cousin Magnus Erlendson returned from exile in Scotland to claim his share of Orkney. Magnus was a committed Christian and reputed pacifist who had served King Magnus as a page on his Irish Sea expedition in 1098 or 1102–03 before deserting; according to the *Orkneyinga saga*, he secretly escaped from the king's warship when it was off Wales after being called a coward, swimming barefoot to shore and running away to hide up a tree from the king's 'sniffer-dogs'. Haakon sent Magnus packing, but he secured an equal division of Orkney in 1108 by appeal to King Sigurd's brother and co-ruler King Eystein; Sigurd was away from Norway on a pilgrimage to Jerusalem. The cousins were uneasy allies for a few years, though the *Orkneyinga saga* says that assorted troublemakers endeavoured to set them at odds and once they raised their armies and nearly came to blows before mediators arranged a truce meeting. The subsequent uneasy truce broke down, probably at Easter 1116, and Haakon treacherously brought more – armed – men than Magnus to a supposedly peaceful meeting on the island of Egilsay, where he turned up with eight shiploads instead of the promised two. Magnus allegedly urged his alarmed followers not to resist and give an excuse for unnecessary bloodshed, and Haakon's men duly seized and imprisoned Magnus. When Haakon arrived, Magnus purportedly asked to be sent into exile so he could go to Jerusalem or, failing that, be blinded to save Haakon from committing mortal sin by killing him. Haakon refused and ordered his execution, but only a lowly cook would do the deed as 'honourable' warriors refused.

Magnus, already loved for his sense of justice, became the local saint after his murder by Haakon, with a cult based at the Orkney cathedral of Kirkwall, built on the site of his burial on the wishes of his mother Thora. As long as Haakon lived the murder was not officially commemorated, but the new cathedral was built at the site in the late 1120s to 1130s by Haakon's heirs as a 'national' shrine, as requested by popular demand, though Haakon had notably tried to 'downplay' the cult as implicit or explicit criticism of him as a murderer of his kin. The date of Magnus's death is unclear, due to misleading evidence in the *Orkneyinga saga*; this puts it at seven years after his accession (i.e. 1115), but the date of Easter in that year means that the time between the festival and the day of the killing makes a later year more probable. The popular cult of Magnus as a saint who would grant cures (particularly to blindness) was initially ignored and viewed as an embarrassment by both Jarl Paul II, son of the murderer, and Bishop William of the Orkneys, and the latter only agreed to create a shrine and lend the Church's support around twenty years after the killing.

Haakon reformed into a more just ruler later according to the *Orkneyinga saga*, and even made a pilgrimage to Jerusalem. He was succeeded by his sons Paul II 'the Silent' and Harald I 'Smooth-Talker' in 1126; the latter was his illegitimate son by the daughter of a Caithness noble and mostly resided on the mainland. Harald was also an ally of the kings of Scots Alexander (r. 1107–24) and David (r. 1124–53), who had recognised him as Earl of Caithness. The Scots kings' elder brother King Edgar had abandoned their claim to the lands north of the Great Glen to King Magnus in 1098, so this represented a wary move back into northern politics. The brothers' relations were always strained, and were soured by Harald's men (led by Sigurd 'Snap-Deacon', another protégé of King David and at the time involved with the jarls' widowed sister Frakok) murdering Paul's ex-fosterer Thorkell Summerledson, a close kinsman and ally of St Magnus, which nearly led to civil war. Their alarmed nobles managed to patch up a truce and Sigurd was sent back to Scotland. But Harald then plotted to depose his brother, and was accidentally poisoned at his house at Orphir at Christmas 1131 by putting on a poison-dipped shirt intended as a 'present' for his brother, allegedly prepared by his sister Frakok and mother Helga, Jarl Haakon's mistress. (Frakok, whose trail of killings would have been excessive even for a contemporary male warlord, had been married to the bluntly named Ljot 'the Dastard', a nobleman in Caithness).

Paul was left as sole ruler and deported his stepmother and half-sister to the mainland, where Frakok's full brother Jarl Otter ruled at Thurso and they had estates, but Paul later faced attack from forces raised by Frakok across the Pentland Firth in 1136. He was then deposed by his cousin Ragnald (born as 'Kali'), ex-merchant son of St Magnus's sister by a Norwegian farmer called Kol, who had been raised in Norway to be a merchant and had had the luck to make friends with the future King of Norway, King Sigurd's bastard half-brother Gillechrist/Harald (r. 1130–36), on a trading visit to Grimsby in England. Kali had taken service with King Sigurd and been invested with the jarldom of Orkney (only nominally as he did not go there) in 1129, and on Sigurd's death the following spring (1130) he had backed Harald for the throne against Sigurd's son Magnus IV. They had held a rally at Tunsberg and successfully demanded a half-share in the kingdom for Harald, which Magnus had to concede to avoid civil war. Three years later, having mustered more men, Magnus had challenged his rival. Magnus won the initial clash, Harald fled to Denmark to win the support of King Eric 'the Ever-Good' and Kali lost his title, but Kali was restored when Harald seized sole rule of Norway by arresting and blinding Magnus at Bergen in 1135. He sent to Jarl Paul to demand St Magnus's half of the jarldom on pain of invasion backed by Norway, while also sending for help to his kinswoman Frakok in Caithness, who agreed to attack Paul if needed. Paul refused to concede any land despite this double threat. Harald lent Ragnald the ships needed for an attack on Orkney in spring 1136 and he landed on Shetland to demand his rights, but Paul resisted and prepared to attack him from his base on Westray.

Frakok and her son Oliver (an Anglo-Norman name possibly indicating his parents' appreciation of the French epic *The Song of Roland*, where an Oliver appears) now invaded from Caithness with twelve ships to aid Ragnald, but were spotted and intercepted by Paul and his fleet and fought off. In the crucial sea battle off Orkney Paul was felled and nearly killed, but his lieutenant and bodyguard Sweyn 'Breastrope' threw a heavy stone at Oliver, who fell overboard while stunned, demoralising his men, who rescued him and withdrew. The year's campaign ended with Ragnald in possession of Shetland and Paul unable to drive him out but holding the Orkneys, and he returned home to his father's farm in Agdir, Norway and won more support from King Harald. His second invasion in 1137 had greater success, as he landed on Westray at a time when the strong easterly currents prevented Earl Paul on Hrossey/Rousay from sailing with his fleet to intercept him and the locals rallied to him there. He may also have been helped by a promise to build a magnificent new church on the Orkneys to the popular late jarl (St) Magnus, victimised by Paul's father.

Paul held on to Hrossey/Rousay and the Church under Bishop William mediated a truce, with the two men likely to share the jarldom. But Ragnald secured sole rule by surprise and luck when one of his kin, the exiled landowner Sweyn Asleifsson, unexpectedly returned to Orkney to aid him. The ferocious Sweyn, a roving warlord said by the *Orkneyinga saga* to maintain eighty warriors as his war band, was in trouble with Paul over a typically 'Viking' episode that shows that the 'modern' world of twelfth-century Christian western Europe had not penetrated the local habits very far. The previous Christmas Sweyn Asleifsson had had a quarrel with one of Paul's men at Paul's feast at Orphir over the allocation of ale, ambushing him outside the jarl's hall and killing him. He had been outlawed, fleeing to Egilsay where Bishop William arranged for him to go to an acquaintance on the Outer Hebrides. Sweyn now sailed back to Orkney and opportunistically kidnapped Paul while the jarl was hunting otters on Rousay early one morning after hearing that he had very few guards with him, then sent him off as a prisoner to his ally, Paul's sister Countess Margaret of Atholl, at her home in central Scotland. Margaret's husband Earl Maddad was the nephew of the late King Malcolm III of Scots and first cousin of King David, and possibly David as well as the ubiquitous meddler Frakok was involved with the Atholl/Sweyn plot to attack Paul. Sweyn Asleifsson later murdered Frakok herself sometime in the 1140s for her part in his own father's death, burning down her homestead in Helmsdale in Sutherland, but her son Oliver (the real killer of Sweyn's father) escaped his ambush and fled to the Hebrides and thence the Scots court. Sweyn then resumed his accustomed practice of going on spring and autumn raids from his Orkneys farmstead, before and after the harvest, and later raiding adventures took him to Man, where he married. The complex stories of feud and counter-feud among the nobility in Orkney in these decades show that this was a Scandinavian rather than a settled, legalistic Anglo-Norman world and more unruly than most of King David's Scotland. Sweyn indeed featured in the final 'Viking' action in Dublin in 1171, shortly before the Anglo-Norman invasion, when he turned up on a – by now rather anachronistic – plundering voyage with a few shiploads of Orkneymen and tried to storm the gates and loot the city. According to the sagas he had asked Jarl Harald 'the Old' for permission for this voyage as he was bored with farming, though he was probably well over fifty; he now ended up ambushed and killed by the angry Dubliners as his men blundered into a series of pits dug outside the gates.

Ragnald/Kali now ruled Orkney, but in 1140 he voluntarily shared rule with Paul's and Harald's underage nephew Harald II, son of their sister Margaret and the Scottish mormaer or earl Maddad of Atholl, so probably a nominee of the Scots King David I. The long-serving Bishop of Orkney, William, backed Harald's claim successfully after the Scots envoy, Bishop John of Atholl, turned up at his residence and asked him to help, and the jarldom was divided up into two equal portions; as Harald was only around six he did not exercise any power for another decade or so. In 1151–55 Ragnald was absent with Bishop William and many of his nobles on a prolonged voyage to the Mediterranean and the Holy Land, suggested to him by pilgrims he met on his visit to the new young king Inge (Harald IV's son, reigned 1136–61) in Norway. He left his cousin Thorbjorn, grandson of the murderous princess Frakok (son of her daughter Gudrun by Thorstein 'the Dribbler'), and great-nephew of Jarl Paul II, as effective chief minister to Harald.

Ragnald voyaged to Galicia in Spain to winter there and then on to the Holy Land, and returned after visits to Rome and Constantinople, meeting the Emperor Manuel Comnenus at the latter (1153). In his absence Harald I's son Erlend, who had secured Caithness by grant from the King of Scots as his earldom, invaded Orkney by sea in 1154, and ejected Harald II (who still ruled part of Caithness). His coup thus represented a major Scots intervention in the region, setting Erlend up as a conduit of Scots royal power in its expansion under Scots kings David (d. 1153) and his grandson Malcolm IV (d. 1165). It was agreed that Erlend would take over Ragnald's half of the jarldom if the kings of Norway would confirm this to him, and he left for Norway – where he proceeded to secure full rights to both Ragnald's and Harald's lands from Inge's brother and co-ruler King Eystein II of Norway. He then returned to fight Harald, who had to flee to Norway after being defeated and forced to surrender at Kiarrek-Stadir in September 1154. Erlend offered half of the jarldom to Ragnald when he returned in 1155 in order to obtain his help against Harald II, but failed to deliver. Harald now returned from Norway to invade Orkney; Ragnald considered changing sides and when he went south to Sutherland to marry off his daughter to one of Harald's supporters Harald made haste to nearby Thurso to accept Ragnald's invitation to a meeting. Ragnald and Harald II now agreed to share the jarldom and crossed the Pentland Firth to Ronaldsway to war on Erlend, who had initial success in a surprise attack on Harald's base on 24 October 1156 and drove him into flight. The unsuspecting Ragnald was away from the fleet on a private visit to his home at Orphir, and Erlend's men went in pursuit and turned up at the house where he was spending the night to ask his host if he was there. The latter sent them off on a wild goose chase and alerted Ragnald, who made his escape and duly got back to his troops safely. On 21 December 1156, Ragnald's men killed Erlend by a sudden swoop on his camp while his main commander, Sweyn Asleifsson, was away, finding him and his men lying hopelessly drunk around their beached warships and butchering them.

Harald II became sole ruler when Ragnald was murdered in a private blood feud by his banished cousin Thorbjorn in August 1158. According to the *Orkneyinga saga* the two jarls went in pursuit of the latter, who had earlier murdered one of Ragnald's officers in a private feud. Thorbjorn ambushed and killed Ragnald; Harald refused the cornered Thorbjorn's appeal to accept that the killing had done him a service but let the killer go – to be cut down later by Ragnald's men. Harald was left as sole ruler. He had the longest rule in any Scottish realm, as earl from 1139 to 1206 and sole ruler from 1158. The middle decades of his rule seem to have been unusually peaceful after recent civil wars, or else the oral/written evidence of any feuds has been lost. He later shared rule with Ragnald's grandson Harald III 'the Young', a protégé and nominee of King Sverre of Norway and son of Thorbjorn's nephew Erik by Ragnald's daughter Ingibiorg, in the 1190s. Harald III had secured a grant of the earldom of Caithness from the Scots king William 'the Lion' back in the 1170s, probably while he was still a boy, and had also secured the backing of King Magnus V of Norway, but this was not acted upon until around 1193. King William, newly interested in the far north of his realm after the end of his enforced vassalage to the kings of England in 1174–89, gave Harald III his backing and Caithness to keep the jarldom divided. Harald II's second marriage, to Hvarflod MacHeth – of an obscure but politically important northern Scots dynasty which claimed rule over both Ross/Moray and Scotland – probably led to him making claims on Ross and being seen as a threat by King William, who had faced a MacHeth rebellion in 1181.

Possibly Harald III was also spurred on by the difficulties that Harald II suffered with King Sverre of Norway (r. 1184–1203) for allowing a pretender, Sigurd Magnusson, to invade Norway from Orkney in 1194. Sigurd was the son of the former king Magnus V (k. 1184), overthrown in a civil war by Sverre, and his backers included a substantial party from Orkney and Shetland; Sigurd's uncle Hallkjell, husband of Magnus V's sister, established an army there in 1193 with Harald II's backing then led them on to Norway to proclaim Sigurd king. Sverre was absent in Trondjheim as the rebels advanced on and took Bergen, but their coup was resisted by a force of the so-called 'Birkbeiner' ('Bark Shoes', i.e. very poor) faction, enemies of Magnus V and his line, who held out in the city's fortress. Early in 1194 Sverre moved south with his fleet to help them and both Sigurd and Hallkjell fell in battle – along with many Orkneymen and Shetlanders – at the Battle of Florvag on

3 April, Palm Sunday. After Sigurd's defeat Harald II was summoned
to Norway by King Sverre to explain himself and had to pay increased
tribute, and possibly Harald III hoped that the angry Sverre would
back him as a safer vassal ruler. However, it is not clear if Harald III's
visit to Sverre in Norway preceded or followed Sigurd's invasion. By
1195–96 Harald III, based at Thurso, seems to have been planning to
attack Orkney and he may have been backed by King William of Scots
as a weaker and more amenable ruler. In 1196 Harald II's son by his
first marriage, Thorfinn, invaded and took over Caithness (possibly as
a move to check Harald III) and marched south into Easter Ross, aided
by an obscure noble called Ruadhri, and they fought a battle with royal
troops near Inverness. Subsequently King William intervened in person,
the first royal campaign this far north, with troops sent by his ally King
Ragnald of Man. Harald II, outnumbered, had to agree to talks, came
to do homage at Nairn, and was held hostage until Thorfinn handed
himself over; Caithness fell into royal hands and Ragnald installed
Manx officials in part of the territory.

Harald III now ruled as William's protégé in Caithness, but was killed
in battle by Harald II who attacked him at Wick as he was fitting out
a fleet ready for invasion in 1198. Harald II then seized and mutilated
Bishop John of Caithness at Scrabster Castle, for stirring up trouble
between him and William. As a result he faced invasion from the Scots
king again in 1202 and had to hand over Caithness and do homage. He
was succeeded in 1206 by his sons David (d. 1214) and John, notably
with Anglicised rather than Norse names, who were unable or unwilling
to prevent assorted contenders in the early 1200s civil war in Norway
from using the Orkneys to gain supplies and recruits. As a result they
had to go to Norway and pay homage to the suspicious victor, King
Inge (r. 1205–17), in 1210. John was required to leave his son and heir
Harald at Inge's court as a hostage; the youth's subsequent death left
the jarldom with no clear heir. Another Norse expedition under King
Haakon IV (r. 1217–63) passed through the Orkneys en route to the
Hebrides in 1230, collecting troops on the way.

The death of Harald II's younger son John in 1231 is something of
a mystery, with two alternative versions reflecting the lack of clear
sources. He had been challenged for the jarldom by Snaekoll Gunnison,
a descendant of Ragnald II (d. 1158), and an evenly matched civil war
followed. Either both contenders agreed to sail to Norway to get King
Magnus's arbitration and John won but was drowned on the return
voyage, or else he was killed when his hall at Thurso was attacked
by unknown persons. The rule of Orkney passed to another branch
of the family who cannot be definitively placed, falling to Magnus II

(d. 1239), the son of Earl Gillebride of Angus, who was probably a Scots royal nominee. This probably represents a move for control of Orkney by the expansionist king Alexander II of Scots (r. 1214–49), who was similarly involved in gaining control over the Inner Hebrides via loyal subordinates. Magnus was succeeded in 1239 by his son Gilbert and in 1256 by his grandson Magnus III. The territory remained subject to sporadic indirect or direct control by Norway, depending on the strength of the latter's kings, until the late fourteenth century. Particularly close control was exercised in the period 1098–1103 and by Haakon IV in the 1240s to 1260s, with the latter's great expedition to the Hebrides and the Firth of Clyde in 1263 collecting troops from Orkney en route to the Inner Hebrides and landing on the Firth of Clyde at Largs. Magnus III's death in 1273 was followed by direct Norwegian rule until 1276, when his son Jarl Magnus IV was allowed to succeed by King Magnus 'the Law-Mender' of Norway (r. 1263–80). He ruled both Orkney and Caithness, and died in 1284; he was succeeded by his son John (in Norwegian 'Jon') Magnussen, who was earl until his death in around 1312. His joint Scots/Norwegian role came into focus in March 1286 when King Alexander III of Scots died without a son, falling from his horse in the dark on a Fife beach, and his granddaughter Margaret – offspring of his daughter Margaret and the new Norwegian king, Eric – succeeded to the throne aged three. As Earl of Caithness, a Scots peer, Magnus signed the Treaty of Birgham endorsing the infant Queen Margaret's marriage to Prince Edward of England at Birgham on the Tweed in 1290. The young queen died in his dominions later that year, at Kirkwall in the Orkneys en route from her homeland to Scotland. King Edward of England now acted as overlord of Scotland in choosing and later deposing the new king, Anglo-Scots baron John Balliol; after invading Scotland and defeating Balliol at Dunbar, Edward then took Scotland for himself. On 5 August 1296 John Magnusson of Orkney and Caithness swore fealty to King Edward I's representatives at Murkle, Caithness, probably backing the Norwegian 'line' of not affronting their valuable trading ally England.

Magnus V, last of the direct male line of Orkney, died at an unknown date around 1329 and was succeeded by his cousin Malise, son of Earl Malise of Strathearn. The new Jarl Malise's great-grandmother had been Maud/Matilda, daughter of Jarl Gilbert, who had married Earl Malise of Strathearn (d. 1271); their son, Jarl Malise's grandfather Earl Malise of Strathearn (usually known as 'Malise III', d. 1317), in 1290–96 had been a partisan of King John Balliol, and after his deposition joined the William Wallace rebellion but made peace with Edward I. The earl was usually loyal to England but was eventually deported there by Edward

I, and his son Earl Malise 'IV' of Strathearn (the Jarl of Orkney's father) joined the Bruce cause in 1308. His father was returned from England to help the waning English cause by Edward II in 1310 and ended up besieged and captured at Perth in 1313 by his son, who secured his pardon from King Robert. The younger Malise ('IV') then inherited the earldom of Strathearn in 1317; he died in 1329 just before his eponymous son, usually known as Malise V, took over Orkney. Malise 'V' backed the Balliol cause as John Balliol's son Edward invaded Scotland with an English army under King Edward III in 1333, fought for him at the Battle of Halidon Hill, but lost his earldom of Strathearn to the more important Balliol partisan John de Warenne, Earl of Surrey; he later returned to the Bruce cause but did not get his earldom back. He presumably resided largely in Orkney after this, but his rule is obscure and devoid of interest; he died around 1353, leaving only daughters. Even the name of the daughter (Agnes?) who transmitted the title of earl to her husband – the senior Swedish noble Erengisl Suneson, who was one of the councillors of his sovereign King Haakon VI (King of Norway from 1344–80, and briefly Sweden) – is unclear, as is whether Erengisl ever visited his new lands. The existing dynastic union of all three Scandinavian kingdoms was weakening rather than strengthening the Crown, and giving considerable powers to nobles like Erengisl at the monarchy's expense. King Haakon V of Norway died in 1319, leaving his kingdom to his daughter's son Magnus, who ruled 1319–44; the latter was the son of Prince Eric of Sweden and later inherited Sweden too. Once his son Haakon VI was adult in 1344 the nobles made Magnus hand over Norway to Haakon, but he kept Sweden. Haakon VI now married Margaret, daughter and heiress of Waldemar IV of Denmark, who died in 1374; their son Olaf was King of Denmark in 1375–87.

Erengisl, a distant relative of the powerful Bonde clan and of St Bridget of Sweden (d. 1373), came from a family based in Smalland – his father was also hereditary constable of Viipuri/Vyborg Castle in Carelia at the eastern end of the Gulf of Finland, later in Russia – and was probably too preoccupied with court duties to bother with the Orkneys beyond using their revenues. He was one of the 'kingmakers' who had raised up King Magnus of Sweden's son Eric, Haakon VI's brother, as a rival King of Sweden in 1356. Meanwhile most of Caithness passed to another son-in-law of Malise, the Scots noble Alexander d'Ard, who was a family ally of the Stewart dynasty and so was in a good position once they inherited the Scots throne in 1371. Erengisl was deprived of the lands of Orkney by a judicial decision by his sovereign, Magnus VI of Norway, in 1379, his title having been challenged by a number of locally based Scots contenders including Henry St Clair and Malise Sparre. Probably the death of his wife (Agnes? of Strathearn), before 1377, and his remarriage led to arguments that he now had no claim on the title. Erengisl, however, continued to use the title of jarl until his death in Sweden in December 1392.

On 2 August 1379 at Marstrand in Norway, King Haakon VI made a ruling on rival claims to Orkney and it finally acquired a Scottish lord in the person of Malise's grandson, Henry St Clair of Roslin/Rosslyn in Lothian. The main defeated candidate was his cousin Malise Sparre, a Sutherland noble, who may or may not have been killed by the St Clairs later after trying to take over Shetland by force. Henry, probably in his thirties, was the son of William St Clair (d. *c.* 1358) by Isabella, one of Malise's daughters. His grandfather Henry had been one of Robert Bruce's close advisers, and was killed by the 'Moors' of Granada at the Battle of Teba in Spain in 1330 as a group of knights was taking the late king's heart on Crusade. The younger Henry St Clair, first Earl of Orkney from his dynasty, was also the possible re-discoverer of America according to the theory identifying him with the northern sea-lord 'Zichmi', who voyaged there with the Zeno brothers around 1383, as stated in the 'Zeno narrative', published in Venice in 1556. The identification was first made in 1786 by Anglo-Prussian scientist John Forster on the grounds that 'Zichmi' was said by the Zeno narrator to rule a large, fertile island north of Scotland, which sounded like the mainland of Orkney, and he clearly had a fleet of experienced sailors used to the north Atlantic. He was campaigning in the northern islands (the Shetlands?) when the Zenos arrived there, which may refer to St Clair's real-life campaign there against his rival Malise Sparre, and accompanied them to America via the island of 'Friesland', possibly the largest of the Faroes.

The identification of St Clair as 'Zichmi' has always been contentious, though a voyage by him as far as Greenland is not impossible as the Norse colony there still existed until the early fifteenth century. The identification became popular in the 1980s–90s as the St Clairs and their mysteriously decorated Rosslyn Chapel in Lothian were linked by controversialists to the Templars and the Holy Grail, and the claim was made by Henry Lincoln and others in a BBC documentary that the Templars had custody of mysterious early Christian secrets which they took into exile after their suppression by the Pope in 1307. Supposedly one of their destinations was Argyll in Scotland – 'proved' by Templar-style marks on local knightly gravestones – as Robert Bruce had been excommunicated by the Pope and so could defy his orders. The best-selling book *The Holy Blood and the Holy Grail* then had the Templars guarding the secret 'bloodline' of Jesus Christ – the *'sang real'*, 'royal blood' – in the Languedoc until the Albigensian Crusade in the 1210s and surviving their suppression to exist as an 'underground' organisation that turned into the early Freemasons. Supposedly the St Clairs had not only built a chapel featuring 'Masonic' and 'Templar' imagery (the two becoming linked in the popular imagination, with the early eighteenth-century Freemasons deriving their rituals from the Knights Templar) in the 1440s, but Henry St Clair, protector of the 'extinct' Templars in Lothian, had even voyaged to America – using Templar geographical knowledge? The naval resources attributed to the northern 'sea-lord' 'Zichmi' by the story might suggest the lord of Orkney rather than some minor chieftain (in the Faroes or Norway?), and contemporary Orkney merchant ships still traded with Iceland and probably the declining 'East Colony' of Norsemen in Greenland. St Clair has even been linked with the apparent carving of a Scots-style knightly figure with armorial bearings (of the Scots Gunn family?) discovered on a rock face at Westford in Massachusetts in the 1930s. This, of course, could have been a later fake but was enthusiastically hailed by some in the 1990s as 'proof' of Norse/Scots presence in North America. The 'Zeno narrative' never explicitly names Orkney or St Clair and there is no local tradition of a voyage, which leads sceptics to deny that it refers to him. Indeed, the whole story may be a romance despite the hopeful modern claims that St Clair was a patron of the descendants of refugee Templars who had fled to Scotland.

The kingdom of Norway now had no time to supervise Orkney as closely as in the thirteenth century, with King Haakon and his son Olaf both dying in the 1380s and their widow/mother Margaret succeeding as Queen of Norway, Denmark and Sweden in 1387–1412. This 'Union of Kalmar' left Orkney effectively autonomous, and Henry St Clair had more connections to the Scottish Crown as its Earl of Caithness. In 1388 he served in the royal campaign to invade Northumberland, organised by King Robert II's son and heir John, Earl of Carrick (later King Robert III, the name 'John' being considered unlucky for a Scots king on account of King John Balliol) and led by the lame Earl John's military deputy, James, Earl of Douglas. The Scots army was unable to take well-defended Newcastle and turned back, and around 5 August it was intercepted by the pursuing English led by the main local noble dynasty, the Percys of Alnwick. The Earl of Northumberland's heir, Harry 'Hotspur' Percy, attacked Douglas's army by surprise while it was besieging Otterburn Tower and was defeated and captured in an epic battle, commemorated by poets and chroniclers alike, in which St Clair probably fought. (Although Douglas won the battle he was mortally wounded, so the campaign was a draw.) St Clair was probably a political ally of John of Carrick against his ambitious younger brother Robert, Earl of Fife and later Duke of Albany, who, thanks to John's ill health as heir and king, was to be 'Governor' of the realm for most of the 1390s; St Clair had married a local Lothian girl, Jean Halliburton of Dirleton, and his son and heir Henry appears to have mostly resided in Lothian on his behalf as a royal stalwart after Douglas's death weakened royal power on the Borders. Also significant was St Clair's daughter's marriage to John Drummond, a brother of Robert III's Queen Annabella Drummond, whose family were foes of the 'Governor'. St Clair died around 1400, possibly in the English naval raid on Orkney of that year although this (like so much about him) is debated; his son by his second marriage (to Jean Halliburton), Earl Henry, succeeded him to Orkney. Henry, a close aide of the embattled elderly Stewart king Robert III (r. 1390–1406), with his sister married to a relative of Robert's queen, was one of the courtiers who emerged as a leader of the faction opposed to the 'Governor', Duke Robert of Albany, around 1403–04. He had previously served on the new Earl of Douglas's expedition into Northumberland in September 1402, which ended in a disastrous defeat by the Percys at Homildon/Humbledon Hill under a shower of English arrows; Douglas (later nicknamed 'the Tyneman', 'the Loser', from the number of battles he lost), St Clair and many others were captured and held to ransom. St Clair first appears as a witness to a charter in the south of Scotland late in 1404, significantly with the king's ally Bishop Wardlaw of St Andrews, who had guardianship of the king's young son Prince James (later King James I). In 1405 he appears as a witness to court documents (one of them the creation of Prince James as titular lord of the ancestral Stewart lands in Renfrew and Arran) and was from time to time in attendance on the king. He also led a small force to Wark Castle across the Border to help save his ex-foe, the now rebel Earl of Northumberland (Henry Percy), from an English attack by King Henry IV's troops. He was then one of the men who tried to save Prince James from the hands of ambitious rivals by smuggling him out of Scotland to France in 1406 after a blatantly treasonous attack by Albany's allies on a military force, led by Sir David Fleming, acting on James's behalf under the royal banner in Lothian. Possibly the king's ambitious brother and regent Albany intended to kill James and take the throne – James's headstrong elder brother Prince David had already died mysteriously while in his hands at Falkland in 1402.

The ship that took James abroad, the *Maryenknight*, picked their party up at the Bass Rock in the Firth of Forth but was captured off Flamborough Head by the English; James ended up as a hostage 'guest' at the court of kings Henry IV and Henry V from 1406 to 1424 but Earl Henry was allowed to go home (temporarily, on a pledge to return to custody at Durham by a fixed date) in September 1407. His ransom was evidently paid, as by 1409 he was again in England as an ambassador from the Duke of Albany. He married a daughter of Sir William Douglas, 'knight of Liddesdale', by King Robert III's sister Egidia, and died in 1422. He married his daughter Beatrice off to the son of his ex-commander at Homildon Hill, the sixth Earl of Douglas, and she was thus consort to the seventh earl, who was regent of Scotland in 1437–39. It was his son William St Clair, third Earl of Orkney (*c.* 1410–80), who built the chapel at Roslin/Rosslyn on his lands from 1446 onwards. A minor at his accession, his lands were held in trust by Bishop Tulloch of Orkney, who was later to present a document containing the family lineage back to Viking times (drawn up or just owned by him) to St Clair's overlord, the King of Norway, when he did homage to him in 1446. By 1436 William St Clair was adult, as in that year he acted as the King of Scots' admiral in escorting his daughter Margaret to France to marry the Dauphin, later King Louis XI. The Scots ships were apparently magnificently decorated, possibly a sign of William's showmanship given his commissions at Rosslyn/Roslin, but when they arrived in France they felt insulted by the minimal expense the parsimonious King Charles VII spent on the wedding. In 1446 William travelled to Bergen to do homage to the new King Christopher of Norway and Denmark (r. 1440–48), a distant relative chosen by election to succeed the deposed King Eric (Queen Margaret's great-nephew, ruled 1387–1439). A close adviser to King James II, he became his Lord Chancellor from 1455–60 and was later ambassador to Edward IV under James III. More likely than patronage of Masons or Templars is his link to contemporary Arthurian romance as a patron of Scots authors, and it has been suggested that it was the Lothian–Orkney link of his time that led to Arthurian writers such as Sir Thomas Malory having Sir Gawain, a figure based on the sixth-century prince Gwalchmai ap Llew of Lothian, rule Orkney.

Orkney was finally alienated to Scotland under a treaty of 28 September 1468 whereby King Christian of Denmark (and Norway)'s daughter Margaret was to marry James III; this ruler of a large but poorly administered multi-state realm could not pay the dowry of 60,000 Rhenish 'guilders' due to his financial weakness, so he pledged his rights and lands in Orkney for part of the sum (50,000 guilders). He was to pay the other 10,000 in cash, but next May (1469) found that he could only raise 2,000 guilders so he pledged the Shetlands for the other 8,000. The money was never paid. The islands were technically only leased and Norway could have bought them back later; nor did the king's rights of ownership extend to the lands of other, lesser local lords and farmers under Norse law so legally he only handed over his own land there rather than the entire islands. Scotland understood it to be the latter, and acted thus. Earl William renounced his earldom in 1470 and lost his lands in Orkney to the Scots Crown, which annexed Orkney formally by Act of Parliament on 20 February 1472, and in return was given more lordships in Lothian and Fife. He retained Caithness as its earl and in 1476 passed it on to his eldest son by his second wife Marjory Sutherland, Earl William (k. 1513 at the Battle of Flodden). His son by his first wife, William, Lord St Clair, was disinherited as a wastrel.

Orkney was placed under direct royal rule, though the earldom was to be revived in the sixteenth century (21 October 1581) for Queen Mary's half-brother Robert Stewart (1533–93) who was resident there for a time but was more involved with court politics as half-brother to the queen and uncle to King James VI. The son of James V by Euphemia, daughter of Lord Elphinstone, he was initially the lay 'abbot' of Holyrood Abbey in Edinburgh – which amounted to living off its revenues as its lord rather than any monastic role – and retained these lands at the Reformation in 1559–60, which he enthusiastically supported. He was granted funds out of the revenues of Holyrood to support his legitimate and illegitimate children in 1566. He was an ally of his 'ultra'-Protestant half-brother James, Earl of Moray, at Mary's court after her return home in 1561 and after the latter's marginalisation, failed revolt and exile in 1565 was linked to the disgruntled Protestant nobles who opposed the Catholic queen and her vain, feckless husband Henry Stuart, Lord Darnley. He thus backed the attempts to induce Mary to rid herself of her husband – linked to the murder in front of her in June 1566 of her secretary David Riccio/Rizzio, of whom Darnley was jealous – by divorce or worse in early 1567. Nevertheless Robert is said to have warned Darnley, as the latter returned to Edinburgh and moved in at the isolated house of Kirk O'Field, that violence was intended if he stayed on there, and Darnley reported the warning to Mary; Robert was called on to explain but denied saying anything and exchanged heated words with Darnley, both men touching their swords. Moray had to separate them. Did Robert panic lest his fellow conspirators think he had betrayed them? Had Darnley listened to Robert and left Kirk O'Field early, history might have been different and Mary might have escaped the worst scandal of her reign. Darnley was murdered at Kirk O'Field, found strangled in the garden after the house was blown up, so Robert had evidently heard rumours of the plot or been involved initially and backed out of it.

Robert backed the overthrow of his half-sister and elevation of his infant nephew James VI to the throne under Moray's regency later in 1567, but in 1570 exchanged his secularised Holyrood estates for the 'temporalities' (lands) of the bishopric of Orkney and moved there. It was a shrewd move to get away from the feuds and instability of the regency, with his ally Moray soon to be assassinated, but his thorough if not illegal seizure of lands and their accompanying rights in Orkney led to complaints by the threatened Bishop Adam Bothwell that Robert was acting illegally, taking lands to which he was not entitled by force via his henchmen, and trying to ruin him. Robert was remembered in tradition as ruling like a gangster with a posse of thugs, though this was hardly unique for a sixteenth-century Scots landowner. Robert was at odds with the eventual winner in the struggles over the regency, Earl James Douglas of Morton (his uneasy and far more ruthless partner in the anti-Darnley plans of 1567), who in 1576 accused him of planning to sell Orkney to its ex-owner the King of Denmark and threw him in prison at the castle on Mainland, Orkney. He remained there despite attempts to bribe Morton for his release until Morton's overthrow in 1578, and participated in the ex-regent's arrest, trial and execution in 1581. Rehabilitated by James VI and given the islands' earldom in 1581 to confirm his pre-eminence there, he died in 1593 and was succeeded as earl by Patrick (b. *c.* 1566), his second but only surviving son by Janet Kennedy of Cassilis. Patrick, owner/'prior' of secularised Whithorn Abbey in Galloway, also lived on Orkney for much of his career after he succeeded his father as earl, having been a close companion of his contemporary and cousin James VI in his youth. He also exploited the locals shamelessly, extorted excessive rent, had a brood of illegitimate children, and built Scalloway Castle on Shetland and the Earl's Palace at Kirkwall on Orkney. He was accused of misrule, albeit by the not exactly unbiased figure of his family's rival Laurence Bruce (a distant relative of the royal Bruces from Perthshire), who was sheriff/bailiff of Orkney in the 1570s and was just as oppressive. Suspected of wanting to declare independence by James VI, Patrick was arrested – traditionally by a royal expedition to the islands – in 1609 and imprisoned in Edinburgh Castle. His illegitimate son Robert raised a revolt in his name in May 1614 and led a force of seventy or so retainers to seize Birsay, followed by the occupation of his father's fortified palatial residence at Kirkwall where he withstood a five-week siege by a royal army in September–October. The latter was led by George Sinclair, Earl of Caithness and descendant of the islands' ex-lords, whom the king sent over as a figure with a rival claim on local allegiances. The thick walls deflected the royal cannon, but eventually the defenders had to surrender and Robert was sent back to Edinburgh and put on trial for rebellion in November. Earl

Patrick was accused of sending him instructions to revolt so the islands could be held 'hostage' for his release, and although no documentation for his putting Robert up to the revolt was produced a maidservant at the Earl's Palace on Orkney testifed that she had seen a letter, in Patrick's handwriting, which Robert had destroyed. Both men were executed in February 1615 and the islands were annexed to the Scots Crown.

Lords of Orkney, 850 to 1471

Name	Date of accession	Date of death/dep.	Years ruled
Ketil 'Flatnose' (extent of realm unclear)	c. 850?	<890?	30/40?
Ragnald/Rognvald	c. 870/75?	?875/80	?4/5 (abd.)
Sigurd 'the Mighty' (brother)	?875/80	?892	?12/17
Guthorm (son)	?892	?893	?1
Hallad (son of Ragnald)	?893	?894	?1
'Turf' Einar (brother)	?894	?920	?16
Arnkel (son)	?920	954	?34
Erlend (brother)	?920	954	?34
(King Erik 'Bloodaxe' of Norway, overlord 937–54)			
(Queen Gunnhild of Norway, overlord 954–55 and 976–77)			
Thorfinn 'Skull Splitter' (brother of Arnkel and Erlend)	?947	?977	?30
Arnfinn (son)	?977	?980	?3
Havard (brother)	?980	?982	?2
Liot (brother)	?982	?985	?3
Hlodvir (brother)	?985	?987	?2
Sigurd 'the Stout' II (son)	?987	Apr. 1014	?37
Somerled (son)	Apr. 1014	?1018	?3
Brusi (brother)	(i) Apr. 1014	1018	4
	(ii) 1020	?1031	?11 (Total: ?15)
Einar (brother)	Apr 1014	Oct 1020	6 years 6 months
Thorfinn 'the Mighty' or 'Raven Feeder' (brother)	?1018	1064/5?	<47
Ragnald (nephew)	1038	Dec 8 1046	
Paul (son of Thorfinn)	?1064/5	1098	<33
Erlend (brother)	?1064/5	1098	<33
(King Magnus 'Bareleg' of Norway, direct rule 1098–99)			
Sigurd, prince (1103 King of Norway)	1099	1105	7
Haakon (son of Paul)	1103/5	1126	21

Name	Date of accession	Date of death/dep.	Years ruled
(St) Magnus (son of Erlend)	1108?	16 Apr. 1116/17/18	8/10?
Paul II (son of Haakon)	1126	1137	11
Harald (brother)	1126	Dec. 1131	5
Ragnald III (nephew of Magnus)	1137	Aug. 1158	20/21
Harald II (nephew of Paul II and Harald)	1139	1206	67
Erlend III (son of Paul II)	1154	21 Dec. 1156	2
Harald III (grandson of Ragnald III)	?1195	1198	?3
David (son of Harald II)	1206	1214	8
John (brother)	1206	1231	25
Magnus II (desc. of Ragnald III)	1231	1239	8
Gilbert (son)	1239	1256	17
Magnus III (son)	1256	1273	17
(Direct rule by Norway 1273–76)			
Magnus IV (son)	1276	1284	8
John II (brother)	1284	1312	28
Magnus V (son)	1312	?1329	?17
(Orkney to the husband of Magnus's daughter Margaret – Malise, son of the 7th Earl of Strathearn.)			
Malise	?1329	?1353	?24
Erengisl (Swedish son-in-law)	?1353	1379 (d. 1392)	?26
(Effective rule by Norway as Erengisl was absentee, *c.* 1359–79)			
(1379: Orkney awarded to the son of Malise's younger daughter by William de St Clair, lord of Roslin.)			
Henry (St Clair)	2 Aug. 1379	1400?	21?
Henry II St Clair (son)	1400?	1422	22?
William St Clair (son)	1422/34	1471	37/49

3

Lords of the Isles, I: The Hebrides to Robert Bruce

The Lord of the Isles controlled the southern section of the jarldom of Orkney, excluding the Isle of Man; the territory was centred on the island of Islay and contained most of the Inner Hebrides (the 'Sudreys', 'South Islands' as seen from Orkney) along with the mainland territories of Argyll (Somerled's ancestral lands) and, until 1308, Garmoran, Morvern and Lochaber, and Kintyre.

Before Somerled: the southern Hebrides and the links to Man and Dublin

The region was probably settled by the Scandinavians in the later eighth and early ninth centuries; the records of the sacking of Iona in 795, 802, 806 and 825 indicate a local Viking presence but it is not clear if this was only summertime raiding at this date. The islands of the Gall-Gaedhil were apparently more orientated towards military leadership from the Scandinavians of Dublin or the Isle of Man in the ninth century than to leadership from Orkney, but local 'kings' are only sketchily known. Godred MacFergus, king of Airgíalla (Oriel) in northern Ireland and unusually the son of an Irish father and Scandinavian mother – most known 'mixed-race' warlords were the reverse – was recorded in Irish annals as 'Ri Innse Gall', 'lord of the islands of the Gael', and died around 853. He was probably ruler of the Hebrides, and in later legend was supposed to have come to Scotland to offer his military support to King Cinaed/Kenneth MacAlpin – possibly a 'back-dating' to give respectable antiquity to the idea of the Hebridean lords as loyal dependant allies of the kings of Scots. (The date for this event is also suspect, as it is supposed to have occurred around 835, when Kenneth was not yet king of either the Picts or the Scots; he died in 858 after a reign of around sixteen years.)

The actual terminology used by the Irish *Annals of the Four Masters* (early seventeenth century) for naming Godfrey's lordship is post-ninth century, which has led to sceptics claiming it is an unhistorical claim. His possible successor as local overlord was Ketil 'Flatnose', possibly the same as the Gaelic Caitill 'the Fair' who was active in Ireland in the 850s. Ketil, as seen in the previous chapter, was a Scandinavian warrior who was father-in-law and local viceroy to King Olaf 'the White' (probably but not definitely 'Amlaith') of Dublin in the 850s and 860s, and operated in the 'Sudreys' and possibly Man too. Olaf married Ketil's daughter Aud 'the Deep-Minded', a pioneering female Scandinavian adventurer who ended up leading a group of emigrants to Iceland around 900 to join her relatives; after Olaf divorced her and died or left Dublin for Norway around 871, their son Thorstein 'the Red' set up a lordship in Caithness in alliance with Jarl Sigurd of Orkney. Ketil may have lasted as ruler into the 870s and 880s, or else his daughter inherited his role and presided over the 'Sudreys' in person. It is unclear if Ketil was succeeded in the Hebrides by any one leader or if political chaos resumed; Thorstein chose to pursue his career on the mainland, where he possibly conquered Ross and was eventually killed in battle around 885/90. After his death Aud left Orkney for Iceland and the family lordship apparently lapsed, though Thorstein's daughter was to marry a subsequent Mormaer of Caithness so she presumably acted as its heiress.

The first known 'ri [i.e. 'king'] Innse Gall', king of the Hebrides, was another Godfrey or Guthfrith, son of Harald, who raided Wales in the 970s and 980s, fought with the king of Man, and in *Njáls saga* was a rival of Jarl Sigurd 'the Stout' of Orkney in the 980s. His father Harald or 'Arailt' may have been a Norse ruler of the kingdom of Limerick in western Ireland, descended from Ivarr 'the Boneless', king of Dublin and co-leader of the Scandinavian invasion of England in 865/66 (d. 873). Godfrey was killed in Ireland in 989, and was brother of Maccus (Magnus?), king of anonymous islands and probably Man, who was one of the seven kings who met (and, according to twelfth-century English sources, submitted to) King Edgar of England at Chester on the River Dee in 973. Edgar had an Irish Sea fleet and established local naval supremacy, so Maccus was probably an Irish Sea ruler – presumably of the Isle of Man (see also chapter 5). The title used for 'king' in the Hebrides and Man was notably Gaelic/Celtic, not the Scandinavian word 'konung' – implying that the concept was adopted from local practice. The probability is that Godfrey's sons ruled the Sudreys as well as Man around 1000, but as vassals of the Viking ruler Olaf 'Cuaran' ('Sandal', from his Gaelic-style footwear) of Dublin. Hebrideans were recorded as fighting in the army of Jarl Sigurd against Irish 'High King' Brian Boru at the Battle of Clontarf near Dublin in April 1014, and so were presumably his allies and/or vassals; the unusual degree of centralised power which Brian, king of Munster, was asserting in Ireland was a threat to the autonomous Viking settlements of Waterford and Dublin and potentially to the Irish Sea islands. Then another hiatus in local leadership probably ensued as Sigurd's four sons divided the jarldom. The Viking mercenary captain who killed Brian Boru at the battle (traditionally in his tent away from the fighting), Brodar, was a Manxman though probably not its ruling lord.

Some sort of overlordship of Man (and the Hebrides too?) seems to have been taken in the 1020s by the ruler of Dublin, Sihtric 'Silkenbeard' Olafsson (abd. 1036). By 1031 an Irish/Scandinavian Irish Sea warlord, Echmarcach, is recorded as a 'king' when he joined Malcolm II of Scots to submit to the invading King Cnut of England and Denmark. He was probably king of the Hebrides, possibly also of Man and the mixed Celtic and Scandinavian settlements in Galloway, and from 1036 to 1048 ruled at times in Dublin. Lesser successors in Man and the Sudreys included Margad Ragnallson (*c.* 1052–61), ruler of Dublin, and Muirchaid/Murchad MacDiarmait (*c.* 1061–70), ex-ruler of Dublin and son of the king of Leinster. At this point Man was certainly part of the extended kingdom of Leinster, which now had Dublin (with its fleet) as a junior partner, and possibly some of the Hebrides came under this overlordship too. The next ruler of the Irish Sea region was Godred/Godfrey Sihtricson, ruler of Dublin around 1070–74, and his probable son and deputy Fingal (called after the legendary Irish hero Fionn MacCumhaill) – though it is not clear if they ruled more than just Man. Fingal was in a weak position after his probable father lost Dublin, and was expelled in 1079 by his rival Godred 'Crovan' ('White Hands', called from his gloves). Godred 'Crovan', who became famous in Manx folklore as 'King Orry', had apparently fought in the Norwegian army of King Harald 'Hardradi' against the English at Stamford Bridge near York in 1066. He set up a long-lasting dynasty and held authority in parts of the Hebrides and coastal Ireland too (see chapter 5). But after his death in 1095 his son Laghman, his deputy in the Hebrides since 1091 and called 'lord of Uist' by the Norse sources, was in dispute with his brother Harald, murdered him, was overcome with remorse and abdicated to go on pilgrimage to Jerusalem sometime in the late 1090s.

The year 1098 saw a first and overwhelming Norwegian naval

expedition by the ambitious King Magnus 'Bareleg' to conquer the Hebrides and Man, bringing the region temporarily under direct Norwegian rule. Laghman was still ruling the Outer Hebrides at this date and had to submit or else abdicated; the *Manx Chronicle* refers to one of the ephemeral regional rulers of the mid-1090s, a nominee of Magnus, being killed on Lewis by the locals en route to Man thanks to his plundering. King Magnus led a large fleet from the Orkneys via the Hebrides to Man in 1098, and traditionally transported his longship over the isthmus at Tarbert ('the narrows') in Kintyre to show that the peninsula was an 'island' and so under his control. All of the Hebrides was duly ceded to him by King Edgar of Scots, a half-Saxon ruler only precariously holding onto Scotland from 1097 as the nominee of King William II of England (who had lent him troops to overthrow his uncle, King Donald 'Ban'/'the Fair'). Probably Edgar, son of St Margaret and in exile in England in 1093–97, had little interest in the Hebrides as well as lacking local allies; however, his half-brother Duncan II (r. 1094), overthrown by Donald 'Ban', had been the son of an Orkney princess and would have been in a better position. Magnus's precarious long-distance 'empire' of the Hebrides, Orkney and Man lasted until his death in battle in Ireland in 1103, with one of his many sons, the underage Sigurd, brought to the region as his client ruler aged eight. When Magnus died Sigurd and his Norwegian councillors returned home, and Man fell to an obscure Domnall MacTeige, who appears to have been acting as regent for Laghman's younger brother Olaf (under Norwegian supervision). Domnall and his eventual supplanter, King Olaf (r. 1114?–53), may or may not have ruled the Hebrides too, but were probably only nominal suzerains; centralised control seems to have lapsed with the end of the first Norwegian incursion in 1103. Olaf, whose rule was long remembered as a time of peace, was murdered by three disgruntled nephews in 1153 and succeeded by his son, Godred II. It is possible that Olaf's mother had been a daughter of the late King Harald 'Hardradi' of Norway (k. 1066), and so he and his son would have had a claim on the loyalties of Norse chieftains in the Sudreys.

Somerled and his heirs

A lordship was carved out of the Viking settlements in the area in the late 1120s and 1130s by Somerled, son of 'Thane' Gillebride of Argyll, the first to use the title of 'Lord of the Isles'. His name in the then current Norse meant 'summer voyager', i.e. a seasonal seaborne campaigner who would farm in the winter and go off trading and plundering in the summer or else in the spring and autumn in between the sowing and harvest – as many Hebrideans of Norse descent did at the time. In the Gaelic used at the time the name was 'Somhair-lidh', the latter part meaning 'champion'; the name may mean 'to become a champion on the grassy slope' – his later admirers, opposed to Norwegian cultural influence on the medieval Hebrides, have claimed that this was his actual contemporary name, to minimise his Norse heritage. (The 'grassy slope' was said to be a reference to his first victory, a hillside ambush of some Vikings in Argyll.) His name was generally translated by the Anglicised historians of the sixteenth century from Hector Boece onwards as 'Somerledus', which was then assumed to be from the Norwegian for 'summer voyager', but this does not prove that this was its twelfth-century context or meaning. The first ruler to use this name had been a son of Jarl Sigurd of Orkney in the 1010s, definitively Norse. The dynastic origins of Somerled of Argyll are unclear, and recent DNA studies of his MacDonald descendants show his patrilineal line as having been Norse, not Celtic or Irish – though his Irish-named father may well have had an Irish mother or grandmother and was supposed to be from Fermanagh (see below). Somerled was probably a 'new man' and self-made warlord in an era of dislocation and turbulence, like his mainland equivalent Kenneth MacAlpin, the first King of Scots; rather than any prestigious ancestry, it was his success as a leader that attracted warriors. In the usual manner for great dynasties, his descendants' eulogists needed to prove that he had heroic noble ancestry, preferably from an ancient line of kings. Thus his father Gillebride, a name meaning 'servant of St Brigit' in Gaelic, was supposed to come from the ancient line of the kings of Airgíalla/Oriel in northern Ireland; as late as 1411 at the Battle of Harlaw the warriors of his descendant Donald, 'Lord of the Isles', were exhorted into battle against the army of the Scots monarch with the reminder that they were descended from the historic 'Clan Colla', that is the family of a semi-legendary mid-fourth-century 'High King' of the dynasty of the great king Conn of the Hundred Battles (*fl. c.* AD 200).

The oldest known written pedigree for Somerled's family is Irish and fourteenth-century – that in the *O'Cianain Miscellany* drawn up for 'Lord of the Isles' John MacDonald's cousins Toirdelbach and Eoin/ John MacAlexander in around 1344. A later one, but more closely linked to the main MacDonald family, is that in the fifteenth-century poem 'Gaoidheal di Chlain Colla', now in the family's 'Black Book of Clanranald'. These all gave him Gaelic male ancestry. The former gives a line of fourteen generations from Colla to Somerled, the latter gives twelve; this would indicate a period covered of a maximum five hundred years, which is too short for a descent from a fourth-century ruler to around 1130. Both of these genealogies, and a pedigree in the Irish 'Book of Lecan', agree on Somerled's father Gillebride being son of 'Giolla' (Giolla 'Adamnan' in the Irish sources, 'Oghamnan' in the Clanranald one) son of 'Solam' son of 'Suibne'(?). The earlier names in the list differ, but scholars agree that most seem authentic Gaelic; the mention of a 'Fergus' may mean the father of the 850s northern Irish ruler Godred MacFergus, who may have been linked to Airgíalla. The DNA evidence, however, indicates an omission of at least one transmission of the Irish/Gaelic bloodline via a female, if the list is anywhere near accurate. One or more of Somerled's Gaelic-named male ancestors must have been Norse in ethnic origin – and the 'Viking' name and Hebridean lordship of Godred MacFergus might indicate he was the paternally descended 'Norseman' in the pedigree. The later medieval MacDonald poets' references to the family as the descendants of 'Godfrey'/Godred are not clear evidence of a perceived allegiance to this man as the defining 'clan ancestor'; the Godfrey in question may be Godred 'Crovan' of Man, grandfather of Somerled's wife.

According to Irish legend, only written down centuries later and dated in extant early seventeenth-century annals, Colla 'Uais', who ruled for three years around AD 321–24 according to the *Annals of the Four Masters*, was a prince of the ruling family of the 'High Kings' who broke a taboo that anyone of the family who killed and replaced the reigning king would be punished by his descendants never ruling. He overthrew and killed his uncle 'High King' Fiachra, aided by his brothers – the trio were known as the 'Three Collas' – and as a result his own overthrow led to Fiachra's son sending his brothers off to conquer Ulster from the 'Ulaid', the people whose past great rulers had included the legendary Cormac MacNessa (employer of the Homeric-style warrior hero Cú Chulainn). The Collas won the battle of 'Achaidh Leithdeircc' (dated to AD 331) and sacked the Ulster 'capital', the hill fort of Emain Macha – thus bringing an end to the heroic age of Ulster – to set up their own kingdom of Airgíalla. But they and their descendants never ruled as 'High Kings' in Tara in Midhe, hence the tradition that this was due to Colla 'Uais' breaking the sacred taboo, and later some of their family relocated to Argyll – formerly part of the kingdom of the Collas' maternal grandfather, the 'king of Alba' (i.e. Scotland). In fact, modern DNA shows that the traditional close kinship of the descendants of the Collas, such as the MacDonalds, to the ruling Uí Néill dynasty of Ireland from the 400s is fictional unless it was by maternal descent, and the kingdom of 'Alba' did not exist in the 300s though a Pictish kingship may have done so. The legends probably rationalise a genuine close link between the early settlers of Argyll and the Late Iron Age kings of Ulster, though modern Irish historians would doubt that there was any genuine wide-ruling 'High Kingship' at Tara to be usurped as early as 300. The earliest definitive king is Niall 'of the Nine Hostages', ancestor of the Uí Néill, as king of Midhe and central Ireland in the early fifth century.

MacDonald family traditions written down in the seventeenth-century 'Book of Clanranald' had it that Somerled's father Gillebride, 'of the Cave' (implying that he was at one time reduced to living or hiding in one), went to his ancestors' land of Fermanagh in Ireland in or around 1110 to recruit military support but was unable to drive out his Argyll lands' occupiers. This task was passed on, more successfully, to his son. Logically Somerled came from a mixed Norse/Gaelic background, probably in Mull or Lochaber, and unified local lords and warriors from both peoples in a new kingship. The local tradition speaks of him as being a minor local resident content to spend his time fishing when a deputation of lords came to him to ask him to lead them in rebellion against the men of 'Lochlainn', that is the Scandinavian settlers. One of the deputation, Ruadhri, grumbled that the salmon Somerled was fishing for would jump out of the stream before Somerled would become a leader – and it promptly leapt out as a miraculous sign of Somerled's destiny. This has echoes of the legends of Fionn MacCumhaill, the great mythical third-century AD Gaelic warrior leader of the 'Fianna' bodyguard of the Irish 'High Kings', who in Irish/Scots legend also (unhistorically) fought the 'Lochlainn'. Fionn acquired his skills and wisdom by licking his fingers after touching a magic salmon which his druid mentor had asked him to catch. Fionn, Scottified as 'Fingal', was a hero to the Irish-descended Gaels of Argyll too, hence the location of 'Fingal's Cave' on the Inner Hebrides island of Staffa. Was there some identification even in the twelfth century between Somerled, 'liberator' of Argyll and creator of a sense of regional identity, and Fionn?

One source refers to his descendant Angus 'Mór', lord of Islay (d. 1294/95), as being of the kin of 'Gofraidh' – i.e. Godfrey, probably Godred 'Crovan' ('White Hands') – who was the founder of the main dynasty of the Isle of Man. But this may be due to the ancestry of Somerled's wife, not of himself; he is first recorded in 1140, marrying Ragnhild, the daughter of King Olaf of Man (who died in 1153). The native *Chronicle of Man* indeed reckoned this marriage as the cause of the downfall of the kingdom of Man in that it gave Somerled and his sons a stake in its future and so brought war with their kingdom (in the entry for '1156'). As brother-in-law of King Godred II of Man, Somerled used his wife's support against the autocratic Godred in that kingdom to make a claim on it on their sons' behalf as revolt broke out, led by a chieftain called Thorfinn. The latter took Somerled's son Dugald – the grandson of Godred's father Olaf, so Godred's rival heir to the Manx dominions – around the Hebrides taking pledges of allegiance from the local lords, but Godred was tipped off and collected his fleet. Given the location of the subsequent clash, Somerled attacked first, daringly in midwinter. On 5–6 January 1156 Somerled fought a naval battle off Man with Godred, allegedly involving hundreds of ships and a severe defeat for Godred (who had possibly lost valuable men recently in his attempt to invade Dublin). Godred bought him off by ceding the southern Hebrides to him and his son Dugald, whose new 'kingship' as his father's deputy possibly reflects memories of the similar rule by Sigurd of Norway on his father King Magnus's behalf. Godred held onto Skye and the Outer Hebrides. In Godred's absence in Norway in 1158 Somerled landed on the Isle of Man and took it over too, and his foe had to retire into exile and went off to complain to the King of Norway. Thenceforth Somerled ruled most if not all of the southern Hebrides south of Skye. A former lieutenant of King David of Scotland in his invasion of England in 1138 and participant in his defeat by King Stephen's troops at the Battle of the Standard near Northallerton, the 'summer voyager' (a nickname for Vikings) created the most powerful fleet in the northern seas and was accepted as 'king' by the Scots and Norse sovereigns. Dugald ruled as 'king' of the southern Hebrides (including Godred's former islands) from 1156. Somerled's ethnic origins and politico-cultural orientation – mainly Gaelic or Norse? – have been hotly disputed, with enthusiastic historians allied to his MacDonald descendants claiming him as leader of a Celtic or Gaelic revival aimed at expelling Norse influence from the Hebrides. He was also declared to be the inventor of the small and mobile Hebridean galley, the 'birlinn', which could outmanoeuvre the larger Scandinavian longships, and the ship duly appeared on his family's official seals. He has even attracted a modern fictionalised biography, by Nigel Tranter (*Lord of the Isles*, 1983).

Certainly he was the first lord of the Hebrides for centuries to have a definitively local origin as opposed to dynastic or personal links with the Scandinavians in Man or Dublin. He was from an Argyll family and by family tradition linked to Fermanagh in Ulster (see above). From the seventeenth century onwards, anachronistic accounts placed him in 'national' Gaelic terminology probably unlikely for the fluid situation of the twelfth century; the accuracy of the (probably originally oral) MacDonald traditions have also been disputed, and their dates are probably less accurate than their overall tenor. Contemporary evidence is entirely annalistic apart from one poem, written by an eyewitness, on his invasion of Renfrew in 1164 – and hostile, being written by monastic Scots (Holyrood and Melrose abbeys) and Manx sources.

To complicate matters, Somerled's sister married the obscure Malcolm MacHeth, a claimant to the Scots throne and probable descendant of King Macbeth's stepson Lulach (reigned 1057–58). Lulach's origins lay in the northern kingdom of Moray (presumed by mainstream historians since the nineteenth-century Skene and Robertson to be the northern half of the old 'Pictish' kingdom, originally one of the two halves of the Pictish realm and ruled by a separate dynasty from the south); he was the son of Mormaer Gillacomgain, killed in 1032, and Gruoch (the real-life 'Lady Macbeth'), daughter and heiress of Boite, the son of the Scots king Kenneth III (reigned 997–1005). Lulach, probably then in his twenties, briefly succeeded his stepfather Macbeth when the latter was killed at Lumphanan by Malcolm II's grandson Malcolm III, son of King Duncan, in summer 1057 but was killed by Malcolm III within a year. His son, however, held onto Moray, as mormaer, until driven out by Malcolm in 1078. Malcolm MacHeth was connected to (perhaps brother of) Angus/Oengus, Mormaer of Moray in the 1120s, who had revolted against King David (the youngest son of Malcolm III) in his absence in England in 1130. Angus, maternal grandson of Lulach and so great-grandson of Mormaer Gillacomgain (k. 1032), clearly represented a 'Gaelic' threat to the line of David and his brothers, sons of the English princess St Margaret (d. 1093) and introducers of Anglo-Norman administration, towns, culture, religious life and personnel to Scotland. Logically Lulach's line represented a 'northern Pictish autonomist' stand by the men of Moray against the house of Malcolm III, and what would later be called a 'Highlands' resistance to 'Anglicised' rule of the main, southern Scots kingdom – but some historians see this as unproven. The province or ex-kingdom called 'Muref' in medieval records of the eleventh and early twelfth centuries was presumably geographically coterminous (more or less) with the later province of Moray and, like the Hebrides, was resistant to central control from the kings ruling in the Lowlands – at least when challenged. The 1130 revolt would thus have been a clash of 'north' and 'south' in the kingdom of Scots or 'Alba', with an added genealogical challenge by the ancient line of Moray to Malcolm III's dynasty.

But Angus was defeated and killed and his ally Malcolm, illegitimate son of David's brother King Alexander (d. 1124), was captured in the Battle of Brechin in April 1130 by David's – English – general Edward Siwardsson. David then confiscated Moray and probably gave it to his nephew, William FitzDuncan (d. 1147), son of his elder half-brother King Duncan II (reigned 1094). Technically William FitzDuncan had a superior claim to the Scots throne over David as his father had been Malcolm III's eldest son (by his first, Orkney marriage) and David was his seventh son (his sixth by his second marriage). However, he remained loyal and was now given the task of taming the rebel 'heartland' Moray. Malcolm MacHeth then probably succeeded William in 1147 as mormaer – or, as the Anglicizing David and his heirs translated the title, earl. If William left any sons who lived in Scotland, such as the mysterious 1187 rebel 'Donald MacWilliam', they did not inherit titles; his known son only inherited his Cumbrian and Yorkshire lands in England. The 'MacHeth' threat to the ruling dynasty of Malcolm III remained, and now Somerled became involved in it. His interventions in Scots affairs against the young Malcolm IV (reigned 1153–65), David's grandson, in 1153–54 and 1164 posed a threat to the incumbent dynasty of Malcolm III and implied that Somerled threatened to install a MacHeth ruler as his own client. Was Somerled involved in Malcolm MacHeth's initial attempt to replace the Anglicised Malcolm IV in 1153–54 and distracted by the easier prize on offer in Man? Notably, Somerled kept out of the next attempt to unseat Malcolm, by a formidable coalition of six earls/ mormaers led by Earl Ferchar of Strathearn, in 1160. (This is recorded by the English chronicler Roger of Hoveden rather than any Scots source, and the other participants are not named.) This rebellion saw a move by southern Highlands-based Ferchar and his allies to attack Malcolm on his return from an expedition to help his ally King Henry II of England in his war with Toulouse – where Malcolm, who held lands as Earl of Huntingdon in England and so had to do homage to King Henry to keep them, had acted as a loyal vassal to Henry and received knighthood from him. It is plausible that Malcolm IV's 'Anglicised' love of knightly chivalry as well as his doing homage to the King of England infuriated his nationalist-minded great lords as a 'betrayal' and he was seen as too close to Henry and uninterested in the Gaelic part of his realm. (The Scots kings now usually lived at Roxburgh Castle on the Borders, in the far south.) Malcolm was besieged at Perth by the coalition, but managed to fight off his attackers – probably as they had no siege engines to tackle the walls and he had plenty of supplies – and forced their submission, apparently on easy terms which were kept. This rebellion may well indicate a Gaelic *versus* Anglicised fault line among his senior lords, as it is not specifically recorded as being in the dynastic cause of the MacHeths; possibly Malcolm was regarded as Henry's puppet. Somerled's MacHeth dynastic alliance seems to indicate his sympathies – though he had fought loyally for David in England in 1138. At the least, he used the MacHeths as a threat to aim at Malcolm IV if he was challenged.

Did Somerled see Malcolm's invasion of Galloway and deposition of its semi-independent lord, Fergus, in 1160 as implying that he was next on the centralising Scots king's list? The massive lordship of Galloway, still Gaelic in its cultural orientation and inheritance laws in the early to mid-twelfth century like the Highlands, also had a degree of Scandinavian settlement and was similar to Somerled's realm in that an impressive 'centralised' lordship had emerged in this period, based on a dynasty of obscure Gaelic/Scandinavian origins. Fergus was a similar figure to Somerled, and like him was not definitively opposed to all 'modern', Anglo-Norman innovation as such – he founded a new Cistercian monastery and abbey at Dundrennan, and Somerled has been suggested on unclear evidence as the founder of Saddell Abbey in Kintyre, where debateable traditions have it that he was buried. If Somerled did not found Saddell himself, his son Ranald certainly did. (One thirteenth-century French list has 'Sconedale' Abbey, probably Saddell, in existence in 1160 but abbey documents of 1398, 1404 and 1498 and the MacDonald 'Book of Clanranald' refer to Ranald as the founder.) Fergus was as much of a threat to Malcolm IV with his large army of local tenants as was Somerled, and was more vulnerable as his territories were all on the mainland and could be invaded without a fleet. He was overwhelmed by the King of Scots' army in a series of three campaigns (a sign of royal persistence) in 1160, and was forced to abdicate and become a monk at Holyrood Abbey outside Edinburgh, i.e. under royal control to prevent him changing his mind and rebelling again. Galloway was divided between his two sons, the elder but illegitimate (by Catholic canon law) Gillebride and the legitimate Uhtred, to weaken it. If normal Gaelic inheritance laws had prevailed, the elder son would have had a strong chance of gaining all the lands. Following this, the *Holyrood Chronicle* records for 1163 that Malcolm 'moved' the men of Moray, that is to say transferred potentially disloyal or turbulent locals (MacHeth supporters?) out of the region and replaced them with loyal men so these would not aid any future rebellions. Moray had aided a successful revolt against the incumbent king (by Macbeth) in 1040 and unsuccessful ones in 1078 and 1130; from now on, Moray resistance to central control (or aid to pretenders) ended and the 1187 and 1212 MacHeth revolts were centred on Ross to the north. In political if not cultural terms, the traditional Gaelic order was now replaced as far as the Moray Firth by a relatively stable 'modern' European feudal kingdom. But this only applied to the elite who could challenge the king; 'lower-level' society would not have altered.

Possibly the royal 'taming' of Galloway reactivated Somerled's antagonism to the king, or else he had time to tackle the mainland now that the situation in Man had stabilised. His subsequent invasion of Scotland in 1164 may have followed news of Malcolm's deteriorating health – the young king had been seriously ill in 1163 and was to die aged twenty-four in 1165. (Given the nickname 'Canmore', 'Big Head', which may originally have referred to him rather than to Malcolm III, he may have had Bright's disease.) Somerled may have aimed at the throne for his MacHeth protégés, as seventeenth-century historian George Buchanan reckoned, and the chronicle of Fordun has it that the greedy Scots nobles encouraged King Malcolm to confront Somerled in the hopes of obtaining his confiscated lands. But this is far from certain. A long-running dispute with the king's new Renfrewshire 'strongmen', the Stewarts – a branch of the Anglo-Norman family of Fitzalan from Shropshire installed by King David as hereditary 'High Stewards' of Scotland – over the ownership of Bute is more likely as an immediate cause. Indeed, the installation of the Stewarts in Renfrew (and Strathgryffe) as Anglo-Norman neighbours of Somerled was part of the same process of 'hemming in' the fearsomely-well-resourced 'Gaelic' lords as that carried out by David and Malcolm IV against Fergus of Galloway by installing the ancestors of Robert Bruce (the Norman family of De Brus) in Annandale. Other new lords in the region included the De Morevilles in Cunningham, facing onto the lower Firth of Clyde. The Stewarts, as lords of the nearest section of the Clyde coast opposite the Firth of Clyde islands, were probably intended by the king to try to wrest control of these from the 'Lord of the Isles'.

Both the hostile Glaswegian *Carmen de Morte Sumerledi* and the chronicles say that Somerled took a huge fleet of 160 ships (some from as far afield as Dublin, i.e. Scandinavian mercenaries) up the Clyde to invade Renfrew, the centre of the Stewart estates. The sources differ as to whether the landing took place near Renfrew or Greenock, but the lower Clyde was evidently the target. Killing, looting and burning followed, causing the people of nearby Glasgow to flee, until Somerled was killed at or near Renfrew – possibly at 'the Knock' between Renfrew and Paisley, where the traveller Thomas Pennant was shown a memorial stone at the site in 1772. The violent death of Somerled halted the attack, and was ascribed by Glasgow church traditions to the intervention of the local saint, their founding bishop Kentigern (late sixth century). One version of the killing, recorded by MacDonald historians in the seventeenth century, had it that he was murdered by Scots envoys sent by King Malcolm – Somerled's nephew Malcolm MacNeill – during a parley in his camp by the Clyde. But the contemporary Irish sources, e.g. the *Annals of Tigernach*, and the Glaswegian *Carmen de Morte Sumerledi* say that he was killed in battle, probably against Walter Fitz Alan (Stewart)'s royal army – possibly stabbed in the leg and then beheaded. One of his sons (Gillebride) was also killed in the clash, which nationalist historians claimed as a 'Celtic' attack on the 'Anglicised' Scots monarchy. Somerled's demoralised sons then embarked their men and returned home; the contemporary sources have Somerled being buried on Iona but later ones prefer his or his son's abbey of Saddell on Kintyre. In any event Somerled was the dominant and inspiring figure of his era in the Hebrides and changed its political orientation, creating a new polity where Ketil 'Flatnose' and others had failed.

The descendants of Somerled

Godred regained Man in 1164 (and lived until 1187), but the rest of Somerled's kingdom was divided among his sons – Dugald of Lorne, Ragnald of Kintyre and Angus of Islay, the two former of whom were ancestors of the pre-eminent Hebridean lines of 'MacDougall' and 'MacDonald' (called after Ragnald's son). The title of 'Lord of the Isles' was shared at first by Ragnald, the most powerful of Somerled's sons due to his inheritance of the family's fleet, and Dugald, and thence passed down their descendants; a charter described Ragnald as 'king of the Isles and lord of Argyll and Kintyre'. An apocryphal family legend ascribed Ragnald's nickname 'of the red (i.e. bloody) hand' to his having won a swimming race among the brothers off the island of Kerrera, ordered by their father – the victor to have seniority – by cutting off his hand and throwing it ashore to touch the land first. (The use of the 'Red Hand' symbol by the MacDonalds more likely came from their Ulster descent, this being the heraldic symbol of Ulster.) It is not even clear who was the elder brother, and thus genealogically senior, but it was probably Dugald ('dubh-gall', 'dark stranger') who succeeded his father as 'ri Airer Goidel' (king of Argyll) and ruler of the Gall-Gaedhil. The *Orkneyinga saga* names the brothers, probably in order of age as this is the usual tradition, as Dugald, Ragnald and Angus. As the main local vassal ruler of the King of Scots, Dugald accompanied King William to York to do homage to Henry II of England in 1175.

Ragnald, however, was politically and militarily more powerful in the Hebrides, and he was the son who organised the re-foundation of St Columba's monastery on Iona – the spiritual centre of the Hebrides – as its main patron. The restoration of the abbey marked the re-emergence of a (Gaelic not Anglo-Norman) realm of the Hebrides to match that of Dalriada in Columba's time and was a highly significant act; the adjoining new Augustinian nunnery had Ranald's sister Bethoc/Beatrice as its first abbess. Not much is known of later twelfth-century Hebridean history, but it is apparent that Ragnald and Angus fought a battle in 1192, the result probably in Angus' favour according to one source.

But this was evidently not decisive; nor was the dispute between Dugald and Ragnald over Skye recorded in MacDonald tradition. Either the brothers had the sense and family solidarity to avoid pressing disputes to extremities – heavy losses in an internecine battle would only benefit outside predators – or their resources were too evenly matched. No one brother was able to continue Somerled's united realm, or to annex Man and so obtain added military resources. The multiplicity of Somerled's sons was poetically called the ruin of their kingdom, at least in the long term. Ragnald, the most forceful of the brothers and called the most generous and militarily successful by the 'Book of Clanranald', took over Dugald's main islands (Mull and Tiree) after his death while Dugald's family retained mainland Lorne and the lordship of Argyll. Ragnald ruled as 'ri Innse Gall' (king of the Gaelic Isles, i.e. Hebrides) and died around 1210, according to family tradition having been on pilgrimage to Jerusalem earlier. The 'Book of Clanranald' dates his death at 1207, but this is disputed as it got the date of Somerled's death (1180 not the actual 1164) wrong. The _Annals of Ulster_ refer to a dispute between Ragnald's sons and the people of Skye in 1209–10 but do not mention him so he was probably dead – or possibly retired to a monastery, as he was a member of the 'confraternity' of Paisley Abbey – by then.

Donald, son of Somerled's son Ragnald, had to cede Garmoran to his younger brother Ruadhri, and centred his realm on Islay and the southern Hebrides. This probably followed the death of Ragnald's brother Angus, whom the _Annals of Ulster_ say was killed with his sons in an obscure war against the Norsemen of Skye in 1210. Dynastic tradition has it that the main clan ruling on Skye, the MacLeods of Dunvegan, were descended from Leod or Liot, a son of the Norse Manx king Olaf 'the Black' (d. 1230). This is now seen as unlikely (see chapter 7), but the DNA of most Skye residents confirms their Norse orientation, as does their use of names. Skye was thus politically orientated more towards its trading 'contacts' along the sea lanes, Man and Orkney, than to the mainland; the struggle between the two foci of its loyalties would continue for centuries. When Angus was killed, his nephew Donald inherited the lands centred on Islay from him or else now took them by force – the Irish records have the sons of Ragnald fighting the men of Skye (to avenge Angus?) in 1210. From this time the family's lands were split into three principalities. Ruadhri notably joined Alan of Galloway's brother Thomas in a plundering raid on Derry in Ireland in 1214, suggesting that he was seeking to build up a reputation as a source of loot and military success to attract warriors to his allegiance. He may well be the elusive 'Roderick' cited in the Scots chronicles as aiding the rebellious Gillescop MacWiliam, a turbulent warlord from the far north of Scotland, in attacking Northern Scotland (Caithness or Sutherland?) in 1223. More seriously, this 'Roderick' aided the MacWilliams in another invasion that the *Lanercost Chronicle* (Cumbria) believed was aimed at taking the kingdom of Scots, but which was defeated. These MacWilliams may have been the family of the 1187 rebel Donald MacWilliam, who was possibly the son of King David's nephew William FitzDuncan (the grandson of Malcolm III and Ingibiorg of Orkney), but this is uncertain. Given that the MacWilliams had joined Kenneth MacHeth in a previous revolt on King Alexander II's accession (1215), this may represent Ruadhri taking on the cause of the MacHeths that his grandfather Somerled had supported – but this was the last time such a revolt was to threaten the kings of Scots.

Donald MacRagnald either shared the Inner Hebridean lordship with or was partially dispossessed by his ambitious cousins Duncan and Dugald MacDugald (MacDougall) of Lorne. Donald was regarded as the founder of the line of 'MacDonalds', lords of the Inner Hebridean islands/Lochaber section of the dynasty, but no evidence of him exists beyond his name in the genealogies. His mother was supposed by the seventeenth-century clan historian Hugh MacDonald of Sleat to be related to the earls of Moray – not through the suggested Bruce dynasty ally Earl Thomas (d. 1333) as this is wrongly dated, but possibly through the twelfth-century MacHeths, relatives of Earl Angus (k. 1130) or the later De Moravia clan. According to the 'official' delineation of spheres of sovereignty between kings Edgar of Scotland and Magnus 'Bareleg' of Norway in 1098, all the Hebridean Sea islands were Norway's; thus the MacDonalds were Norwegian vassals, though this was only sporadically enforced. Occasionally, as in 1098 and 1161, a Norwegian King would 'show the flag' with a personal naval expedition to the Hebrides and the ruling dynasts would be expected to come to do homage; at other times he sent his commanders there, as in 1210. The MacDugalds, based on mainland Lorne and founded by Dugald MacSomerled, were Scots subjects – but Norse ones too if and when they had control over islands. Their principal castle, Dunstaffnage in Lorne, was founded by Dugald's son and successor, Donnchadh/Duncan, who was old enough to accompany his father on pilgrimage to the shrine of St Cuthbert at Durham in 1175 so he may have been born around 1160/65. His date of accession is unknown, but was probably early thirteenth century. He was recognised as king of Argyll by Alexander II of Scots in 1221–22 after a first Scots royal expedition to Argyll, and first appears as 'de Argadia' (i.e. 'of Argyll') in a Lennox charter of 1225. He also founded Ardchattan Priory, for the 'up-to-date' new religious order of the Valliscaulians. He died around

1244–48; he last appears as a witness in a letter of Alexander II to the Pope in 1244 and may be the 'Mac Somhairle', 'king of the Isles', killed at Ballyshannon in Ireland in 1247 but this is disputed on account of his age. The degree of the MacDugalds' cultural and political orientation towards mainland Scots, as opposed to island 'Norse', is unclear, but was logically greater than that of their island cousins (whose realm became centred on Islay). Duncan and Dugald's undisciplined piratical ravages of their neighbours' lands led to protests to the local overlord, Haakon IV of Norway (reigned 1217–63), and his intervention on behalf of their relative Gillespie (Uspak) Osmundssen in 1230. The latter – possibly a brother of Donnchadh/Duncan MacDugald, as said by the Norse saga of King Haakon – was promised the rule of the Isle of Man too by King Haakon, according to the Manx and Norse sources. He may have been intended as supreme Norwegian sub-king in the region, as the overlord of the MacDugalds and MacDonalds; as with Orkney, Norway was seeking to reassert its early twelfth-century rights. But this was difficult without a permanent patrolling fleet; Gillespie/ Uspak's Norse fleet secured control of Skye for him in 1230, but he was soon killed (probably in a siege on Bute).

The 'kingship of the Isles', shared between the feuding princes of the Somerled clan without Norway recognising any ruler as legitimate, was finally settled by King Haakon of Norway in 1249 on Ewen/Eoghan MacDougall (son of Duncan MacDugald, above) of the Lorne line. His visit to Norway to gain the title in 1248, plus his claim to Man, had aroused the fears of King Alexander II of Scots, who objected to a leading Scots royal vassal doing homage to his rival for control of the Hebrides. Ewen's MacDugalds, unlike the other branches of Somerled's line, were based on the mainland (in Argyll) – so was Ewen meant by Norway to be their vassal for mainland territories too, not just for the islands? Ewen was probably given Norwegian permission to take over various castles in Mull and Lochaber, including Cairnburgh off the west coast of Mull, in the power vacuum following the drowning of King Haakon's local viceroy, Jarl Harald of Orkney, in 1248. But King Alexander summoned him to a meeting – Ewen insisted on four Scottish earls serving as sureties for his safe conduct so he would not be arrested there – and demanded that he abandon his homage to Haakon and do it to him instead. Ewen refused and insisted that he could perfectly well serve two masters at once. The Scots king proposed to invade the Hebrides and bring him back under control and sailed a large fleet into the Sound of Mull – the first recorded royal intervention there. But he died in July 1249 at the island of Kerrera before he could sail with his fleet to attack Ewen's lands, and the officers of his underage heir

Alexander III returned home, leaving Ewen unmolested. In 1250 Ewen attempted to secure Man with an invasion, apparently linked to local opponents of the current usurper King Harald, and a claim that he was 'king of the Isles' (i.e. Man) too. But he was driven out after a battle at Ronaldsway and had to give up (see chapter 5). He may well have married his daughter to Magnus, the last native king of Man (d. 1265), with political ambitions in Man in mind; his grandson's failure to regain Man, having been defeated by King Alexander III in 1275, may thus have been a blow to the MacDougalls. Notably, his exiled MacDougall descendants were to try to seize Man in 1316–17 as English allies – due to a hereditary claim?

As with Orkney, there were problems with Norwegian claims to overlordship of the various Hebridean territories held by Somerled's family. Trying to balance between two masters, Ewen found it easier to defy young Alexander III's weak regency government in Scotland after 1249 and to keep in with the aggressive Haakon of Norway instead. Refused pardon by the Scots government for his defiance in 1249, he spent a few years in the early 1250s as a naval mercenary captain in Norway and on his return home in 1255 was able to go to the Scots court to make his peace and receive ratification of his mainland territories in return for homage. Haakon IV re-enforced his rule with his huge fleet in 1263 and most of the local lords, led by Donald's son Angus 'Mór' MacDonald, submitted. The first of the family to do so was Dugald MacRuadhri of Garmoran, who joined King Magnus of Man to meet Haakon as he arrived on Skye from Orkney and was chosen to lead the fleet's detachment to attack Kintyre ahead of the king's arrival there. Angus 'Mór' submitted next, on Islay, as Haakon moved south, and received his lands back on the same terms as he had held them from Scotland to date. Ewen MacDugald/MacDougall evaded doing homage when he came to meet Haakon at Kerrera, according to the chronicles to avoid another breach with the Scots by contradicting his previous oath to their king. He was promptly arrested by Haakon, but at least he had avoided battle with Haakon's much larger army. Luckily for him the Norwegians moved on southwards in September round the Mull of Kintyre rather than attacking his lands. Probably the MacDonalds sent troops to aid Haakon's subsequent attack on the Scots kingdom via the Firth of Clyde, and the Norwegian saga of King Haakon alleges that Dugald MacRuadhri led an incursion up Loch Long to raid the Stewarts' Lennox lands.

The Norwegian expedition up the Clyde led to a drawn battle at Largs on 1–2 October 1263, although in reality this was not a deliberate invasion but a successful Norwegian landing to recover ships blown across the Firth from their nearby position on Great Cumbrae by a westerly gale. The series of muddled skirmishes on Largs beach led to heavy casualties but no decisive outcome, and Haakon chose to sail back to the Inner Hebrides rather than invade so the Scots had at least deterred him. He retreated via Kerrera, where he and the now released Ewan MacDougall exchanged messages but Ewan still did not come to do homage, and then Skye (where Kyleakin was named after Haakon; 'the Narrows/Kyle of Haakon') to Orkney. Norwegian power lapsed after his death at Kirkwall in December 1263, and Haakon's infuriated grant of the untrustworthy Ewan's lands to Dugald MacRuadhri of Garmoran was never implemented. Instead, Dugald stayed loyal to the Norwegian cause as long as practicable, and in 1264 Norwegian sources record him as driving the Scots king's men out of Caithness. That year also saw an attack on the Hebridean mainland by the Scots king's ex-regent and senior general Alan Durward to punish those chiefs who had defected to Haakon in 1263, possibly including the MacRuadhris. Dugald died in 1268, the Irish annalists referring to him as 'king of the Isles and Argyll' (i.e. recognising Haakon's grant of the latter to him); his son Eric fought for the Norwegians in 1264 too but his younger brother Alan was to serve the Scots king in his invasion of Man in 1275. (The MacDougalls, as seen above, were marital allies of the native dynasts on Man whom Alexander had replaced.) Ewen meanwhile transferred his allegiance to Alexander III of Scotland as the Scottish–Norwegian treaty of Perth (2 July 1266) saw King Magnus IV, Haakon's son, hand over his claim to the area to Alexander. He also married his son John to a Scots noble lady from the Comyn dynasty and remarried his daughter Mary, previously wife of King Magnus of Man, to the Earl of Strathearn.

The former Norwegian vassals were promised immunity for all previous acts hostile to the Scots kingdom, but the eldest son of Angus 'Mór', Alexander, was among MacDonald hostages deported to the Scots court by Alexander III in 1264/65 to ensure the dynasty's good behaviour. Alexander duly succeeded his father as head of the MacDonald dynasty in 1294–95, but died young in 1299 – according to the Irish *Annals of Ulster*, killed in battle by his kinsman and rival Alexander MacDougall. He was succeeded by his younger brother Angus 'Og'. His main fame in Highland history lay as patron and ally of his nephew Angus, sixth chief of the then minor Mackintosh clan, who in 1291 married the heiress of the sixth chief of Clan Chattan. By this marriage the Mackintoshes from Angus onwards were to claim the headship of the Clan Chattan confederation, and Angus and his bride took over Tor Castle near Loch Arkaig as their home. But after Alexander died his brother Angus 'Og' MacDonald took against the Mackintoshes, possibly during the Wars of Scottish Independence as MacDougall/Comyn allies, and sometime around 1310 called in the Camerons to expel them (to Rothiemurchus) and take over the Loch Arkaig region as his allies. The younger brother of Alexander and Angus 'Og', Ian/John 'Sprangach', was the founder of the line of 'MacIains' of Ardnamurchan, and seems to have been at odds with Angus in the 1300s as he was an English ally. He may have received Ardnamurchan from King John Balliol or Edward I of England as a local loyalist, but if so negotiated his pardon by Robert Bruce after 1307. He held onto his lands and died in 1340; his grandson traditionally led the clan levies for his kinsman Donald, 'Lord of the Isles', at the Battle of Harlaw in 1411.

4

Under Scots Overlordship: MacDonald *versus* Stewart 1329–c. 1600

(i) The wars of independence and the realignment of the Highland political system: from a network of great lords to a multiplicity of clan chiefs and one MacDonald lordship

The realignment to Scots vassalage was disputed by Ewen MacDugald's pro-Norwegian cousin Dugald MacRuadhri of Garmoran (grandson of Ragnald MacSomerled), a piratical plunderer, until he died in 1268. While Ewen's family held the mainland territories, Alexander III recognised Angus 'Mór' (the Great') of the MacDonald line, son of Donald MacRagnald, as ruler of the islands. The death of Alexander in March 1286, the vacancy in the Scots kingship when his granddaughter Margaret of Norway died at Kirkwall on Orkney in 1290 and the choice of Galloway lord John Balliol by Edward I as the new king in 1292 brought his MacDougall allies into the English camp in the national Scots crisis. By contrast, Angus MacDonald and his son Alexander joined the September 1286 'Turnberry Band' of magnate allies of the rival Bruce claimant to the Scots throne, Robert Bruce ('the Competitor'), lord of Annandale. This meeting was possibly as much to do with an imminent expedition to Ireland as with the Scottish throne, but it showed which nobles were natural Bruce allies. Their presence at the Turnberry 'summit' and the oath of the Bruce faction's leading members would have seen them meet Bruce's grandson, the future (1306) King Robert, whom their family was to back; traditionally Angus had married into the Argyll family of the Campbell chief 'Mac Cailean Mór' ('Son of Great Colin'), another leading Bruce ally in the

coming wars. Angus himself refused to do homage to Balliol as king in
1292–93 and died in 1294–95, and when Edward invaded Scotland and
deposed John Balliol in 1296 the MacDougalls under Ewen's son John
rallied to the rebel cause in Balliol's name. But the sons of Angus 'Mór',
Alexander (killed by the MacDougalls in 1299) and Angus 'Og' (head
of the family at the time of the Bruce/English wars after 1306), were
initially allies of Edward I after 1296, Alexander asking him for military
help against MacDougall attacks, and both accepted local offices from
him to govern the Inner Hebrides. In 1301 Angus was asking his lord
Edward I for permission to attack Alexander MacDougall, who had not
yet recognised the English king as his lord (probably out of loyalty to
the Balliol–Comyn alliance). Edward's local official Hugh Bisset wrote
that Angus had been fighting the MacDougalls – i.e. on Edward's behalf
– in Bute and Kintyre. Probably as a reply to this MacDonald naval
assault, Alexander MacDougall and his sons John and Duncan received
permission from Edward I in June 1301 to make their submission to his
representative, the admiral of the 'Cinque Ports' in south-east England
(implying that the latter had brought his ships up to the Hebrides to form
part of Edward's largely hired navy of privately owned ships). Evidently
the MacDonalds had the naval edge over the MacDougalls, probably
due to their ownership of the main islands and their skilled sailors. In
September 1305 Alexander was to be appointed to the advisory council
of Edward's lieutenant in Scotland, John of Brittany, and in 1304 he was
excused attendance at Parliament in St Andrews due to illness.

The collapse of the Balliol cause in the late 1290s forced the two
rival lines of the isles to make a choice between the causes of Bruce
and Comyn as the next heir to the national cause, while recognising
the military might of Edward I and doing homage to him for the
moment. The MacDougalls backed their kinsman Comyn; Alexander
MacDougall, fourth lord of Lorne, was married to the daughter of
John 'the Black' Comyn (d. *c.* 1300), lord of Badenoch, the sister of
Robert Bruce's arch-rival John 'the Red' Comyn (assassinated February
1306). The two rivals, the younger Bruce and the younger Comyn,
cooperated uneasily as joint 'Guardians' of Scotland after the rebellion
led by William Wallace and Sir Andrew Moray (unusually for the era,
not noblemen) raised the possibility of expelling the English in 1297,
but the exiled and ageing John Balliol refused to return home as the
royal leader. The MacDougalls thus ended up on the side of the Comyns
when relations between Bruce and Comyn soon broke down and their
guardianship lapsed; but by 1301 King Edward was in control of most
of lowland Scotland and the two rivals, plus Comyn's ally Alexander
MacDougall, accepted Edward as their king. The MacDonalds, their

isolated island and mountainous lands safer from English attack, stood aloof from the anti-Edward plots at first, but in 1306 Angus 'Og' backed the younger Bruce, who rose in revolt against Edward that year. Bruce famously confronted and murdered Comyn in the Greyfriars church at Dumfries, after which there was no going back as he was now not only a 'murderous rebel' to Edward but likely to be excommunicated by the Church too. Bruce now had himself crowned King of Scots at Scone – possibly earlier than he had intended and spurred on to revolt by his treacherous 'ally' Comyn threatening to tell Edward of his plans. But English loyalists closed in on his small army at Perth and defeated them at Methven in June, and he was forced to flee west into the Highlands, where the MacDougalls sent their army east from Lorne to trap him. The (1370s) epic poem *The Bruce*, by John Barbour, recorded its hero as seeking sanctuary in Angus Og's Kintyre lands in September 1306, after he lost the Battle of Dalry in Strathfillan to the MacDougalls and their allies (probably led by Alexander's son John MacDougall) and was chased across Argyll into hiding. Bruce sent his womenfolk to safety in Ross at the remote shrine at Tain but the local Earl Uilliam, a Comyn ally, handed them over to Edward.

The assassination of the Comyn claimant to Scotland, John 'the Red', by Bruce at Dumfries in February 1306 put the latter at feud with the MacDougalls, who no doubt hoped by their eager aid to Edward I in hunting him down to gain English backing for their rule of Argyll. Bruce was apparently besieged at the castle of Dunaverty by the English – on 25 September Edward I wrote to the English commander of the siege complaining that he had heard that the refractory locals were not sending them supplies. Thence Bruce escaped to the island of Rathlin off the Ulster coast (scene of the alleged encounter with the spider), according to *The Bruce*, and thence the Outer Hebrides or Ulster. Logically Angus 'Og' was his protector at this point, and probably also loaned him the ships that took him back to his earldom of Carrick early in 1307 to resume the war. It was a MacDonald fleet, joined by the ships of their kinswoman Christina MacRuadhri of Garmoran, who escorted the small Bruce army up the Firth of Lorne to Loch Linnhe to invade the Great Glen region later in 1307; the MacDougalls dared not intervene. It would also have been the threat of attack from the MacDonalds that held the MacDougalls back from sending aid to the Comyns in Buchan in 1308 as Bruce ravaged their lands, defeated Earl John of Buchan at the Battle of Barra (May 1308), and forced the Comyns and their allies to flee to England. The notorious 'Harrying of Buchan' thus neutralised the pro-English lords in north-east Scotland. Once the Comyns were dealt with, Bruce returned to tackle the MacDougalls in Lorne.

After Robert Bruce defeated the MacDougalls for backing his Comyn rivals at the Battle of the Pass of Brander in August 1308(?), sending his men under Sir James Douglas up the mountainside to attack would-be ambushers from above, he dispossessed them of Lorne. The campaign was dated to the week after the 'Feast of the Assumption of the Virgin' (i.e. 15 August 1308) by John of Fordoun and Walter Bower (fifteenth century). The exact sequence of events is unclear; the Battle at the Pass of Brander was certainly in 1308 not 1309, and family 'head' Alexander MacDougall apparently surrendered or was captured despite the claim of John of Fordoun that he fled directly by sea to England. Barbour, a slightly earlier writer, says Alexander submitted, and he was definitely at the St Andrews parliament unmolested in March 1309, so it was probably his son John who fled to seek English help – a letter of his in this vein dated 1308 is extant. King Robert besieged their Dunstaffnage Castle in autumn 1309; the fortress fell and the family were dispossessed. Alexander's son John fled to England and ended up as a mercenary naval commander, becoming admiral to Edward II to command in the Irish Sea in 1311 and dying in 1317, and King Robert granted the lordship and lands (minus Argyll) to his ally Angus 'Og' MacDonald, younger son of Angus 'Mór'. They passed down his family, with his son John claiming to be 'Lord of the Isles' from 1336. Angus 'Og' duly commanded one of the Scots battalions at Bannockburn in June 1314, and remained a loyal Bruce ally. He was granted the ownership of Lochaber, Morvern, Ardnamurchan and (in Argyll) Duror and Glencoe, in charters by King Robert.

The triumphant progress of King Robert in the Hebrides in 1315, commemorated by his ceremonial 'voyage' in an oared galley across the isthmus of Kintyre between East and West Loch Tarbert (recorded in Barbour's *The Bruce*), confirmed and cemented the Bruce–MacDonald alliance. Angus 'Og' or his elder son Alexander (granted Mull and Tiree by King Robert) appears to have joined the Bruce expedition to conquer Ireland for King Robert's brother Edward Bruce around 1318. Like the MacDonalds, the Bruces could claim 'High Kingly' blood – by distant descent from the 1170s Anglo-Norman warlord Richard de Clare, 'Strongbow', Earl of Pembroke, and his Leinster bride. One Alexander MacDonald, 'ri Airer Goidel' ('king of Argyll'), died in battle at Dundalk in Ireland in 1318 according to the Irish *Annals of Innisfallen*; this is presumably Angus Og's eldest son, who did not succeed his father (or did so only briefly). MacDonald manpower was vital to the Bruce cause, and Bruce had distant Irish ancestry via his Anglo-Norman ancestors, which enabled his brother Edward to pose as the new 'King of Ireland' in a Scots–Irish Gaelic alliance in 1315–19. Unfortunately the invading

Bruce army proved as ruinous to the inhabitants of the land they crossed as the English and Anglo-Irish lords' armies, the bad weather caused famine several years running, and Edward Bruce's defeat and death was generally welcomed in Ireland as bringing peace. Angus' younger son John MacDonald, who succeeded his father sometime around 1320 (or his brother Alexander in 1318?), married secondly the daughter of King Robert II (Stewart), Bruce's grandson who succeeded to the throne when King David II died childless in 1371. John secured the majority of the Hebrides by royal grants – the first from usurper Edward Balliol (ex-king John's son), who was briefly reigning as an English nominee in 1333–41, as his terms for recognising Balliol as king in 1336. This recognised his rule of Islay, Kintyre, Knapdale, Mull, Skye, Lewis, Ardnamurchan and other lands, with the 'ward' of Lochaber. After Edward was driven out by the Bruces' armies, John made another treaty with his restored rival David II Bruce at Ayr in June 1343, which recognised his rule of the southern Inner Hebrides and also of Lochaber, Duror and Glencoe (i.e. part of Argyll) but not of Skye or Lewis, which David's brother-in-law and ally Earl William of Sutherland also claimed. Nor was John supported over his claims to Kintyre, then held by Robert Stewart, or to Knapdale, which the Stewart's kinsman Sir John Menteith had seized. John's (first) wife Amy's brother, Ranald MacRuadhri of Garmoran and Arisaig/Knoydart, who actually held Skye, was also present and had his mainland territories plus Uist, Rhum, Barra and Eigg guaranteed. John soon gained Garmoran, by his first marriage to its heiress, Amy MacRuadhri, shortly after her brother Ranald MacRuadhri, lord of Skye, was assassinated at Elcho nunnery near Perth by his enemy William, Earl of Ross, in October 1346. He assisted his rival Robert Stewart (later King Robert II) in governing northern Scotland after King David was captured by the English at the Battle of Neville's Cross in 1346, and improved relations between them despite the Kintyre dispute were to lead to his second marriage, to Robert's daughter.

The complex nature of the northern and western Highlands elite – some 'outsider' Anglo-Norman barons from further south married into old Gaelic/Scandinavian families, some still ancestral lords – was further complicated by the struggles of Bruce and Balliol for the crown after Robert Bruce died in 1329, leaving a five-year-old son, David. John MacDonald was not the only local great lord whose family had benefited from backing the Bruces in 1308–14 but who realistically abandoned his young son's cause as (temporarily) hopeless when Edward III's army helped Edward Balliol to destroy the Bruce army at Halidon Hill and take the throne in 1333. With the weight of military manpower on Balliol's side, resisting only invited the destructive attentions of the English army – which marched as far as Moray on several occasions – and their Scots allies, the 'Disinherited' whom Robert Bruce had expelled as Comyn or English partisans and who now returned to their confiscated lands as Edward Balliol's nominees. John was in a better position than most Highland lords as his lands were too remote for an easy English attack, and after a prolonged guerrilla war in central and southern Scotland saw Balliol expelled and David restored with French help in 1341 he returned – at his own pace so as not to seem too accommodating? – to the Bruces' side. The preoccupation of Edward III with his war in France from 1337 in effect ended Balliol's hopes and solved the question of who was to rule Scotland. But now the childlessness of David and his English wife Joan raised the question of the succession again, albeit less urgently, and David's only full sister, Margaret Bruce, was married off around 1343 to John MacDonald's powerful neighbour, William 'de Moravia', fourth Earl of Sutherland. (William's mother, Mary or Marjorie, who secondly married Kenneth, third Earl of Sutherland, was the daughter of Earl Domnhall of Mar and sister of Robert Bruce's first wife, Isabel of Mar.) This raised the possibility of their son John (1346–61) as the next King of Scots until he died young; the alternative was the son of David's half-sister Marjorie Bruce (d. 1316), Robert Stewart, hereditary 'High Steward' and head of the Stewart family ruling Lennox. The Stewarts also owned the Firth of Clyde islands of Bute and Arran and, as seen above, had been clashing over them with the MacDonalds' ancestor Somerled as far back as the 1160s. David II seems to have resisted his nephew's succession as late as the 1360s and married a second time (and possibly planned a third marriage too when that failed) in an effort to provide an alternative heir after John Sutherland died, and Robert Stewart was in and out of the king's prisons for rebellion in the 1360s. In addition, he was eight years older than David II and the latter's sudden death at the age of forty-seven in 1371 was unexpected. Nor were Robert's sons by his first, probably 'common-law' marriage to Elizabeth Mure of Rowallan (including the future King Robert III) seen as fully legitimate so his succession could cause a civil war with his sons by his second marriage in future. Accordingly John MacDonald kept his options open as to who to back as the next King of Scots, though Robert Stewart's second marriage in 1355, to Euphemia of Ross, daughter of his neighbour and ally Earl Hugh of Ross (and widow of the Earl of Moray, Robert I's great-nephew John Randolph), brought him closer local connections. The Ross marriage also gave Robert a claim via his wife's first marriage on lands in Moray, bringing this Lowland magnate into central Highland politics – it was probably this link that gave Robert the lordship of Badenoch, which he assumed around 1360 and which he was to pass on to his third son, Alexander.

This was an era of major structural change in the Highland lordships, with many of the old families (especially the MacDougalls of Lorne and Comyns of Buchan) destroyed in the civil wars and English invasions and 'new men' awarded the lordships. The fall of the Comyns was an especial bonus, as their large family had held both Buchan and Badenoch and lands in Galloway too and had matched the MacDonalds in manpower. In their place Robert Bruce had installed his own men in 1307–14, mostly either non-locals with smaller resources of manpower or men caught up in politics and war in the south and so unable to devote all their energies to their Highland lordships. Thus the evicted pro-Comyn Strathbogie family, earls of Atholl, were replaced as the main landholders in Atholl by the Campbells – Bruce's close companion Neil 'Mac Cailean Mór' ('son of Great Colin') and after him his son John, who acquired the earldom of Atholl, but this dynasty was cut short when John fell in battle for David Bruce at Halidon Hill in 1333. Neil also gained the lordship of Loch Awe in Argyll from King Robert in 1308, and this remained in his family (unlike Atholl) and was to be the centre of Campbell power for many centuries – but as of the fourteenth century the Campbell lordship was still small and no threat to the lordship of the Isles. The crucial earldom of Moray went to King Robert's own nephew Thomas Randolph, who had been captured by the English in Robert's defeat in 1306 and had taken service with Edward I but defected back to his uncle after being captured fighting for the MacDougalls at the Battle of the Pass of Brander in 1308. (He allegedly then taunted his uncle for fighting a 'cowardly' guerrilla war rather than a chivalrous one of open battles, but this did not do him any harm long-term.) He then commanded one of the divisions at the Battle of Bannockburn, and was one of King Robert's main commanders as well as the second person to sign the Declaration of Arbroath affirming Scotland's right to independence. He was both the main Bruce lieutenant in the Highlands and a major player at court and the ongoing war with England (to 1328), taking on embassies to the Pope and to France, and the nation's needs took priority over his local role. Indeed, when the king died in 1329, leaving a five-year-old son (David II), Thomas Randolph assumed the regency of Scotland, only to die suddenly (probably only in his forties) in July 1332 precipitating the invasion by the 'Disinherited' (see below) on behalf of the Balliol cause. His elder son and successor Thomas Randolph, second Earl of Moray, was killed rashly leading a frontal charge on the Balliol/'Disinherited'/English invaders at Dupplin Moor near Perth a month later. His younger brother Earl John

succeeded, and was distracted from Highland affairs by the long war
with the Balliol/English invaders in 1333–41, in which he served as
'Lieutenant of Scotland' for the absent David II with Robert Stewart in
1335, and was later captured and deported to England until 1341. He
was killed fighting for David against the English at the Battle of Neville's
Cross in 1346, leaving no heirs; both Atholl and Moray thus lost their
new, Bruce-era dynasties in the mid-fourteenth century. This vacuum
aided the emergence of the MacDonalds in the west Highlands – and
the devolution of leadership in the central Highlands to 'lower-level'
local lords rather than the pre-fourteenth-century system of great earls.
Arguably much of the 'clan' system's success in the fourteenth century
and fifteenth century was due to the politico-military rifts among the
Scots elite between 1290 and 1341.

Some of the older earldoms of the Highland region survived under
the original dynasties, including the earls of Sutherland – known by the
Anglo-Norman name 'De Moravia', i.e. 'of Moray', but probably Gaelic
in descent. The earldom (originally 'mormaership') of Ross also had
local, Gaelic-descended holders – firstly the MacHeths (or MacAeds,
that is 'Sons of Hugh/Aed'), possibly descended from the royal house
of Moray in the tenth century and probably from King Macbeth's
stepson Lulach (r. 1057–58). Their representative Malcolm MacHeth
had claimed the crown of Scotland in a revolt against King David with
his brother or other relative, Earl Angus of Moray (Lulach's grandson),
in 1130; they may have been the sons of 'Mormaer' Maeslnechtai of
Moray, Lulach's son, who had revolted against King Malcolm III in
1078 and been driven out of Moray. As early as 1078 it seems that the
line of Moray had been in revolt against Malcolm III and his family
on dynastic grounds, and they evidently had some hereditary right to
the crown – possibly from King Aed 'Wingfoot' of Scots (d. 878), son
of Kenneth MacAlpin, if he was the eponymous ancestor 'Aed', and
certainly from Lulach's mother Gruoch's grandfather Kenneth III (k.
1005). This encouraged the extant dynasty to remove the threat that
they posed in the twelfth century, leaving the lords of the Hebrides
with one less challenger to the rule of the north-west. The ninth- and
tenth-century Scots crown had indeed rotated among the descendants
of Kenneth MacAlpin (d. 858) until Malcolm III's time, so they could
appeal to ancient custom in rebelling. After their extinction or removal
from Ross, the 'new man' Lord Ferchar or Farquhar, known as 'Son
of the Priest' ('Mac an tSagairt') and possibly descended from the
hereditary abbots of Applecross as surmised by W. F. Skene in the
nineteenth century, ruled as Earl of Ross from the 1220s to his death
in 1251. He received that title from a grateful King Alexander II (r.

1214–49), who came as far north as Inverness in 1221, after defeating the invasion of Ross by Kenneth MacHeth in 1215. His son Earl Uilleam/William (d. 1274?) acted as Alexander III's main commander in challenging Norwegian rule of the Inner Hebrides by raiding the Skye region in 1262, thus sparking off Haakon of Norway's 1263 attack, and received Skye and Lewis from their new lord Alexander in 1266 (hence the rivalry with the MacDonalds over this region).

Uilleam married into the Comyn dynasty, and thus his son Uilleam/William (d. 1323) backed the Comyns against the Bruces and after his capture by the English at the Battle of Dunbar in 1296 was held hostage in London until his wife secured his release in 1303. Thereafter he fought for Edward I in the independence wars, clearly unwilling to arouse his wrath again. His capture and surrender to the English of Robert Bruce's wife, sisters and daughter Marjorie at the shrine of St Duthlac at Tain (of which he was hereditary keeper) as they took refuge from Edward there in 1306 put him at risk of being expelled by the vengeful Robert Bruce as the latter regained local control in 1308. Bruce's sisters were imprisoned in cages, his wife Elizabeth de Burgh (daughter of the Earl of Ulster, who luckily was Edward's close ally) and daughter Marjorie sent to castles/nunneries, and their escort, Bruce's brother Neil, executed, so the new King Robert had every reason to feel aggrieved at Earl Uilleam. However, he prudently surrendered to the new king on this campaign and secured pardon – the realist Robert could not take on Ross as well as the Comyns' Buchan in a campaign of burning and expulsions – and later fought for Robert at Bannockburn with his levies. His son Earl Hugh, a Bruce loyalist, was killed at Halidon Hill in 1333.

Thus both Sutherland and (for the moment) Ross survived under their original, Gaelic but Anglicised lords, who unlike the MacDonalds were often involved in court politics and warfare with England in the south. But other major Anglo-Norman dynasties ruling wide lordships in the north had become extinct or been exiled, most crucially the Comyns, whom Robert Bruce drove out in 1308–09, and some smaller Gaelic lords who had been their tenants re-emerged to play a crucial role as providers of their own tenants as well-armed and mobile mercenary troops, 'caterans', to their social superiors in the frequent internal Scots conflicts or foreign wars. This helped the emergence of what became known and organised as the 'clan system', with small, family-based lordships replacing the large pre-1300 Anglo-Norman peerage system created by David I and his brothers and grandsons. All the main sub-tenants of the lord, and probably other lesser ones, were the descendants of a common ancestor, with the most senior patrilineal line of the founder as the overall clan chief – and the lord had a duty to his tenants just as they had a duty to fight for and pay their dues to him. The smaller family-based 'clan' units were virtually autonomous in some areas where there was no major local landowner, and in others clustered round the latter – who was often of the same family lineage as some of the major new 'clan' chiefs – as their leader in war.

John MacDonald had a built-in advantage in his region, as both the only surviving great lord of ancient lineage in the Inner Hebrides (with his rival MacDougall kinsmen evicted) and the richest landed member of his dynasty, with his numerous sons by two marriages available to divide up the family inheritance and provide a number of allied lordships. Given the number of sons he had before his second marriage in 1350, he was probably adult and married (in his late teens) by around 1336/38, though the date of his accession is unclear. He had more men at his immediate call than most of his neighbours or the hard-pressed kings of Scots except in a major campaign, plus a fleet used to difficult waters in the Hebrides, so he could auction off his support to the rival Bruces and Balliols. In addition, the shaky state of usurper Edward Balliol's throne in 1333–41 meant that the new king could not afford the distraction of a Hebridean campaign despite the submission of most of the Scots nobility, led by David's nephew and heir Robert Stewart, at Perth in 1335 as Edward III led a large army across southern Scotland ravaging and burning.

The main threat to John MacDonald came from the 'Disinherited' Comyn lords; Edward Balliol had restored them to their confiscated Buchan/Mar lands and Edward III backed them up with impressive but ephemeral English expeditions in 1335–36. One of the two leaders of the 'Disinherited' in the north-east was the Englishman Henry de Beaumont, who was the husband of Alice, heiress of Buchan, daughter of Alexander Comyn (ex-sheriff of Aberdeen) and niece of Earl John Comyn of Buchan, whom Robert Bruce had evicted in 1308. The other leader was David of Strathbogie, claimant to Atholl as son of Earl David, whom Bruce had also evicted. David of Strathbogie's mother had been daughter to the 'Red Comyn' killed by Bruce in 1306, putting him at feud with the Bruces. Both men had gained military experience in England in service of its kings. These men were competent generals and capable of invading the Hebrides – Beaumont had fought for Edward I at Falkirk in 1298 and made mincemeat of the incompetently led Bruce army at Dupplin Moor – but never had the opportunity as they faced resistance from those still loyal to David Bruce. The latter, led by Sir Andrew Murray, eventually drove their enemies out; the Balliol cause in the Highlands was probably doomed once David of Strathbogie, lieutenant of Balliol's backer Edward III in the Highlands, fell in battle against Murray at

Culblean in November 1335. David II's lieutenant John Randolph, Earl of Moray, visited John MacDonald in June or July 1335 to attempt to secure his support, but John clearly thought his cause doomed and in September allied to Edward III and Balliol instead. He was recognised as lord of the Isles and Skye and warden of Lochaber, commencing the MacDonald/England alliance as a threat to the Scots kings which was to be revived in the 1460s and 1540s. Edward III marched as far as Lochindorb Castle in Moray in 1336 to rescue David's widow from a Bruce faction siege and sacked Aberdeen, but could not sustain his position and had to withdraw; he also recognised John MacDonald as well disposed in this year and ordered seized ships of his to be released and allowed to trade with English-held lands. By 1339 the 'Disinherited' had given up their claims to the north-eastern Highlands and fled south, where Edward III was too busy preparing for war with France to do more than attack 'rebel'-held Dunbar Castle (unsuccessfully).

The most obscure and youngest branch of the 'MacSorley' clan was that of the 'MacRuadhri' branch of Garmoran, founded by Ruari/ Ruadhri – the younger son of Somerled's son Ragnald. They never claimed to be 'lords of the Isles', but were in practice as autonomous as their senior cousins. Even their dates are unclear, with Ruadhri being succeeded by his son Dugald – who backed Norway rather than Scotland in the 1260s, as seen above – around 1240. Dugald (d. 1268) and his son Eric were followed in the late thirteenth century by the former's younger brother Alan (d. by 1296), who had two sons and a daughter. The latter, the famous Christina of Garmoran, married to Duncan the son of the Earl of Mar, was a unique example of a female ruler of a Hebridean maritime realm, a more peaceful equivalent of western Ireland's sixteenth-century Grace O'Malley. She lent valuable support to the refugee Robert Bruce (ex-husband of her husband Duncan of Mar's sister) as he hid from Edward I in the Hebrides in 1307–08 and thence launched his reconquest of the mainland, helping him to defeat her MacDougall cousins at the Pass of Brander and gain control of the Highlands. Her elusive half-brothers Lachlan and Ruadhri were piratical 'chancers' who were complained of for ravaging Skye and Lewis in 1297 and had no stable loyalties. Lachlan ended up fighting for his MacDougall kinsmen's relative Alexander Comyn in an attack on northern England in 1299 and then signing up for lands in England under Edward I, before returning to Scotland in Edward II's service; in 1308 the Earl of Ross gave him lands in the Isles at the king's request but complained that he was withholding their revenues from the earldom. Ruadhri also served the English temporarily, but ended up being killed at Dundalk fighting for Edward Bruce in 1318.

The dynasty ended with Christina's half-brother Ranald MacRuadhri, who secured his lands in the northern Hebrides by charter from Edward Balliol around 1334 and then from David II in 1343/44, probably at the meeting of David II and John MacDonald 'of the Isles' at Ayr. The fact that David accepted his rule of Garmoran apparently annoyed the Earl of Ross, who had a rival claim arising from Robert I's recognition of his lordship of the island of Skye and adjacent territories. He was killed as a result of this feud by the Earl of Ross at Elcho nunnery, Perth, in spring 1346, as he led his levies to join David's army for the invasion of England. Apparently David's senior adviser and general Sir William Douglas advised the king to call off the invasion and attack the murderous Ross instead, and much of the army was in sympathy, but David pressed on into England – to be defeated and captured by Edward III's troops at Neville's Cross. The MacRuadhri family's lands reverted (via his daughter Amy's marriage to 'Lord of the Isles' John, probably in the mid-to-late 1330s) to the senior line of MacDonalds of the Isles. Amy was a renowned local patron of the Church who built several churches in the Isles, and was also said to have extended the family seat at Castle Tioram, where she may have lived after John 'of the Isles' divorced her.

(ii) The MacDonalds and the Scots monarchy – Bruce and Stewart – after 1341

When David Bruce was restored to power in 1341, an inexperienced teenager nervous of imminent English attack from the south, he had other priorities too. Unlike southern barons, John MacDonald was relatively safe from eviction as a Balliol ally; he could negotiate recognition of the new king on relatively easy terms at Ayr in November 1341 and had his rule of disputed Kintyre (claimed by the Stewarts) and Skye (claimed by the earls of Ross) recognised. In 1342 he sent the king a gift of falcons, but at a second meeting at Ayr in June 1343 David excluded Kintyre and Skye from his grant to the MacDonalds to appease the Stewarts and Rosses. At this point, as ever since the time of Somerled in the 1150s–60s, the MacDonalds and Stewarts were on poor terms – this had implications with Robert Stewart as the childless David's heir. In 1347 Edward offered military support to John as he was fighting Robert over control of Kintyre. Following David's capture in battle invading England at Neville's Cross in Durham in 1346, complex negotiations took place for either his release or else Edward securing the Scots Parliament's recognition that Edward Balliol should be king either immediately or as the childless David's heir. When Edward finally gave up his hopes of this and agreed to ransom David, John MacDonald was one of the noble hostages sent to England on David's release in 1357 to guarantee that the money would be paid. But John's second marriage, to Marjorie Stewart, Robert Stewart's daughter, in July 1350 showed his settlement of the long-running rivalry with the Stewarts over control of the Clyde estuary islands and potential backing for Stewart as successor to Robert Stewart's nephew David II. His refusal to pay any part of David's ransom was enshrined in David's treaty with Edward III at Berwick in 1357 – probably as a result of John's good relations with Edward since 1335, as John was included in the general military truce between old rivals – but aroused David's hostility. If he was not paying anything for David's ransom like the rest of the realm's peers, was he claiming to be of a higher rank than them and even an autonomous dynast not a feudal subject of the Crown?

There was also the matter of David's use of John's hereditary foe and rival as lord of Lorne, John MacDougall 'the Foreigner' – the long-exiled son of Alexander MacDougall whom Robert I had driven out in 1309. A Balliol partisan, John had clearly given up hope of his ally gaining the Scots crown once Edward III came to an agreement with his prisoner David in 1357. In January 1358 David invited John MacDougall back to the Scots court and gave him custody of his late father's castles along the Firth of Lorne, followed by the king's cousin Joanna Bruce as a wife. By implication, John was to replace the untrustworthy MacDonalds as royal viceroy in the southern Great Glen and northern Argyll. In summer 1366 Parliament included the MacDonald lands in the territory to be assessed for tax, but the king's tax assessors were refused admission. The steward (David's probable heir but lacking in mutual trust as the childless David could remarry) promised to bring John to heel either by a military expedition or by persuading him to come to court as an obedient vassal in 1368. When neither followed, David suspected him of intending to use the MacDonalds as a military asset in a revolt and arrested him. In March 1369 Parliament included the MacDonald lands in the list of places to be required to pay tax, and in the summer David launched his first major campaign in the western Highlands to bring John to heel. The latter had to come to the king at Inverness that November and on 15 November sealed a treaty of submission as David's feudal vassal, subject to the normal requirements to his lord. Robert Stewart acted as guarantor that John would carry out his duties and signed with him and among the hostages that John had to hand over as pledges of his good behaviour were his son by Robert's daughter, Donald MacDonald, and his illegitimate grandson Angus. They were imprisoned in Dumbarton Castle.

Robert succeeded David as king on 22 February 1371, the late ruler having unexpectedly succumbed to the after-effects of a head wound which he had received at Neville's Cross twenty-five years earlier. As he was John MacDonald's ally and father-in-law, the position of the 'Lord of the Isles' improved, and in Parliament at Scone on 9 March 1372 the new king recognised John's acquisition of the lands of the MacRuadhris of Garmoran. In January 1373 he also recognised that John's eldest son by Amy MacRuadhri, Ranald, would inherit them – this marked the creation of the new lordship of 'Clanranald' and the division of the huge lordship of the Isles among John's children. The weak rule of Robert II in 1371–90 saw a great deal of autonomy for the great lords of the north of the kingdom, and in this respect John MacDonald was of the senior rank of feudal vassals of the remote and ineffective king, along with his neighbour Alexander Stewart, 'Wolf of Badenoch', the king's younger son and now lord of Badenoch and Moray. Alexander also acquired the governorship of Urquhart Castle in the Great Glen, as 'stand-in' for his underage half-brother David Stewart (one of Robert II's sons by Euphemia of Ross, dowager Countess of Moray), and by 1377 David, now Earl of Strathearn, had also been made Earl of Caithness. (Alexander de Ard, the local claimant, was bought off with Stewart backing for his claims to the earldom of Orkney; *q.v.*) David Stewart was thus intended, once he reached adulthood, to be the new Stewart 'strongman' in the far northern Highlands, as Alexander Stewart was in the central northern region. David was then married to the daughter of local lord Alexander Lindsay of Glen Esk.

Unfortunately for Robert II's plans David died young in 1388, and his Caithness title was transferred to his full brother Walter Stewart. When Earl William of Sutherland, David II's ally, died around 1371 his underage surviving son, Robert, was placed under Alexander's guardianship and was later married off to his daughter, Margaret; Alexander was also granted the lieutenancy (i.e. military and judicial supremacy) of all Scotland north of Moray to the Pentland Firth in October 1372. Meanwhile the clear-out of the old order in the far north also involved the fallout after the death of Earl William of Ross, without a son, in February 1372. David II had forced him to marry off his daughter and heiress Euphemia to the royal courtier and champion jouster Sir Walter Leslie, a renowned knightly Crusader but not locally connected, but the earl hated him and had tried to disinherit him. Now the new Stewart regime tried to prevent Leslie taking over Ross while the latter sought support from his English Crusading friends and interested Edward III's government in his cause, and a long-running dispute followed for control of Ross. Leslie established some degree of legal right to it despite Alexander Stewart's animosity but then died in February 1382, whereupon Alexander married his widow Countess Euphemia and took over the earldom. The legal agreements that covered the marriage laid out that the lordships of Skye and Lewis and the 'thaneships' of Dingwall, Glendowachy and Deskford plus Euphemia's own personally inherited lands would go to Alexander and Euphemia's children and if they had none would revert to Euphemia's other heirs, i.e. her son by Walter Leslie, Alexander Leslie, and her daughter Mariota. Alexander Stewart was made Earl of Ross for his lifetime (he probably died around 1404, though early historians put it a decade sooner), and when he died it would revert to Alexander Leslie. This aggrandisement of the 'Wolf of Badenoch' across the northern Highlands thus guaranteed the enmity of both the Leslies and of their allies the Lindsays of Glen Esk, and destabilised the area – though the Wolf's formidable army of 'caterans' and alleged fondness for committing atrocities warned smaller rivals off challenging him. In contrast with the struggles in Alexander's lands, the MacDonald lordship was to appear stable and relatively peaceful in the weak reigns of Robert II and Robert III and the captivity of James I (1371–1424).

John was buried at Ardtornish in 1386, and was succeeded by the elder son of his second, Stewart marriage (Donald, d. 1420/23) in the Isles. The latter was probably in his late twenties or around thirty, given that his parents had married in 1350. (One family tradition has it that his half-brother Ranald acted as his 'tutor' for a year or two, but this seems unlikely as Donald would have had to be born a full twenty years after his parents married.) The mainland territories of Garmoran, Kintail, and much of western Lochaber had gone to Donald's half-brothers, as the sons of the MacRuadhri heiress. The likeliest ally and lieutenant for Donald among them seems to have been Godfrey, the next brother after Ranald who died in 1386/87. (See separate chapter on them.) Donald's younger full brother John 'Mór' was given a small appanage, centred on Dunaverty, but was not content and raised rebellion in 1387; by 1395 he had been driven out of his lands and fled to Ulster, where he married the daughter of MacEoin, 'Lord of the Glens', and entered English service. He was back in the Highlands by 1411, when he fought for Donald at the Battle of Harlaw. John (d. 1386) also had an illegitimate son called John (aka Ian) 'of the Heather', founder of the junior line of MacDonalds or MacIains of Glencoe – his location away from the Isles implying that he was kept out of the main family lands.

The sons of John's (d. 1386) less prestigious first marriage, Ranald and Alastair, inherited the mainland territories of what became known as 'Clanranald' and Keppoch. They duly founded long-lasting dynasties. Ranald ruled Garmoran, acted as the underage Donald's regent for the first months of his rule as Lord of the Isles, and died soon after his father in 1386/87, with his elder son Allan (d. 1419 or 1430) eventually succeeding Ranald's brother Godfrey to Garmoran as lord of Clanranald and his younger son Donald succeeding to Glengarry as its first lord. Alastair, Ranald's brother, ruled Keppoch and was succeeded by his son Angus, second lord, and then his grandson Donald (d. 1496). Garmoran was seized from Allan by his uncle Godfrey, another son of John and Amy who had been given what he considered an inadequate portion of the family lands; it reverted to the Clanranalds on his son's execution by James I in 1428. The main Isles lordship became very powerful again and was practically autonomous under the weaker early Stewarts, especially the aggressive Donald (d. 1420/23), John's elder son by his second marriage, and his younger brother Alexander of Lochaber. Alexander secured a royal grant for his 'protection' of the royal and episcopal estates in Lochaber and Ross at a time of weak central government under Robert III (r. 1390–1406) and his brother and deputy, the 'Governor' Duke Robert of Albany, and expanded his control to include the Loch Ness area including Urquhart Castle. The brothers had ambitions in the central Highlands too and Donald married the well-connected Mary/Mariota, daughter of Countess Euphemia of Ross (heiress to the earldom) and her first husband Earl Walter (Leslie). When Euphemia, who had married secondly King Robert III's younger brother Alexander (the notorious 'Wolf of Badenoch') and thus given the latter – ruler of Moray and Buchan – effective control of the Ross lordship, died around 1394 she was succeeded by Mariota's brother Earl Alexander in Ross, but he died in May 1402. Donald 'of the Isles' backed Mariota's claims to the rule of Ross against those of Earl Alexander's daughter Euphemia – maternal granddaughter and protégé of the Regent/'Governor' of Scotland in 1402–20, Robert Stewart, Duke of Albany. Albany was believed to be intending to add Ross to his lands in her name. Donald's brother Alexander of Lochaber had already quarrelled with the government and marched across the Great Glen into Moray to sack Elgin Cathedral in 1402, but was excommunicated by Bishop Spynie and was forced by threat of invasion to sue for pardon and come to Elgin to beg for absolution. Now the illegitimate son of the 'Wolf of Badenoch', Alexander, married the widowed Countess Isabella of Mar and took over her earldom, thus becoming the MacDonald brothers' eastern neighbour.

David II's restoration of the MacDougalls' heir, John 'the Foreigner', son of Robert I's exiled foe Alexander MacDougall, to the control of castles on the Firth of Lorne was an implicit threat to the MacDonalds, and John's marriage to David's niece Joanna Bruce showed his role as a close royal ally. In February 1369 David's parliament at Perth gave him the lordship of Glen Lyon on the eastern borders of Argyll with Atholl, extending his power eastwards, but he seems to have been seen as a royal 'trusty' in Atholl as much as in Argyll and was most noticeable in Atholl affairs in the 1370s and 1380s. Unfortunately for the MacDougalls he had no son, so their return to favour at the MacDonalds' expense was short-lived, and his daughter and heiress Isobel was married off by the new Stewart regime to a distant relative, Sir John Stewart of Innermeath, around 1380/84. Thus a Stewart would succeed to the MacDougall inheritance, and the latter would be orientated towards Atholl and Perthshire not Lorn. Robert II's second son and effective deputy for much of his reign, Earl Robert of Fife (later Duke of Albany/'Governor'), married his daughter Marjory off to Sir John's son by a previous marriage, Robert, and thus Stewart of Innermeath as the MacDougall heir entered the 'inner circle' of the Fife affinity in the turbulent world of late fourteenth-century court politics. It would seem that Fife was intending rule of Argyll to pass to another closely associated family, the Campbells. As we have seen, it was Robert I who raised up his close friend Neil Campbell to prominence and first established his family in Argyll, but only as one among a group of middle-ranking lords; it was under Robert II that the then head of the family, Sir Colin Campbell of Loch Awe, became hereditary lieutenant of Argyll between Loch Gilp and Loch Melfort in July 1382. Sometime in the early 1390s Fife, now 'Governor', arranged the marriage of his daughter Joanna to Duncan Campbell, son and heir of Sir Colin. In a document of 1395 relating to a judicial 'perambulation' of Fife by the 'Governor's local strongmen (including Duncan Campbell), Sir Colin is called 'lord of Ergadia', i.e. Argyll. This title had normally been held by the pre-eminent hereditary lord of Argyll, that being a descendant of Somerled (MacDougall or MacDonald) as 'Ri Innse Gall', and had then been held in tandem with lordship of part or all of the Inner Hebrides. Fife now clearly intended it for the head of the Campbells, and the latter as his mainstay in the region; the Fife/Albany dominance or rule of Scotland between 1388 and 1425 thus marked the final transfer of seniority in Argyll to the Campbells.

Donald invaded eastern Ross and seized control of Dingwall after a successful battle with the defending Mackay clan in 1411. He then invaded Moray with around 10,000 men (according to the account in the *Scotichronicon*), marched east across the Grampians in a daring foray far from his power base, and fought inconclusively against a smaller Stewart army (led by Alexander's son Alexander, Earl of Mar, and nephew John, Earl of Buchan) at Harlaw in Mar, probably on the

'Eve of St James's Day', i.e. 24 July. Subsequent centuries saw this as a classic 'Highland *vs* Lowland' encounter. The lightly armed Highlands and Hebridean 'kern' thus faced Lowland troops and, as at subsequent encounters, relied on the momentum of the charge to overcome the enemy's better weapons, discipline, and protective clothing. Earl John was a knight trained in modern Continental warfare and would later lead the Scots mercenaries fighting for Charles VII of France against the English, being killed at the Battle of Verneuil in 1424; the commander of his main body of infantry was Sir James Scrimgeour, hereditary 'Standard-Bearer' of Scotland and Constable of Dundee, who drove back wave after wave of Highlandmen. The Stewarts held possession of the battlefield overnight, and woke up to find that Donald had retreated to Lochaber. Though the Stewart 'victory' was not clear-cut, Donald was unable to expand further and lost control of eastern Ross. Mariota claimed all of Ross until her death in 1429, while Euphemia sold her claim to Earl John of Buchan, so on his death at Verneuil, followed by Euphemia's death, Mariota had a stronger case that she was now rightful countess. King James I ignored it. Donald died sometime between 1420 and 1423, probably in his mid- or late sixties.

The lordship's power was gradually eroded by the kings of Scots in the fifteenth century after the return of the captive James I in 1424 and the reassertion of central power. Donald's son Alexander chose to press his late mother's claim to Ross on the king, but James I marched an army into Moray to assert his power. He had already been implicated in the 1427 assassination of John 'Mór' MacDonald, Alexander's uncle and a potential challenger to the new Campbell rule of Argyll, and clearly wanted to weaken the great MacDonald lords. Now he arrested Alexander and his entourage of prominent lords as they arrived at Parliament at Inverness (a rare show of royal power this far north) in late August 1428. He held them captive for either a month or so or a year, and may have planned to replace Alexander as 'Lord of the Isles' with his uncle and heir John, who was among those arrested with him but who died inopportunely in 1429. If so James may have released Alexander once he did not have a replacement to hand. The fact that the king rounded up and imprisoned men who had come into his presence under a traditional 'safe-conduct' probably also dented James's reputation in the Highlands and Islands.

The lesson he had been taught did not warn Alexander off challenging the king, and he appears to have hoped to make use of James's cousin James Stewart, 'The Fat', son of the disgraced and executed ex-regent Murdoch Stewart (Albany's son), as a pretender to Scotland. (Stewart had escaped to Ireland after most of his family were arrested and executed for treason in 1425.) If so it was a dangerous game to threaten the paranoid king, who had reason to believe that Murdoch and his father had left him in English custody for eighteen years (1406–24) to keep their hands on the government in Scotland. James 'the Fat' had had his brothers as well as his father executed by the king in an inter-Stewart bloodbath in 1425, and was out to replace the 'tyrant' as well as to claim his kin's confiscated lordships. As the pretender returned from Ireland with a force of hired mercenaries but died suddenly, Alexander subsequently attacked and burnt the town of Inverness in May/June 1429 but could not storm the castle. His probable intention was to overrun the eastern Highlands in a repeat of the 1411 campaign, but this time he was unable to risk advancing into Moray with the garrison of Inverness holding out. The king brought his large and well-armed army north again and chased Alexander across Lochaber, catching up with him at an unknown site, on marshy moorland, somewhere around Fort William. In this 'Battle of Lochaber' on 23 or 26 June the king unfurled his royal standard to show the clans in Alexander's army that they would be fighting their king in person, thus committing treason to their ultimate lord, and by tradition that caused most of Clan Cameron to defect to him; others (Cameron of Lochiel?) did not, so the clash became known as the 'Battle of Split Allegiances'. The Mackintoshes defected too, and Alexander was either defeated or fled without a serious clash. Short of men and facing relentless royal assault, he sued for pardon, was ignored and turned up at Holyrood Abbey later in 1429 or early in 1430 to make a show of his submission, wearing only his underwear and handing over his sword like a felon. The king imprisoned him at impregnable Tantallon Castle in Lothian, keeping him there for two years, until late 1431, and allegedly let his wife Queen Joan talk him out of executing the prisoner. In the meantime the son of John 'Mór', Donald/Domnhall 'Balloch', led a MacDonald revolt in the Hebrides and invaded Lochaber. The king sent a huge army under Alexander Stewart, Earl of Mar and ex-commander at Harlaw, and Alan Stewart, Earl of Caithness and son of the king's uncle Walter Stewart, and as the local clans (e.g. the Camerons, Mackintoshes and Frasers) joined them Donald had to retreat. But he launched a surprise attack on the royal army's camp at Inverlochy in 1431, and scored a major victory as Mar was forced to flee. Around 1,000 royal troops were killed along with Alan Stewart and the royal troops had to evacuate Lochaber again, but weight of numbers by the reinforced royal army eventually helped Mar to prevail in a second invasion later and he drove Donald back into the Hebrides. Thence Donald fled to Ireland leaving his family's lands occupied but restive; the overstretched Mar had his own lands to rule and could not stay in the Western Highlands for long with his troops, lordly tenants rather than professional mercenaries, only hired for a few months and keen to go home to their farms. As so often before the emergence of a central government army able to occupy garrisons in a rebel area for years on end, the Edinburgh regime could defeat but not occupy the western Highlands long-term and even the autocratic James I had to negotiate with its elite – once he had taught them a military lesson.

(iii) The end of the Lordship: to 1493 and after

Alexander was released by James I in 1431 and was subsequently allowed to regain control of Ross and Inverness, with his rival Alexander of Mar dying in 1435. He did not challenge the Stewarts again, was appointed 'Justiciar' (i.e. senior judicial figure in the country) under James II's regency in 1438/39, and died at Dingwall in May 1449. His son and heir by Elizabeth Seton of Huntly, daughter of the first Lord Gordon (Alexander Seton, d. 1440/41, who took the name of Gordon after marrying the Gordon heiress Elizabeth in 1408) and sister of the first Earl of Huntly (d. 1470), was John (*c.* 1444–1503), who succeeded him in 1449. Alexander also had a younger son called Celestine who became lord of Lochalsh, but the sources differ over whether his mother was Elizabeth Seton or else a mistress (or possibly wife) of Alexander's, probably descended from the earls of Ross. (He is referred to in some charters as John's brother, in others as his half-brother.) John was a complex and unsuccessful figure who seems to have had poor judgement and to have been a political gambler as a young man and contrastingly cautious after the 1470s, alienating his clansmen by not standing up to the king. Was he a rare political realist, seeking to avoid inevitable defeat and bloodshed, or the coward that his antagonised son Angus called him? He succeeded aged around five; his marriage to Elizabeth, daughter of the royal chamberlain James Livingston, was arranged by King James II and took place just before the Livingston family were arrested and forfeited by the king in September 1449. John's father-in-law escaped arrest and fled from Dumbarton to the Isles to join John, who harboured him in defiance of the king. John then joined a league of James II's principal foes, the Earl William Douglas of Douglas (leading lord of the southern Uplands) and James Lindsay, the 'Tiger Earl' of Crawford (leading lord of the central Highlands), in 1450 to challenge the young king's expanding power. Already he was seeking to constrain the threat of Stewart centralism by appealing to the monarchy's greatest real or potential foes, thus risking a violent reaction; his father and grandfather had steered clear of risky southern Scots alliances. James decapitated the threat by personally stabbing Douglas at an interview in Edinburgh Castle when he refused to cancel the bond, and Earl John thereafter ineffectively tried to aid a Douglas rebellion by Earl William's brother James in 1452–55. He managed to seize Inverness and Urquhart castles in a northern offensive, and provocatively installed his father-in-law Livingston (a fugitive from royal justice) as castellan of Urquhart. Glenmoriston was annexed to MacDonald-held Lochaber, and John met the new Earl James of Douglas in Knapdale to plan war on the king. In 1453 John sent his fleet to ravage the Stewarts' ancestral estates on the islands of Bute and Arran plus the Cumbrae islands, besieging Brodick Castle and on 10 July sacking Inverkip, but the king held on to Glasgow and overran the Douglas lands in Clydesdale and the MacDonalds could not link up with them. The king put the Douglas revolt down and from then on it was the writ of Stewart rather than Douglas which ran in southern Scotland; but the Highlands and Islands were not yet tackled. John returned to his allegiance to the king, probably in 1454 when his father-in-law Livingston was pardoned and restored as chamberlain, and in 1456 he was granted the 'life-rents' of Glenmoriston and Urquhart castles to confirm his occupation of them. He was made one of the honorary wardens of the Border 'Marches' in 1457, and in 1460 took 3,000 men to assist in his invasion of England in support of the Lancastrian cause in the current succession dispute, the so-called 'Wars of the Roses' (not a contemporary term). James II, a formidable ruler who might have taken on the MacDonalds next and who was the son of one of King Henry VI's Beaufort cousins, was killed in a freak accident in this campaign when a cannon blew up as he was besieging English-held Roxburgh Castle. John accompanied the army under Queen Margaret of Guelders back to Edinburgh to pledge allegiance to the eight-year-old James III at Parliament in February 1461. But he was now at feud with the royal loyalist and stalwart of the regency, Colin Campbell, first Earl of Argyll, and refused a summons to Parliament to explain his private war with the latter. In June 1461 the bishops of St Andrews and Glasgow visited him on Bute to mediate, but the dispute was not solved. He now took advantage of James III's minority to claim full independence in alliance with England at an Isles council meeting held in July 1462 at Ardtornish, sending envoys to King Edward IV, who had on the same date authorised his representatives to treat with John.

In March 1463 John signed with the English envoys the 'Treaty of Westminster–Ardtornish', whereby he did homage to Edward for all of Scotland north of the Forth as its rightful king but divided the territory with the exiled rebel Douglases. This implied an extension of his father's playing with Stewart pretenders to claiming to be one himself (via female descent), implying that the current royal line were illegitimate due to the disputed second marriage of Robert II, and pledging himself to the King of England as Scotland's overlord. It was a formidable gamble, and showed John's confidence in his power but also his fear of the Scots government – possibly it was intended as much as a means of blackmail to force the regency to accept his autonomy as a serious plan for rebellion. At the time the Scots government was giving sanctuary and recognition to Edward's ousted predecessor Henry VI, so Edward had reason to threaten the Scots regency, but he did not take any action to implement the treaty and attack Edinburgh and concentrated on reasserting his claims to lands once held by his grandfather Donald in the north. The only major success John achieved was the conquest of Inverness from the regency sometime in the minority of James III, probably 1463/64. John sent orders to the inhabitants of the sheriffdoms of Inverness, Nairn and Moray to pay their taxes to him rather than the king, and subsequently he advanced with an army of Islesmen as far south as Blair Atholl, where he was said to have captured the castle and kidnapped the earl, James III's half-uncle James Stewart (whose family claimed that saintly intercession by St Brigit caused John to release him later). But John never followed up his Atholl campaign and was driven back into Lochaber, with the possibility that either his army wanted to go home with their loot or he lacked the nerve to venture into the more dangerous Lowlands and tackle a royal army with cannons to hand. (An Atholl family tradition had it that the earl helped the king's forces to rescue him and drive the MacDonalds off by getting his captors drunk by spiking their drink.) In 1464, Parliament demanded that John be outlawed for his part in aiding the 'rebel' Alan McCoule, his lieutenant, who had murdered John Stewart, lord of Lorne and Innermeath – as the heir of the extinct MacDougalls to Lorne and holder of the former title and (some of the) lands of the MacDonalds and MacDougalls in Argyll, a major foe to the MacDonalds. Clearly removing Stewart by violence was seen as a way to reassert MacDonald power in Argyll, but John did not invade – perhaps held back by the power of the Campbells – and the regency did not invade his lands either though in July 1464 the royal court was at Inverness. John was accused of wilfully ignoring royal letters instructing him to hand McCoule over, but clearly the regent, Bishop Kennedy, felt war too risky or costly. In 1467 John came to terms with the young king's government, possibly helped by the new pre-eminence of his Livingston kin in it; he was allowed to keep the lands and rents of Urquhart Castle (as its castellan) and Glenmoriston, and had to admit a new royal castellan to control Inverness but was allowed to keep the borough's revenues which he had seized. Once the royal succession war in England had ended (temporarily) with Henry VI's and his son's murders in 1471 Edward restored relations with Scotland. John was left high and dry to possible Stewart vengeance, as someone more practical should have expected in 1462–63, and was embroiled in trouble with the king over a private war with his cousin George Gordon/Seton, second Earl of Huntly and the new royal castellan of Inverness. In February 1474 James III sent letters to John and to Huntly ordering them to stop feuding, to no avail. James then backed Huntly, who led his Moray/Buchan levies with royal authority to take Dingwall Castle, seat of John's earldom of Ross, in 1474 or 1475 and then invaded Lochaber to reassert royal authority over the MacDonalds in the lower Great Glen.

In 1475 Edward IV probably revealed the hitherto secret Treaty of Ardtornish–Westminster to James III's regime, thus exposing John's past claim on the throne and promise to divide up Scotland with the national enemy. John MacDonald was summoned before the Scots Parliament at Inverness for treason (by plotting with Edward IV and Douglas and invading Bute) by royal heralds at Inverness and Dingwall on 16 October 1475, refused to come on the due date of 1 December and was outlawed. On 4 December the Earl of Argyll was given a commission of 'fire and sword' to invade his lands, as were the earls of Atholl and Huntly. However, the swift resolution to the crisis suggests that once John had found that he would gain no English help he quickly backed down rather than face invasion from the king's main official in Argyll, Colin Campbell, first Earl of Argyll. Apparently his pardon was negotiated by his hitherto hostile cousin the Earl of Huntly – as the head of the Gordons and main lord of the north-east, he was possibly wary of giving the Campbells too much power in the Highlands if they evicted John and were given most of the MacDonald lands. John had to return to his allegiance to Scotland in order to keep any of his lands in the subsequent 'climbdown' which lifted his outlawry and restored most of his lands when he appeared before Parliament at Edinburgh on 10 July 1476. He was deprived of the earldom of Ross, the sheriffdom of Inverness, the castles of Inverness and Nairn, and his lands of Kintyre and Knapdale as a punishment – the first four kept him at a distance from Inverness from now on, and the other two kept him out of Argyll. From now on he would only hold the lordship as a normal Scots peer, by the king's permission and subject to forfeiture at the king's whim, not by hereditary right. Allegedly his pardon was arranged by James's formidably competent and sensible queen, Margaret, who restrained her vengeful husband. He came out of the crisis in possession of most of his patrimony, albeit legally on terms of dependence on the Scots

Crown and thus unequivocally subject to confiscation in the case of a further dispute. But from now on the king's writ would run in his lands (provided it could be enforced), and the future lay with figures with influence at court and a hand in the turbulent politics there. Colin Campbell, first Earl of Argyll (d. 1493), was the most prominent of these in the region, and was married to Isabella Stewart – the daughter of Lord Lorne, so his heirs had a MacDougall ancestry too. The Campbells, like the thirteenth-century and fourteenth-century MacDonalds, had the advantage of various loyal junior cadet lines to support the main dynast too. Colin's father Gillespic/Archibald Campbell had been the predeceasing son of Duncan Campbell ('Donnchadh na-Adh', 'Duncan the Fortunate') by his first marriage, to Marjorie Stewart, the daughter of the 'Governor' Robert, Duke of Albany – hence the close alliance of Campbells and Stewarts. Duncan's second marriage, to Margaret Stewart of Ardgowan, provided the founders of the junior Campbell lines of Glenorchy (Colin, granted Glen Orchy in 1432 and died around 1475) and Ormidale (Otter). The Glen Orchy lords in particular acted as the main agents of Campbell expansion into the lands East of Loch Lomond, being based at Kilchurn/Glenorchy Castle; they were initially allied to but later evicted the older local 'Clan Gregor' (MacGregors), legendarily one of the 'Siol Alpin' (the families descended from King Kenneth/Cinaed MacAlpin).

Technically reduced to an ordinary Scots peerage, John was humiliated and the lordship fell into decline and civil strife. The earldom of Ross was given to the king's second son James (only a boy so the latter never actually resided in the region and just took its revenues). The new Earl of Ross – who did have some genealogical claim to the region's rule as son of the Danish/Norwegian princess Margaret, descendant of its early Scandinavian overlords – also became its duke in January 1488 as the king raised him up as a potential successor in place of his older brother (also James). This probably indicates that James III intended his second son as his new northern Highlands 'strongman' once he was adult – but in the interim the politically blundering king was removed by his elder son in a massive revolt of alienated peers in June 1488. The titular Duke of Ross never had the opportunity to act in the Highlands as viceroy for his suspicious brother as Alexander 'Wolf of Badenoch' had done for Robert II and III, and James IV later moved him to be Archbishop of St Andrews – a cleric could not inherit the throne. (He died in 1504.) John MacDonald, meanwhile, failed to reassert his authority even with James III facing revolt from his brother Alexander in 1483 and his elder son in 1488 and thus usefully distracted. In February 1478 he was cited to the king for treason again for aiding a rebel attack on Castle Sween, but was not punished. At some point in the late 1470s or around 1480 he was evicted from his lands by his rebellious illegitimate son Angus 'Mór', who clearly resented his 'sell-out' to the king, and fled to Ireland. He returned around 1480 with a fleet to gain the adherence of some of his ex-vassals, including the Macleans of Duart, MacLeods of Skye (Dunvegan) and MacNeils, and was given a royal contingent under the Earl of Argyll by the king. He secured most of the Inner Hebrides. But after the royal troops went home (early autumn?) he rashly advanced west and fought a naval battle with Angus's adherents at 'Bloody Bay', a few miles along the coast of Mull from Tobermory. The MacDonalds of Clanranald and Keppoch fought for Angus, and traditionally the MacLeods of Lewis, in Angus's fleet, deserted to John after their Skye kinsmen unveiled the fabled clan 'Fairy Flag' in an appeal to their loyalty. But it was to no avail, and John was defeated and had to flee again; he was only able to return when Angus was assassinated by his Irish piper in an obscure crime at Inverness in 1490. The question of the succession to the lordship was unclear, given that Angus was both a bastard (so denied any rights by Church inheritance law) and a rebel against the kingdom of Scots; in a document of 1484 John MacDonald cited his cousin John of Dunivaig (who had also signed the Treaty of Ardtornish with England with him in 1462) as his legal heir. This would imply that the genealogically closer line of Celestine of Lochalsh, John's half-brother, was illegitimate (as the Church saw it).

The role of MacDonald family 'hard-liner' in resisting the increasingly assertive young King James IV passed to John MacDonald's nephew Alexander, son of his half-brother Celestine (d. 1476) and like him lord of Lochalsh, who invaded Ross (whose earldom had been taken from his uncle by the Crown in 1476) and sacked Inverness in a spectacular gesture of defiance in spring 1491. On this campaign Alexander, who had clearly emerged as a magnet for the more determined clan chiefs in taking on the government, was aided by a coalition of both his own vassals in Lochaber (including the MacDonalds of Clanranald, led by their fourth chief Alan, and Keppoch) and their neighbours such as the Mackintoshes. The former included the Camerons of Lochiel, whose (traditionally thirteenth) chief Ewan was married to Alexander's cousin, but also their long-term rivals of the emerging 'Clan Chattan' confederation whom the Camerons had evicted from the Loch Arkaig region the previous century. The two clans had been at feud over the territory of Loch Arkaig in eastern Lochaber since the victory of Clan Chattan, which was hereditarily led by the Mackintosh dynasty, at the Battle of 'Gleann Laoigh' (probably Glenloy) in 1330 or 1337, and had famously fought a 'controlled' inter-clan battle like a more violent form of tournament in front of King Robert III and his court on the North Inch near Perth in 1396. It was thus a rare achievement to have them fighting on the same side, and they and the MacKinnons helped Alexander of Lochalsh defeat the pro-government Mackenzies of Kintail and occupy then garrison Inverness. Complaints were raised about Alexander's being unchecked in Parliament, but for the moment the government left dealing with him to his neighbours the Mackenzies, who defeated him at Park near Strathpeffer later that year. John was more cautious about defying the king, and notably issued very few charters as an autonomous lord (i.e. without permission of or naming the king) unlike his ancestors had done, the last-but-one being in 1486 and the last at Aros in December 1492. The seventeenth-century local historian Hugh MacDonald dated the outbreak of internecine Isles warfare to the 1490s as John lost his grip and his vassals' respect, and this is probably accurate. In the parliament of April–May 1493 James IV abolished the lordship and required John to remove himself to supervised residence in the Lowlands, a move which has been linked not only to complaints by the Crown's local feudatories at rising disorder and to Stewart centralism but to 'clan politics' by the current Lord Chancellor and 'strongman', Archibald Douglas, Earl of Angus. The latter's predecessor Colin Campbell (d. 1493), first Earl of Argyll and the first of the Campbells to significantly expand the family's power beyond their Loch Awe heartland, had been serving the teenage king's regime as one of its leaders since he took a major role in the overthrow of James's father James III (who had sacked him as Chancellor earlier), the late king being defeated at the Battle of Sauchieburn and almost immediately killed in a mystery 'hit' in June 1488. The ambitious earl, married to the daughter of the second (Stewart) Lord Lorne and eventually gaining that title which became the rank of the heirs of the earls of Argyll, was the first Campbell since Robert I's ally Neil to be a major actor on the national stage and set the scene for the Campbells' rise to Highland power. His grandfather and predecessor Duncan 'the Fortunate' ('na-Adh'; d. 1453/54) had married the heiress of Campbell of Glen Orchy and been made Lord Campbell by his patron James II in 1445. Colin Campbell had been involved with the turbulent Angus 'Mór' MacDonald, who married his daughter Mary/Marjorie, and had possibly hoped to use his revolt to overthrow his rival John MacDonald; his Isles plottings and his rank as Chancellor to James III in the 1480s showed his vast ambitions. After Angus's death the latter's infant son Donald 'Dubh' (b. c. 1490), Argyll's grandson, was kidnapped by Argyll and held at his castle of Inchconnel on Loch Awe as a political pawn.

Argyll seems to have hoped to use his grandson to secure control of the

MacDonald lordship when John MacDonald died or was forfeited – and deposing John and annexing the lordship to the Crown in 1493 meant that the king, not Argyll, would control it from now on. Probably the Earl of Angus, Argyll's rival, hoped for rich pickings from the confiscated lands as King James's close adviser – but the strong-willed king kept the lands in his own firm control. In August 1493, following John's removal, James IV led a royal progress to the ancient castle of Dunstaffnage in Lorn, where he probably received the homage of assorted major local lords as within the next year some, such as John Maclean of Lochbuie (lord of southern Tiree) and John MacIain of Ardnamurchan (lord of Islay), were confirmed in their lands by the king in place of their usual direct lord, the 'Lord of the Isles'. He also strengthened the fortress at Dunaverty to strengthen royal power in Argyll – to little effect, as a later story (first recorded in a history of 1836 but possibly based on oral memories) had it that no sooner had the king sailed off with his entourage than local 'strongman' John MacDonald of Dunivaig/Islay took the castle and hung its commander from the walls in sight of the king's ships. James IV then went on to the northern Highlands for a progress to Dingwall, this time 'showing his face' in confiscated Ross to secure loyalty, and apparently Alexander MacDonald of Lochalsh and his rival John MacDonald of Dunivaig/Islay promised allegiance as both were knighted by the king on his visit to Dunstaffnage. In 1494/95, however, Alexander was killed on Oronsay in obscure circumstances by MacIain, and as the latter received a grant of Crown lands and the office of royal bailiff on Islay it is possible that this was either in anticipation of or as a reward for eliminating the unruly Alexander. The death of Alexander apparently followed the defeat of his forces on the mainland at the Battle of Drumchatt ('The Cat's Back', a mountain ridge) in Strathpeffer by the loyalist Mackenzies (and possibly the Munros, though the first naming of them as participants is by Highland historian Donald Gregory in 1836). The battle is dated at 1497 by Gregory, but this is unlikely if Alexander's army was involved as he was definitely killed in 1494/95; it may be a mistake for '1491'. 'Hitman' or not, John MacIain of Ardnamurchan was to be the main conduit of royal power in the western Highlands for decades. In July 1494 or 1499 he rounded up John MacDonald of Dunivaig/Islay – whose local power was such that Irish chroniclers could call him 'king of Insi-Gall' – and his three sons, John Cattanach, Ranald 'the Red' and Domnall 'the Freckled', in a surprise 'swoop' at Finlaggan. They were all executed at Edinburgh on one gallows in August according to the 'Book of Clanranald', thus removing a major obstacle to royal control. (The last such impressive mass execution of a turbulent aristocratic family had been James I's purge of the Albany Stewart family in 1425.)

John MacDonald was required from his surrender to live under royal supervision in the Lowlands, where he died at Dundee in January 1503. The new Lord of the Isles, the king, took a considerable interest in this part of his realm and in May 1495 he made a rare royal voyage to Mingary Castle in the Inner Hebrides, the first such state visit since Alexander II's 1249 expedition. (Robert I had been in the district as a fugitive and then as a contender to the throne in 1307–08.) In 1495–96 the Crown's officials made a formal land assessment for tax of Islay, centre of the Inner Hebrides portion of the lordship. The Macleans of Duart, Clan Cameron and MacNeill of Barra were all confirmed in their lands by royal charter in 1495 – and the moneymaking king then announced in an 'act of revocation' in March 1498 that all charters would have to be legally revised and reissued to be valid and the chiefs would be expected to pay up for the privilege. An equally aggressive tone was taken by the King's Council, possibly due to Argyll and his allies rather than James himself as he was absent, when in October 1496 they decided that all clan chiefs were to be required to see that any royal warrants against persons in their territories issued before April 1497 must be carried out or else they would be cited along with the accused. The chiefs in the lordship were thus made responsible for their tenants obeying the king's laws on pain of being treated as delinquents themselves. But would this centralist intimidation and rule by legal 'fiat' at a distance work?

Between March and September 1498 James IV spent three separate periods at his main Argyll castle, Kilkerran, in southern Kintyre (the third for six weeks in the summer), receiving and obtaining submission from Highland lords and granting out estates and offices in return. From now on, land and office would come from the king and he could revoke either at will – though this depended in practice on an ability to enforce his will. Ominously, only Torquil MacLeod of Lewis (the new earl Archibald of Argyll's brother-in-law, so presumably assured of council goodwill), Ranald Maclean of Uist and Eigg, and Angus MacRanald of Morar and Arisaig (head of Clanranald) among the major chiefs turned up at Kilkerran to pay for and receive their new charters while the king was there. Alexander MacLeod of Dunvegan had turned up at court at Stirling earlier to acquire a charter too – but by some blunder both he and his cousin MacLeod of Lewis were granted the 'bailiary' of Trotternish so they ended up fighting over it. Possibly Argyll disliked the initial grant to his brother-in-law's foe and so had it countermanded. The other chiefs stayed away and defied the king, and in April 1500 Argyll was appointed as the king's lieutenant for three years within all the lordship of the Isles except Islay and Kintyre, empowered to make new laws and to attack and besiege rebels. Already custodian of local Tarbert Castle, Argyll was clearly intended by the king to carry out a 'forward' policy and make examples – the first such use of Clan Campbell, who made the most of this role on and off for the next 250 years. Another grant, in 1501, gave the head of the Gordons of Huntly in Buchan – Alexander Gordon, third Earl of Huntly – powers to receive royal dues in Lochaber and secure bonds of obedience from magnates north of the Mounth (which might include the western Highlands). But now the royal reliance on the Earl of Argyll backfired, as the latter's brother-in-law Torquil MacLeod of Lewis took on the risky task of restoring the Lordship of the Isle by rebellion. Possibly he was afraid of Huntly targeting him for embezzling the royal rents of the bailiary of Skye. Usefully, his wife's sister had been Donald 'Dubh's mother so he could claim kinship to the young man and act as his patron as well as Argyll could. In October 1501 the MacIains of Glencoe, a junior MacDonald line, either rescued Donald 'Dubh', as heir to the lordship of the Isles, from Argyll's men at Inchconnel Castle or else persuaded the castle's commander to hand him over. Donald ended up in the hands of Torquil MacLeod, and the king quickly ordered the latter to send his pawn to the royal court at Inverness that autumn but nothing happened. Fearing that rebellion was intended after Torquil ignored repeated summonses, the council outlawed him in March 1502 and ordered him to pay up the 900 marks due from the royal bailiary of Trotternish which he had embezzled. At around the same time, local chief Kenneth McKenzie of Kintail (an ally of Alexander MacDonald of Lochalsh in his 1491 attacks on Ross) and Farquhar Mackintosh, captain of Clan Chattan, escaped from prison in Edinburgh Castle and fled to Ross to cause further trouble; luckily for the king they were caught en route a few miles from Edinburgh and Mackenzie was killed. Huntly and his lieutenants – not MacLeod's relative and potential ally Argyll – were given orders to take over Torquil's lands in Assynt and Cogeach in Wester Ross and install loyal new tenants, and in August Torquil's Isles domains were confiscated too. In 1501–02 Huntly and his army seem to have overrun much of Lochaber to evict actual or suspected 'disloyal' tenants and replace them with new ones who would obey royal orders and join royally sanctioned expeditions.

The MacLeods remained out of reach on Lewis until the king could spare a larger fleet, and in retaliation for the royal takeover of Lochaber in late autumn 1503 Torquil MacLeod and his ally Lachlan Maclean of Duart ravaged Huntly's own lands in Badenoch. This was the furthest 'rebel' penetration of the loyal eastern Highlands since the early fifteenth century, albeit now by the Macleans rather than the

MacDonalds, although carried out in Donald Dubh's name. Royal estates on the island of Bute were also raided in 1502–03 in seaborne attacks. As John MacDonald now died the king could not use him against his grandson as a loyalist rallying point as he intended, and a new parliament met in March 1504 to raise funds for a Hebridean war. The issuing of another 'act of revocation' by this meant that the king could cancel all previous grants of land and office and so reverse unsuccessful recent ones by himself and by Argyll, and the rebel Macleans were duly forfeited. MacLeod of Dunvegan, MacIain of Ardnamurchan, McNeill of Barra, and the chiefs of Mackinnon and Maclean of Lochbuie were entrusted with helping Huntly and his army put down the rebellion – but oddly only Maclean of Duart, who now had custody of Donald Dubh, was forfeited and the arch-troublemaker Torquil MacLeod was put on the list of chiefs authorised to fight the rebels. Presumably there was a hope of inducing Torquil to join the royal cause now he did not have the MacDonald 'pretender' in his hands, averting the need to waste time and resources on ravaging his remote island domains. The royal fleet sailed down the Clyde and round Kintyre in April 1504, and headed to the castle of Cairn-na-Burgh in the Treshnish Isles, west of Mull, where Maclean of Duart had placed his puppet Donald Dubh. The king did not go on the expedition, probably due to waning interest in the Isles compared to earlier, and though the castle either surrendered (James had impressive artillery) or was taken, Donald Dubh had been moved elsewhere. The war became lengthy, with Torquil MacLeod eventually being added to the list of those forfeited for treason in December 1505, and the Earl of Argyll (now put in charge of Cairn-na-Burgh Castle and so dominating the southern Hebridean seaways) and MacIain of Ardnamurchan slowly prevailed as various chiefs came in to surrender and save their lands. Maclean of Duart was among them, with his principal castle now lost to his foe Argyll, and it was left to Torquil MacLeod on distant Lewis to take on the role of protector to Donald Dubh and lead the resistance. A new parliament in February 1506 raised funds for the next expedition, declaring Torquil forfeit for not turning up to answer the charges of treason, and late the following summer Huntly and a royal force belatedly landed on Lewis to attack Torquil's territories. Stornoway Castle was quickly taken and its occupant Donald Dubh deported to prison in the Lowlands, either in Stirling or Edinburgh Castle, and Torquil fled overseas and lost all his lands. (He died in 1511.) His younger brother Malcolm, however, retook the family lands on Lewis from their occupiers around 1511, and as he was not actively disloyal the government acquiesced in this.

(iv) A shadow of a lordship? Claimants in the sixteenth century: the ambitions of the MacDonalds of Sleat and of Donald 'Dubh'

With Donald Dubh under lock and key and royal 'trusties' in place the MacDonald lordship was firmly legally incorporated into the royal domains. In the meantime some cadet lines of MacDonald 'of the Isles' survived as local lords, with Lord Alexander's (d. 1449) illegitimate son Hugh (son of a lady from the O'Beolan family, hereditary abbots of Applecross in Wester Ross, and half- or full brother of the late Celestine of Lochalsh) founding the line of MacDonalds of Sleat, 'Clan Ùisdean' (after the Gaelic for 'Hugh'). They became known as the 'MacDonalds of the north', the epithet of 'MacDonalds of the south' being taken by the MacDonnells of Antrim in Ulster, who were descended from the MacDonalds of Dunivaig, the main branch of the clan on Islay. Hugh of Sleat, who died in 1495/96 or 1498 and was buried at Sanda on North Uist, received lands on Uist and Skye in a charter from his half-brother John MacDonald in 1469 – which James IV then confiscated in 1495. Originally Sleat itself was held by his legitimate or illegitimate (half-?) brother Celestine of Lochalsh, so Hugh may have inherited it on the latter's death (or Celestine's son's death); his first base was the nearby castle of Dunscaith, known as the 'Castle of Scathach' after the legendary female druid who educated the Irish/Scots hero Fionn MacCumhaill. This would suggest that the Scots version of the legends of Fionn or 'Fingal', imported from Ulster by Gaelic settlers centuries before, located Scathach's education of Fionn at Dunscaith; the hero was to be linked to nearby Skye too. Hugh also helped to negotiate his relative 'Lord of the Isles' John MacDonald's reconciliation with King James III in 1476, for which he received a grant of land worth £20 from the grateful king, and had his lands of Sleat confirmed by the king verbally in 1476 and by charter in 1495. He was succeeded by his son John MacDonald, who (probably weakened by the loss of his Outer Hebrides lands) was dispossessed of Sleat and lands on North Uist by his better-resourced rival Ranald 'Ban' Alansson, head of the MacDonalds of Clanranald, in or preceding a grant of these to Ranald by the king in 1505. He had also had to hand over his lands on the island of Eigg and in Arisaig to the king for transmission to the Clanranalds before 1500. Genealogically, he was closest in blood to the main line of the 'Lords of the Isles' and so may have been targeted by the Clanranalds (senior in rank as the legitimate descendants of the great 'Lord' John, d. 1387, by his first marriage) as a threat. King James evidently backed Clanranald, to keep the MacDonalds divided. James also gave lands in Trotternish on Skye in two contradictory grants to the two rival parts of the MacLeod clan (Lewis and Dunvegan), as we have seen; 'divide and rule' was the order of the day. John of Sleat died in 1505 and was succeeded by his younger half-brother Donald 'Galloch', 'the Stranger', son of a lady of the prominent Caithness clan of Gunn (reputed descendants of a sister of Jarl Harald II of Orkney; *q.v.*), who had formed a valuable connection by his marriage to the daughter of John of Dunivaig (and widow of the rebel Torquil MacLeod of Lewis). He was soon murdered (1506) by his half-brother Archibald, 'Gilleasbuig Dubh', who took over the family lands aided by his half-brothers, Angus 'Collach' (son of Hugh of Sleat by one of the Macleans of Coll) and Angus 'Dubh' (son of one of the Vicar family from South Uist). Holding onto Dunscaith Castle despite its being granted elsewhere by the king and helped by the two Anguses in murdering their half-brother Domnhall on Loch Scapig, Archibald/Gilleasbuig/Gillespie is said by family tradition to have been a pirate who lived outside the law altogether for three years in a career of pillaging local islands, probably in the mid-late 1500s, after the king authorised his rival Ranald 'Ban' of Clanranald to drive him out. He managed to regain Sleat and secure royal legal confirmation of his lands by his pardon around 1510/12 by handing over his rival pirates the MacAllisters of Kintyre to the king, and was clearly accepted as an effective ruler too costly to remove. Archibald served as 'tutor' of the Sleat lands to Donald's son Donald 'Gruamach' (d. 1534) until the latter became an adult, and according to clan tradition was murdered by his nephew while out hunting on North Uist in revenge for the latter's father's killing. Angus 'Collach', Archibald's half-brother and ally, was also said to have met a violent end, having tried to rape the wife of the head of a younger branch of the MacDonalds, 'Siol Ghorraidh', on the island of South Uist during a visit in her husband Domnhall's absence. Her Clanranald kinsmen then kidnapped him from a nearby island and handed him over to the Clanranald chief for execution, leading to retaliatory attacks on them by Archibald.

The claims to local power in the western Highlands by some MacDonalds continued in times of weak royal government, such as the frequent Stewart minorities. James IV, vanquisher of the lordship of the Isles, relied in his later years on John MacIain MacDonald of Ardnamurchan as his 'strongman' west of the Great Glen and the Mackays of Strathnaver in Wester Ross, while overall control of the 'inner' north-west nearer the Glen was given to Alexander Gordon, third Earl of Huntly (d. 1524), who was married to the king's illegitimate daughter Margaret. Huntly was named as hereditary sheriff of Inverness in 1509, and was in charge of choosing and controlling the deputy sheriffs of Ross, Moray and Lochaber. James was killed leading a large army to invade England in support of his French allies at Flodden in September 1513 along with most of his senior nobles, leaving a one-year-old son (James V). This provided an opportunity to reassert the autonomy of local lords and settle old feuds, though Huntly was one of the few peers to survive the battle (where he commanded the left wing) and was to be named lieutenant of the north (except Argyll) again in 1517–18. It was too good a chance to miss for Sir Donald MacDonald of Lochalsh, son of the assassinated Alexander (d. 1494/95), one of the survivors of Flodden, and on his way home he linked up with his kinsman Alexander MacDonell, lord of nearby Glengarry, and the Chisholms to attack and capture Urquhart Castle on Loch Ness. The new regency government was split between pro-English and pro-French factions, and many great nobles who could command military expeditions had fallen at Flodden. As the shrewd Sir Donald had expected, his usurpation of local power and a major royal castle in the Great Glen went unchallenged except by the regency's nominated representatives, the Grants, whom he fought off. He held onto Urquhart for three years, and in 1515 tackled his great foes, his father's killers the MacIains of Ardnamurchan, attacking their stronghold of Mingary Castle. Taking this bastion would make him the main warlord in Lochaber, but he only succeeded at the second attempt in 1517. The following year he avenged his father by killing John MacIain, the royal 'strongman' for over twenty years. But his death in 1519 ended his hopes of using the government's preoccupations in the south to restore the lordship of the Isles; his sister and heiress Margaret had married his ally MacDonell of Glengarry, who inherited his lands.

The local MacDonald lords mostly seem to have regarded Donald 'Gruamach' MacDonald of Sleat (see above) as their honorary senior and the nearest that the Scots kingship would tolerate to a leader of the clan and 'Lord of the Isles', but Donald 'Dubh' did not give up his claims though he was held prisoner in Edinburgh Castle until after the death of James V in December 1542. Donald of Sleat, as ally of the powerful chieftains Campbell of Cawdor (1521), Mackintosh (1524) and Munro of Foulis (1527), was said by tradition to have accompanied Campbell of Cawdor on the expedition by the Scots regent, the half-French Duke John of Albany, to besiege Wark Castle in Northumberland in 1523. En route home (November 1523) he then helped Campbell to murder Alistair 'Cattanach' MacLean, chief of the Macleans of Duart, in Edinburgh in retaliation for the latter's previous attempt to drown his then wife, who was now married to Campbell. He was distracted from 1528 by his feud with the MacLeods of Dunvegan on Skye, whose castle he attacked that year in alliance with their foe Iain MacLeod, son of their rival the MacLeod chief of Lewis. Iain (or John) was the son of the late rebel Torquil MacLeod of Lewis, and had regained his paternal lands after the latter's younger brother Malcolm died around 1515 as the latter's son Ruadhri/Rory was underage. With Iain MacLeod's help Donald recovered the bailiwick of Trotternish on Skye, to which he laid claim, and after MacLeod of Dunvegan complained to the government he and Iain MacLeod of Lewis were summoned to explain themselves to Parliament in 1530 but never turned up. His son and (1534?) successor, Donald 'Gorm' of Sleat, continued his work of building up a local coalition of lords and seems to have regarded himself as rightful 'Lord of the Isles', though any open claim to this would bring down the wrath of – and a probable invasion by – the alert and aggressive young King James V. Luckily James was distracted elsewhere, though he was concerned enough about his lordship of the Isles to mount a naval tour round the northern Hebrides in 1540. This followed a daring challenge by Donald 'Gorm' in 1539, who now felt strong enough to openly claim to be 'Lord of the Isles' in defiance of the king and was backed up by the MacLeods of Lewis, hereditary rivals of his foes the MacLeods of Dunvegan. He attacked the loyalist Mackenzies' headquarters of Eilean Donan Castle on an island off Ardnamurchan, the key to the central Hebrides, but was unfortunately killed in a skirmish there. The siege broke up as his disheartened army went home, and his underage son Donald Gormson (d. 1575) succeeded under the tutelage of the late chief's younger brother, Archibald 'the Clerk' ('Clearaich'). From the land charters in subsequent decades it appears that Archibald and his sons got their hands on part of the family estates, too.

The Ulster link in the mid- to late sixteenth century

Donald Gormson of Sleat was also in trouble with Mary Stuart's regency government in the early 1550s, but this was for general disorderliness and attacking his neighbours rather than for a 'political' move to claim the defunct lordship of the Isles. His 'Clan Ùisdean' (i.e. 'family of Hugh') forces were at feud with the Macleans and he was accused of raiding their lands on Tiree and Coll (for which Queen Mary was to pardon him in 1562). He was using his ships to commit piracy and 'hit-and-run' looting raids around the Minch like his father, and this wide-ranging campaigning now extended across the North Channel to Ulster where other, southern MacDonalds had been settling as their Argyll and Kintyre lands were seized by the Campbells. In 1568 he took 600 of his experienced warriors off to Ireland to fight in Ulster for Somhairle 'Buidhe' ('the Fair', aka 'Sorley Boy' to the English)

MacDonnell (*c.* 1505–90) in Ulster. This formidable Antrim warlord was brother of the head of the émigré MacDonald branch in Antrim (Sir James MacDonnell, sixth lord of Dunivaig) who was also by female descent (from the Bissets) lord of the Glynns or Glens there. Sir James had secured his family's lands on Islay – disputed by claims by a marital connection, Hector Maclean of Duart, who had been granted much of them by James V in 1542 despite the alleged documentary 'proof' being missing – by charter from Queen Mary's regency in 1545, but the focus of their activity was moving to Ulster. Islay was disputed with the Macleans (*q.v.*), and Kintyre was being lost to predatory Campbells. The MacDonnell brothers, aided by their younger brother Angus and with their other brother Alexander (seneschal of the family lands in Kintyre) bringing in regular troops from Kintyre, were the principal Gaelic Ulster rivals of the Irish clan of MacNeill, hereditary kings of Ulster and descendants of its ancient Uí Néill dynasty. As we have seen, they did have presumed ancient Ulster descent via Somerled – but possession was mainly determined by brute force in 1560s Ireland and the O'Neills were split by quarrels over the succession to the late chief Conn O'Neill.

A complex and constantly shifting pattern of alliances and wars were underway between MacDonalds, rival O'Neill warlords, local O'Donnells (the main rival Gaelic lords to the O'Neills as rulers of 'Tir Connaill'/Tyrconnell) and the English government in Dublin. Currently the MacDonalds (usually known as 'MacDonnells' in Ulster), led by Sir James, sixth lord of Dunivaig (unusually for a MacDonald married to Agnes, daughter of the third Earl of Argyll, a Campbell) were having the worst of it at the hands of the O'Neills, who were trying to drive the MacDonnells and other Scots settlers out of their lands. Dunluce Castle and most of the Glynns with it were overrun in 1564 by the great commander Shane O'Neill (a brigand to the English but a nationalist hero to the Gaels). Previously having used the MacDonnells as mercenaries in his own revolt of the 1550s against his father Conn O'Neill, Shane (illegitimate, so in the same legal position of Church disfavour as the MacDonalds of Sleat) turned on them. In a brilliant manoeuvre he launched a sudden attack in 1565 before their Kintyre reinforcements could arrive, pushing aside Somhairle's attempt to hold him up at a pass and capturing Sir James's new coastal 'Red Castle' (with its intended site for the Kintyre MacDonald landing) before taking on and defeating the brothers in a major inter-Gaelic battle. Sir James was mortally wounded and his Maclean nephew and a MacNeill chief killed (a sign of how many clans were mixed up in the Ulster war) with around 300–400 others, and Somhairle was captured and held hostage by Shane until the fortunes of war shifted in favour of the English 'Lord Deputy', the Earl of Sussex, and Shane had to seek MacDonald aid again in 1565. To add to the complications, Shane's mistress was the daughter of the fourth Earl of Argyll, head of the Campbells and Sir James's wife's brother – whose clan were now driving the MacDonalds out of Kintyre. A reconciliation feast was arranged with the MacDonalds, with Shane bringing his prisoner Somhairle along to cement the alliance ahead of his release, but this gathering on 2 June 1565 ended up (whether by accident or design) with the MacDonalds stabbing Shane to death and liberating his prisoner. Either the MacDonalds or the Dublin authorities (or both acting together) had probably planned it.

The O'Neills lost their most effective leader, and Somhairle now reasserted his independence as a sporadic but much more equal ally of Shane's successor Turlough 'Luineach' O'Neill; but he needed more men and this was where Donald Gormson of Sleat and his warriors came in. They played a major role in Somhairle's late 1560s campaigns and acquired more loot and military experience, besides annoying the English government and adding to its suspicion of the Scots government's supposed goodwill and intentions for Ulster. Meanwhile Turlough married Sir James MacDonnell's widow Agnes Campbell, acquiring more west Highland recruits as part of the marriage settlement, and later on Agnes' and Sir James's daughter Fionnuala would be married off to the O'Donnell chief Aodh/Hugh in an inter-clan alliance. In 1569 Donald 'Gormson' was back in Scotland, feuding with the Mackenzies of Kintail. He died in 1575 and his underage son Donald 'Mór' was placed under the 'tutorship' of his great-uncle, James/Seumas of Castle Camus; the latter and the sons of Archibald (Gillespie) 'Cleariach' (as 'Clann GhillEasbaig') divided up the clan lands, with the latter in charge of Trotternish. Meanwhile in Ulster the MacDonnells continued to be preyed upon by the O'Neills and the English settlers, and in 1575 their residents on Rathlin Island were notoriously overwhelmed and massacred by the new 'Lord Deputy', the Earl of Essex (married to Queen Elizabeth's cousin and rival Lettice Knollys). The clan's main problem in these politically quieter years was a dispute with the bishopric of the Isles for failure to pay due rents on the clan territories in Sleat, Trotternish and North Uist; Seumas agreed to pay up the overdue rents in 1575 but the bishop was complaining about non-payment again in 1580 and acquired a Privy Council decision in his favour. The sons of Archibald were declared forfeit in 1581 for their contempt of court in not paying up. By now Donald 'Mór' was involved in another feud with the Macleans of Duart, which traditionally arose from a mishap on his journey to Ulster to assist his MacDonald/MacDonnell kin in

1579. With Sir James killed in 1565 and his son Alexander, seventh lord of Dunivaig, dying in around 1569, the latter's younger brother Angus (d. 1614) was now lord of Dunivaig and Islay but fighting the Macleans over the latter. A storm drove Donald 'Mór's ship to anchor for safety at Jura, an island divided between the MacDonalds of Islay and their Maclean foes, and he mistakenly landed on the Maclean portion; in the night the Macleans attacked his men's camp and butchered them, though he escaped (traditionally due to sleeping on board ship). Possibly the Macleans thought that as Donald was ally to their rivals for Islay, the Dunivaig family, he had invaded on his kin's behalf. As a result war broke out between Donald 'Mór' and Sir Lachlan Maclean of Duart to add to the MacDonalds of Dunivaig-*versus*-Maclean war, and this added to the manpower of, and resulting damage inflicted by, the rival coalitions of clans, with the main MacDonald branches (Sleat, Clanranald, Glengarry, Keppoch, Ardnamurchan) on Donald's side and the MacLeods fighting for Maclean. Around 500–600 MacDonalds on Islay and Gigha are said to have been killed by Sir Lachlan's raids, and Angus was once besieged in Dunivaig Castle by the Macleans and forced to hand over half of Islay to them in a truce. As soon as possible he collected a new clan army of MacDonalds and resumed the war.

The government endeavoured to impose a legal requirement for all clan chiefs to guarantee their clans' peaceable behaviour on penalty of paying large fines in 1587, but imposing it was another matter. The war only ended by a settlement enforced by the Privy Council in 1589. Next year the rival chiefs were summoned to Edinburgh to ratify the agreement, arrested and held prisoner until they paid large sums to be forfeited in the event of any more conflict. Having been forced to keep his clansmen quiet in Scotland, and with the Dunivaig /Maclean war ended, Donald 'Mór' then returned to Ireland to join in the Gaelic 'rebel' siege of Enniskillen in 1594. Back on Islay, Angus's main rival was soon to be his ambitious son (Sir) James, who famously ended up assaulting and burning his home and kidnapping him in a family feud in 1598. In 1608 Angus was attacked by a government expedition led by Lord Ochiltree, whom James VI had sent to enforce royal authority on the Inner Hebrides and who had called a meeting of the local chiefs on Islay to lay down the law to them. From now on the royal writ would run on the islands, and the threat of confiscation and colonisation (as seen on Lewis) hung over objectors. In this attempt to enforce control of the unruly MacDonalds of Dunivaig and their neighbours, Angus was forced to surrender Dunivaig Castle and deported to the mainland to be imprisoned at Blackness Castle until it was felt that he had learnt his lesson. He then tamely helped the conciliatory new Bishop of the

Isles hold a major meeting of the local chiefs (very rare since the end of the 'lordship') on Iona later in 1608 to sort out differences and arrange a general peace – with the Church replacing the 'lord' as organiser and host. But Dunivaig Castle was permanently seized on his death in 1614, and handed over to the pro-government Campbells of Cawdor.

Donald 'Dubh': The finale of the 'Lordship'?

A second attempt to revive the lordship of the Isles was made by Donald 'Dubh', now in his fifties, after the death of James V and the accession of the week-old Mary Stuart in December 1542. There was a dispute over the regency between her mother, the French Marie de Guise, and the Hamilton family led by the Earl of Arran (next lineal heir to the throne and 'Governor'/regent from January 1543), and to add to the complications a number of prominent lords had been captured at the Battle of Solway Moss by the English just before James's death. The predatory Henry VIII, brother to Queen Mary's late paternal grandmother Margaret Tudor, had them (and some hostages for those being ransomed) brought to court and pressurised them to agree to the infant queen being betrothed to his young son Prince Edward for a 'union of crowns', a revival of the 1286–90 scheme of Edward I. In addition, this would save England from the spectre of a Scots regency dominated by its French enemy. The exiled Earl Matthew of Lennox (1513–71), head of the main branch of the non-royal Stewarts and a distant cousin of the queen, was also involved in this as a French ally and was sent home by King Francis I to assist the Francophile queen mother Marie and Cardinal Beaton. The marriage was duly agreed at the Treaty of Greenwich in July 1543 and approved by the Scots Parliament, led by Arran, but Scots opposition to it soon revived as Henry sought to impose a partial religious 'Reformation' to cut off the Scots Catholic Church from the anti-English papacy. Meanwhile Lennox took over strategic Dumbarton Castle, near his ancestral lands, and fought Arran unsuccessfully outside Glasgow in March 1544, after which he fled – to England not France, probably due to seeking Henry's aid against Arran.

The English may already have been dangling the hand of Henry's niece Margaret Douglas – daughter of Margaret Tudor by her second husband, the Earl of Angus – as bait to the ambitious Lennox, and later in 1544 they were married with Lennox now Henry's principal agent for Scots affairs and his intended replacement for Arran. Some time in this complex struggle Donald 'Dubh' either escaped or was released from captivity, and the results of this – another MacDonald revolt in the Isles – were to England's benefit, so it is possible that one of the Anglophile lords was involved (on Henry's orders?). The timing is unclear, but Donald was back in the Inner Hebrides being welcomed by his father's vassals and raising rebellion against Queen Mary by summer 1544 so possibly Lennox or his friends helped him escape by sea via their stronghold, Dumbarton. The revolt was successful as the embattled regency lacked the troops or time to send a force to the Hebrides, and it was known to and supported by the English. The plan was for Donald to co-ordinate an attack by his sixty-five galleys (an impressive force) on the heartland of Scotland with a naval descent by the now exiled Lennox from England, probably with the two forces joining up in the Clyde. As the new husband of Margaret Douglas, Lennox was now her uncle Henry's choice to head the regency and remove Queen Mary to England to marry Prince Edward. But instead Henry chose to divert Lennox to assist the English attack up the east coast on Edinburgh, which was duly sacked in the so-called 'Rough Wooing', designed to terrorise the Scots into accepting the royal marriage. The Clyde invasion was postponed to 1545, and on 28 July 1545 a 'Council of the Isles' – the last one under MacDonald rule – was held on Islay where the chiefs led by Donald 'Dubh' signed up to an alliance with England. In a revival of the plans of 1462–63, Donald renounced his allegiance to the Scots Crown and transferred it to the King of England, whom he pledged to serve when required with an army of 6,000 men. As in the 1460s, a weak Scots regency would now lead to the MacDonalds becoming semi-independent lords and allies of the King of England, hopefully breaking their lands off from the Kingdom of Scots. But this plan collapsed again – this time due to the mercurial Henry deciding to use his new allies in an invasion of Ulster to deal with the king's foes in Ireland rather than in an immediate attack on Scotland. In August 1545 Donald brought an army of 4,000 men to Ulster, leaving another 4,000 or so back in the Isles, and held another council of his chiefs (and local allies) at Knockfergus to confirm his arrangements with Henry and send an envoy to his middleman, Lennox. The earl then delivered the MacDonald documents of allegiance to Henry in London and the treaty of alliance was signed by him in September. But at this point Donald 'Dubh' died at Dundalk, probably in his mid-fifties, and the project collapsed. His lieutenant Sir James MacDonald of Dunivaig wrote to Henry that he was prepared to act as the new commander and the chiefs would accept him, but there was no reply. The MacDonald invasion of mainland Scotland was abandoned, the chiefs went home, and the lordship of the Isles lapsed again. The English plan to enforce the marriage of Edward, who was King of England from January 1547, and Queen Mary continued under his uncle and regent the Duke of Somerset – though as a Protestant the latter was inimical to Catholic Highlanders – but there was now no obvious Isles commander for the north-western Scots part of the project and it was not pursued.

Name	Date of accession	Date of death/dep.	Years ruled
Godfrey/Godred 'Crovan', King of Man (from 1079)	c. 1079	1095	c. 16
Laghman (son) (King Magnus of Norway, 1098 – 1103)	1095	1098	3
Somerled MacGillebride (Division of kingdom among Somerled's three sons)	early 1130s	Apr 1164	c. 30
Dugald of Argyll/Lorn and Mull, Tiree, etc. (ancestor MacDougalls)	Apr 1164	?1192	?28
Ragnald of Kintyre (and Mull, Tiree, etc. from 1192)	Apr 1164	?1210	?46
Donald MacRagnald (son) (ancestor of MacDonalds) (Isles)	?1210	?1230	?20
Duncan MacDougall (son of Dugald) (Lorne)	?1230	1244/8	?13/18
Donald 'Screech' MacDougall (brother) (co-ruler)	?1230	?1235	?5
Uspak/Gillespie MacDougall (brother) (co-ruler) (Norse nominee)	1230	1230	<1
Ewen/Eoghan MacDougall (son of Duncan (Lorne; recognised by Norway from 1249)	1244/8	1270s	?25/30
Angus 'Mór' MacDonald (Isles; recognised by Scotland)	1266	1294/5	<29?
Alexander MacDougall (Lorne)	1270s	<1300	?20/25
Alexander MacDonald (son of Alex) (Isles) (Nephew of Alexander MacDonald, John 'Sprangach', gains Ardnamurchan c. 1300 and founds the line of 'MacIains'.)	1294/5	1299 (k.)	4/5
Alexander MacDougall (depr.) (Lorne) (MacDougalls of Lorne dispossessed by Robert Bruce.)	<1300	1308/9? (depr.)	
Angus Og MacDonald (brother of Alexander MacDonald) (Isles)	1299	?1318/20	?19/21
Alexander MacDonald (son, co-ruler of successor) (Isles)	<1318	1318 (k.)	?
John MacDonald (brother) (Isles)	<1336	1386	>50
Donald MacDonald (son) (Isles)	1386	?1423	?37
Alexander MacDonald (son) (Isles)	?1423	May 1449	?26

Name	Date of accession	Date of death/dep.	Years ruled
John MacDonald (son) (Isles) (b. 1434)	May 1449	May 1493 (dep.) (d. 1503)	44
Angus (illeg. son) (effective ruler of Isles)	c. 1478?	1490	c. 12?
Donald 'Dubh' (grandson of John)	(i) 1503	autumn 1506	3
	(ii)1543	1545	2 (Total: 5)

Lochalsh

Name	Date of accession	Date of death/dep.	Years ruled
Celestine (brother of John MacDonald)	May 1476	1449	26/7
Alexander (son)	1476	1494 (assassinated)	18
Donald (son)	1494	1519	25

5

Lords of Man to 1265

A British lordship until the Viking conquests, Man was supposedly named after the Celtic god of the sea, Manannan MacLir. The names of its rulers are unclear, though later Welsh legend claimed that it was ruled around AD 400 by a son of Emperor Magnus Maximus/'Macsen Wledig', Anhun (?Antonius), which may reflect a claim by the rulers of Gwynedd where Maximus was connected to Caernarfon. It was supposedly Christianised in the early fifth century by St Garmon, an obscure saint who may have been muddled up with the Powys-connected St Germanus (fl. 429), possibly aided by St Patrick from Ireland. It was ruled successively by the leading naval powers in the Irish Sea – Rheged in the later sixth century and Northumbria in the seventh – with a possible dynastic connection for its sixth-century lords with King Tutugual of Galloway/Strathclyde, the British kingdom based at Dumbarton. The line of kings of Man was supposed to be descended from a shadowy 'Ednyfed', son of Anhun, who was nine generations earlier than the mid- or late seventh-century king Merfyn or Mermin. Tradition had it that at one point in the later sixth century Man was ruled by the famous Welsh poet-prince Llywarch 'Hen' ('the Old'), son of an obscure prince called Elidyr (Roman name 'Eleutherius') 'the Stout', who unsuccessfully challenged King Rhun of Gwynedd in north Wales (r. c. 550–80) by raiding his coasts. Elidyr was of the line of King Coel 'Hen' of York, aka 'Old King Cole', whom the Welsh genealogies made ancestor of a large dynasty of northern British kings ruling in separate realms in York, Northumberland/Lothian, Carlisle and Cumbria/Lancashire. Rhun, who probably had a fleet a well as a formidable army and at one point took the latter as far as the northern Pennines in a campaign, overran Elidyr's kingdom (possibly centred on Lancashire) and either killed or expelled him. This was probably around 565/70, and Llywarch was subsequently listed in Welsh literature as one of the princes who lost their father's inheritance. He ended up as a travelling poet serving his cousin Owain ap Urien, king of Rheged and primary warlord in northern Britain, who was killed by the Angles of Bernicia (Northumberland) around 594 after fighting for his father King Urien and witnessing his assassination at the siege of Anglian-held Lindisfarne island in ?589. Llywarch's poems refer to his part in Urien's and Owain's campaigns, either as a soldier or as a celebratory bard. Later he is said – on less clear evidence as these poems textually seem to be ninth century not seventh century – to have served the Mid Wales ruler Cyndylan of Powys in the 630s or 640s (if he lived that long). He supposedly lived in his later life in Powys, and his sons were killed in battle fighting for that kingdom; at least one fathered heirs who were to regain Man according to the later Welsh dynastic lists of rulers. Either Gwynedd or Rheged probably annexed Man in the 570s, but by the late 620s it was part of the kingdom of Northumbria (the union of Bernicia and Deira/York) under its newly Christian king, Edwin. The latter had a fleet, with which he attacked Anglesey in the 620s, and was probably the pre-eminent power in the Irish Sea as well as overlord of Rheged; after he was killed in battle by the king of Gwynedd in 633/34, Man's fate is unclear.

Man presumably remained under Brittonic and Christian rule, and later traditions named its ruler in the mid-eighth century as Sandde (a name shared with other, more well-attested Welsh/Brittonic figures such as St David's father), who came from mainland Britain to marry the heiress of King Iudugual. (This was another attested Brittonic royal name, held in the sixth century by a king in Brittany/Armorica.) Iudugual was son of king Anarawd (a name also used for a king of Gwynedd allegedly descended from him in the later ninth century), and grandson of Merfyn or Mermin who died around 680. In 790 an Anglian king of Northumbria, Osred II, ended up exiled on Man after a rebellion in his kingdom, which might suggest that he had kin or friends there; given the Tyneside location of his overthrow he probably fled via Cumbria. In the late eighth or early ninth century one of Man's princes, King Sandde's grandson Gwriad ap Elidyr, married the daughter and heiress (Essylt/Isolde) of the king of Gwynedd. The latter's kingdom was being fought over by two rival lines of kings, so Manx troops would have been welcome to one candidate. Their son Merfyn 'the Freckled' founded a new dynasty in Gwynedd in 825; he may have been named for a semi-legendary Manx king of the seventh century, Merfyn or Mermin. He was also the sponsor of the propaganda *History of the Britons* written around 830 in Gwynedd, probably by Bishop Nennius, which popularised the role of 'King Arthur' as the national British/Welsh leader against the Saxon invaders around 500. Possibly this reflects an interest of Merfyn's, inherited with his family's historical traditions from the legacy of his learned ancestor Llywarch 'Hen', the poet 'cheerleader' of Rheged's wars. (Merfyn's father had been named after the father of Llywarch 'Hen', so the dynasty's ancestors were clearly important to them.) Notably, this book hardly bothered with the early history of Gwynedd, but dealt with the 'national' British cause after the Romans left; a politico-cultural theme can be traced from Llywarch to Nennius and may have come via Man. The latter was the refuge of the 'Gwyr a'r Gogledd', the 'Men of the North', descended from the great fifth-century ruler Coel 'Hen' and the warrior kings Urien and Owain of Rheged – so Merfyn's patronage of a book stressing the united British fightback under 'Arthur' against the Saxons was logical. Merfyn's son was Rhodri 'Mawr' ('the Great'), ruler of Gwynedd from 844 to 878 and of Powys from 853. By this date the first Scandinavian settlers were setting up a new port and kingdom at Dublin ('Dubh Linn', 'Dark Pool') on the opposite Irish coast and Man was moving into a world centred on rival Scandinavian kingdoms and ambitious warlords around the Irish Sea. It is possible that this increased danger of raids from Dublin in the 810s and 820s encouraged the royal line of Man to move to the safer Gwynedd, where their military experience from fighting Viking raiders was useful to a kingdom itself under threat from the English of Mercia (who raided to Deganwy in 797 and the mid-820s).

The Viking conquest and settlement of Man in the ninth century led to sporadic rule from York, Orkney or Dublin depending on their respective power. The first recorded Manx king of Viking origin was Godred MacFergus, also king of Airgíalla in northern Ireland and 'Ri Innse Gall' ('leader of the Gaelic Islanders') to the Irish, in the 830s or 840s. However, the Irish *Annals of the Four Masters*, which use this term for him, were composed in the early seventeenth century so their accuracy may be suspect and the term is not authentic ninth century. Godred apparently died in 853 – assuming that the dates are accurate. The mixed Norse–Irish community of the Gall-Gaedhil that emerged in Man in the mid-ninth century mostly came under Viking leadership and had an uneasy relationship with their powerful neighbours in Dublin, their rivals to leadership of the Viking settlers of the Hebrides; Caitill 'the Fair', ruler of Man in the 850s–860s, is possibly the same person as the Viking leader remembered in the sagas as Ketil 'Flatnose' (see earlier chapters). The name is, however, a common one for the age, and there may have been two contemporary rulers of that name; the Irish annals present Caitill as leader of the Gall-Gaedhil in southern Ireland and a local rival of the then Norse rulers of Dublin, Amlaith/Olaf and

Ivarr. The latter two defeated him in battle in Tipperary in 857, possibly driving him from Ireland. Ketil, whether or not the same man, was ruler of Man in the 860s and father-in-law of Olaf 'the White' of Dublin. Ragnald 'Uí Ímair', i.e. 'grandson of Imar/Ivarr', whose grandfather may have been Ivarr 'the Boneless', who ruled Dublin in 871–73 (see earlier chapters), probably added Man to his seaborne 'empire' in the 910s, as it was off the island that he and his relative (cousin?) Sihtric defeated a fleet led by Barid, the son of Jarl Ottar/Othere, in 914 according to the *Annals of Ulster*. They then went on to invade Leinster and retake Waterford in 917, driving back the forces of Irish 'High King' Niall 'Glundub', current head of the Uí Néill dynasty whose hereditary lands were in Midhe. Sihtric took over Dublin, which the Irish had recently (902) reconquered from the Scandinavians in a serious threat to their control over their coastal settlements.

For the first time since the 840s it looked as if the Irish might unite and expel the Scandinavians, and the latter's secure base on Man provided useful troops to the 'House of Ivarr' in these campaigns and was by no means a backwater though it rarely appears in the chronicles and sagas. Ragnald appears to have regarded Ireland as less important to his ambitions than northern England, and most likely used Man as the base for his invasion of the latter in 918 when he probably assumed leadership of the new Norse settlements in the Lake District and Lancashire (attested to by their Norwegian-influenced place names) given the location of this campaign. He then went on to the Tyne valley to fight a drawn battle at Corbridge with the local English army of the lordship of Bamburgh (the part of Northumbria north of the Tees not occupied by the Vikings in 867–70) and assume control of York. The latter had been conquered from the Angles of Northumbria in 867 by Ivarr 'the Boneless' and his brothers Halfdan and Ubbe, sons of Ragnar 'Lothbrok' ('Leather Breeches'), so if Ragnald was Ivarr's grandson he had a dynastic claim to it. Ragnald would have needed control of Lancashire and probably Cumbria to link up his new realm to Man and Waterford as the Scandinavians no longer held the Forth–Clyde corridor in Scotland as they had done in the 870s, though his control of this region as well as York and Man is not certain. He died and was succeeded in 921 by his ally Sihtric, who had killed 'High King' Niall in battle outside Dublin in September 919 and thus restored secure Scandinavian control of Dublin for decades to come. Like Ragnald, Sihtric abandoned a prolonged Irish war to take on the conquest of York instead. But the advance North of the new united 'Kingdom of England', a union of Wessex and Mercia, posed a major threat to the 'House of Ivarr', and Ragnald may have paid homage to King Edward 'the Elder' (d. 924) or at least been his ally to avoid attack as the Anglo-Saxons reached the Dee and Humber in 918–19. Sihtric submitted to Edward's son King Athelstan of England in a visit to his court at Tamworth in the Midlands in January 926 and married his sister Edith, but died in 926/7; his heir in Man is unclear though it may have been his brother Guthfrith, who had taken over Dublin when he left for England. Athelstan's conquest of York in 927 broke up this northern empire as Guthfrith fled to Dublin, and by the time of the Viking–British coalition against Athelstan of 937, led by Olaf Guthfrithson of Dublin, Man was ruled by one Gebeachan. It is unclear if Olaf ever ruled Man, but he was probably its overlord at the time of his rule in York and the 'Five Boroughs' in England in 939–41.

A mysterious 'MacRagnall' succeeded Gebeachan, possibly Sihtric's nephew, and then in the 970s Maccus (called 'Magnus' by the Norse sources) and Godred 'MacArailt' or 'Haraldsen' (probably sons of Arailt/ Harald, Scandinavian king of Limerick, who died in 940). Arailt/Harald is a very obscure figure, but may have been a younger son of Sihtric of Dublin (referred to above); the Scandinavian kingdom of Limerick had been as powerful as that of Dublin in the early tenth century but was reduced to vassalage by Olaf Guthfrithson of Dublin in an attack, apparently in 937 so logically intended to coerce the Limerickmen into aiding his invasion of England that year. By the early 970s Limerick was under the control of the elusive King Ivarr or Imar, not of Arailt's family, the city's last Scandinavian ruler and a successful warlord. He was militarily powerful enough to pose a serious threat to the neighbouring Irish kingdom of Munster and was able to kill its rising leader, sub-ruler Mathgamhain of Thomond (brother of Brian Boru), so Maccus and his kin probably left him alone and made no claim to Limerick until they were strong enough. Maccus was apparently the 'MacArailt' who the *Annals of Innisfallen* and the seventeenth-century *Annals of the Four Masters* state as attacking and capturing Ivarr/Imar at Scattery Island (Inis Cathaigh) in the Shannon estuary in 974. This was evidently part of an extended naval cruise around the West coasts of Ireland, and may reflect the reach of this 'king of the Isles' as he was called by Irish sources. Given that his probable father Arailt/Harald had ruled Limerick and the latter's father may have been Ivarr/Imar who ruled it in the 870s (if he was not Sihtric of Dublin), Maccus may have intended to annex Limerick to his empire of the seaways as his father's lordship but was foiled by his victim's escape. Within three years Ivarr had been killed and Limerick annexed by the reviving nearby Irish kingdom of Thomond, a sub-kingdom of Munster, led by the heroic Irish unifier Brian Boru, whose brother Mathgamhain had been killed thanks to Ivarr's treachery. Brian was to go on to become king of Munster and then in 1002 'High

King' of Ireland, in both cases the first of his obscure dynasty to do so, and in 984 Maccus allied to him and the Viking king of Waterford, another Ivarr, in an attack on Dublin.

Maccus was also involved in plundering Gwynedd in north Wales in expeditions in 972 and 984, and was probably the 'Marcus' who attacked Penmon on Anglesey in 971. His brother Godred seems to have assisted Custennin/Constantine, a pretender to Gwynedd, against his cousin King Hywel (r. 979–85) in 979. We can assume with a reasonable degree of certainty that Maccus' main rivals were the Scandinavian kings of Dublin, Olaf 'Cuaran'/'of the Sandals' (expelled 980, d. 981), and his sons Gluniarn (r. 980–89) and Sihtric 'Silkenbeard' (r. 989–1036, with intermissions). In the late 980s the future King of Norway, Olaf Tryggvason, also turned up in Dublin as an ambitious adventurer with a war band, and secured co-rule with the young Sihtric before returning to Norway to take its throne in 994; we do not know if he ever extended his rule to or secured vassalage from Man. Olaf had enough to do in Norway fighting his rivals to hold on to Dublin, and in 1000 he was cornered by a hostile coalition in a naval battle in the western Baltic and notoriously jumped overboard from his longship to evade capture. In this complex world of shifting realms and allegiances Olaf 'Cuaran', though ruling Dublin for most of his career, was the son of King Sihtric of York in England (d. 927), probable grandson of Ivarr 'the Boneless', king of Dublin, and had also ruled York both in 941–44, after the death of his cousin and rival Olaf Guthfrithson, and in 947–52. Olaf was driven out of York on the first occasion by King Edmund of England and on the second occasion by ex-king Erik 'Bloodaxe' of Norway (see first chapter on Orkney). Control of the seaways to Cumbria/Lancashire and thence York was essential for a ruler of both Dublin and York, and we can assume that Olaf 'Cuaran' at least had the goodwill of if he was not ruling on Man during his reigns in York. He and his sons were the chief foes of the 'MacArailt' brothers Maccus and Godred, hence the latter's attempts to secure the resources of Limerick and later alliance with Brian Boru, and Olaf's expulsion from Dublin by Irish 'High King' Mael Sechnaill in 980 would have been good news for them. Sihtric 'Silkenbeard' was a much less formidable proposition, and was dominated by his formidable mother Gormflaith of Leinster – successively married to Olaf 'Cuaran', Mael Sechnaill, and Brian and the latter's main destroyer in 1014. Another bonus was the early death of the fleet-building King Edgar of England in 975; he had enforced Maccus' and the Scots' vassalage in a meeting at Chester in 973 according to twelfth-century English writers, and his naval power was another threat, but his sons Edward 'the Martyr' and Aethelred

'Unraed' had other problems. Maccus' brother Godred's sons Ragnald and Kenneth ruled Man around 1000, possibly as vassals of the great Norse sea lord Sigurd of Orkney, and as nothing is known of it after its leading warlord, Brodar, led a mercenary force to fight for Orkney against Brian at the Battle of Clontarf in 1014, Dublin may have taken over control. (Other Man warriors are said to have fought for Brian at Clontarf.) Sihtric's nephew Imar or Ivarr MacArailt's rival for Dublin, the even more obscure Echmarcach Ragnaldson, seems to have retired to Man when driven out of Dublin by him in 1038, and probably used it as a base for his restoration to power in 1046.

By 1052 Echmarcach/'Margad' was definitely ruling the kingdom of Man, and the coins produced by the new mint on Man are virtually identical to those in Dublin, showing the administrative closeness of the two halves of this kingdom. But Echmarcach was expelled again from Dublin in 1052 according to the Irish *Annals of Innisfallen* and *Annals of the Four Masters* – this time not by a Norseman but by an Irish ruler, King Diarmait 'Mac Mael N Ma' Bo' of Leinster (so called from the nickname of his father Domnhall). Like Brian of Munster, Diarmait was a 'self-made man', ruler of a long obscure branch of the ruling family – in this case the 'Uí Ceinnselaig' – who had risen by ability and warfare to take over the kingdom in place of its failing ruling family and then gone on to attack its Scandinavian neighbours. His son Murchad went on to drive Echmarcach out of Man too in 1061, and the unlucky ruler fled overseas to Rome and died there in 1064/65; Man was ruled with Dublin by its first known Irish mainland dynast, Murchad, until he died in 1070. Logically its warriors would have taken part in the successful Norse expeditions sent by Echmarcach to assist exiled Earl Aelfgar of Mercia in forcing his restoration on King Edward of England in 1058 and by Diarmait to assist the late King Harold Godwinson's exiled sons to raid Norman-occupied Devon in 1068–69. Any direct Dublin control soon lapsed, and in 1070/71 a 'Godred Sihtricson' was in control of Man. Diarmait, who may have ruled Man as its overlord in 1070–72, was killed in battle in Ireland in 1072 and the Scandinavians of the 'House of Ivarr' regained Dublin but not apparently Man. A 'Godred MacAmlaith' was ruling Dublin as viceroy for the Irish 'High King', Toirdelbach Ó Briain (grandson of Brian Boru), in the early 1070s, and it may have been his brother Sihtric who was killed with two of the Ó Briain dynasty in 1073 while raiding Man. If the Ó Briains of Munster were hostile to the current government of Man in 1073, this would link in with the island's continuing alliance with the Munster rulers' rivals in Leinster, Diarmait's family. Fingal, son of one of the two Godreds, was ruling in Man by 1079; if his father was Godred MacAmlaith then his father's expulsion from Dublin by the 'High King' in 1075 would have weakened him.

Eventually a greater degree of historical certainty surrounds the emergence of the first recorded dynasty of kings, founded by Godred 'Crovan' in 1079. Godred, a Viking of Manx origin and a veteran of the Norse army of Harald 'Hardradi' at the Battle of Stamford Bridge in 1066, was nicknamed 'Crovan' – i.e. 'Crobh Bann', 'White Hands' – from the gauntlets that he wore in battle. He was referred to in the Irish *Annals of Tigernach* as 'Mac mic Arailt', i.e. a grandson of Arailt or Harald; either his father or uncle was presumably Imar MacArailt (son of Harald), ruler of Dublin from 1038 to 1046 and nephew of King Sihtric 'Silkenbeard'. Harald, Godred's grandfather, was thus Sihtric's brother. An alternative genealogy for King Ragnald/Reginald of Man (d. 1227), preserved in a Welsh source and in a collection published by P. C. Bartrum in 1966, gives Arailt/Harald as son of 'Ivar son of Olaf Sihtricson', as does a family genealogy of Christina MacLeod, great-granddaughter of the elusive 'Leod' (founder of the MacLeod clan, *q.v.*, and supposed son of King Olaf 'the Black' of Man). This makes Harald's grandfather King Olaf 'Cuaran' of Dublin. On this basis, the MacLeod genealogist Andrew P. MacLeod has suggested that references to Arailt/Harald's father Ivarr as 'rig Lochlan', i.e. 'King of the Norsemen' might mean that he was viceroy for his brother Sihtric 'Silkenbeard' over Norse settlers in either Man or the Hebrides, possibly in the 1020s or 1030s. In any case, whatever the exact link, Godred was probably descended from the Scandinavian family of the father of Sihtric 'Silkenbeard', King Olaf 'Cuaran', and from the Irish – Leinster – family of Sihtric's mother Queen Gormflaith, the turbulent and strong-willed wife of 'High Kings' Mael Sechnaill and Brian Boru. (See chapter on Orkney, section on the Battle of Clontarf.) An alternative *Manx Chronicle* reference gives his father or grandfather as Harald, a ruler of Iceland – which did not actually have any kings, though Andrew MacLeod thinks the confusion may have arisen over Harald having to flee to Iceland from the resurgent jarls of the Hebrides in the 1030s or 1040s. (The mid-eleventh-century material in the *Manx Chronicle* is somewhat inaccurate in its dating anyway.) Godred's ancestry was thus suitable to rule a mixed Gaelic and Scandinavian people. He evicted the current ruler, 'Fingal the son of the King of Dublin' (i.e. Fingal son of Godred), who is not referred to in reliable Irish sources, in a struggle that ended in 1079. Irish sources claim that he had previously lived on Man as a refugee after the Battle of Stamford Bridge, taking service there with its then ruler Godred Sihtricson, who may be the same man as one then co-ruling Dublin with Murchad (d. 1070). In that case

Fingal, named by one record as 'MacGodred', would probably be this Godred's son.

The *Manx Chronicle* recounts that Godred Crovan's success was after three invasions, the first two unsuccessful, and involved laying an ambush for the local army in a wood on the ridge of Snaefell near his landing place of Ramsey. He put 300 men ready in ambush in the wood so that they could emerge and attack the enemy in the rear as the two armies confronted each other, and the Manxmen fled to be trapped by a flooding river. Many of Godred's mercenary army preferred to take their loot and go home, so he gave the Manx survivors the northern half of the island as his tenants (i.e. removable at will) and took the southern half for his own men. He then went on to overrun parts of the Hebrides to form a seaborne empire on the lines of its Orkney rival. From this time the frequent rule of Man by the current Norse kings of Dublin came to an end, and Godred established both a dynasty and the Manx legislative assembly or 'Tynwald'. Temporarily ruling Dublin too until evicted by 'High King' Muirchertach Ó Briain (of the line of Brian Boru as king of Munster) in 1094 and raiding into Leinster, he married a lady of Norse extraction called Ragnhild, 'daughter of Harald', who may or may not have been an illegitimate daughter of his ex-patron, King Harald 'Hardradi' of Norway. If so, his descendants had Norwegian royal blood and were thus kin to their future overlords in Norway. He died in 1095 on Islay in the Inner Hebrides, which was presumably part of his empire, of the plague. His son Laghman (an official Manx rank, i.e. 'lawman', not a personal name in origin but probably a normal name by this time) either abdicated voluntarily in guilt at his part in his captured rebel brother Harald's mutilation and death or was forced out by his new Norwegian overlord King Magnus 'Bareleg' (ruled Norway 1093–1103). If it is correct that Laghman's abdication preceded the Norwegian conquest of 1098/99 by several years, this period saw civil war, a brief incursion by a Norwegian governor sent by Magnus called Ingemund who was killed in battle on the Outer Hebrides, and a battle between the northern and southern Manxmen at Santwat in which the rival commanders, Jarl Othere and Macmarus, were both killed. The chronicle links this latter battle time-wise to the First Crusade and the fall of Antioch to the Christians, i.e. 1097–98.

Now King Magnus 'Bareleg' of Norway, the new master of the northern seas and recent conqueror of Orkney, secured dominion of Man for his family by invading on his first western voyage in 1098–99. Laghman is said by Norse sources to have been captured by him, and is called 'lord of Uist' not of Man – so had he taken refuge in his northern dominions after expulsion from Man or abdication? Magnus imposed his underage son Sigurd as ruler of both Man and Orkney, and constructed new buildings in the capital, Ramsey. Sigurd was married off to the daughter of Magnus's new Irish ally, 'High King' Muirchertach Ó Briain, but Magnus broke off the arrangement after he and her father quarrelled. After Magnus's death while campaigning in Ulster as an ally of the Ó Briain dynasty in 1103, a period of confusion proceeded as Sigurd went home to Norway and Laghman briefly regained the throne. The Manxmen at one point sought a new governor from the most powerful king in eastern Ireland, Muirchertach Ó Briain, who sent out Donald MacTeige/Tadhg. He proved to be a tyrant and was expelled after three years, returning to Ireland (1110–13?). The confusion ended with the emergence of Laghman's now adult son Olaf 'the Red' as lord of Man in 1113/14, his rule lasting for around forty years.

Olaf was a man of peace, unlike most of his warlike family, and in 1134 founded the first Cistercian abbey on Man, Rushen, with monks from Furness Abbey in Cumbria. The first abbot was Wimund 'of the Isles', possibly son of William FitzDuncan, lord of Egremont and Craven (and grandson of King Malcolm III of Scots). Olaf's Norse nickname was 'Kleining', 'the Dwarf', a reference to his stature; the *Manx Chronicle* calls him a mild-mannered and pious ruler whose only vice was the domestic one of kings, i.e. presumably having mistresses. He married Auffrica, the daughter of his powerful neighbour to the north-east, Fergus, lord (or king) of Galloway, who abdicated on the orders of King Malcolm IV in 1160 and died in 1161. Auffrica's mother Elizabeth was the illegitimate daughter of King Henry I of England (r. 1100–35), an aggressive warlord, conqueror of Normandy and possible fratricide who was probably using both his son-in-law Fergus of Galloway and his viceroy of Cumbria, the future King David of Scotland, to act as his agents in extending his power northwards. Did he approve of his granddaughter's marriage (c. 1116–20?) to extend this family network of influence? Olaf's son by Auffrica, Godred 'the Black', was adult and was absent in Norway doing homage as heir to King Inge when a fleet led by Olaf's three disgruntled nephews, the sons of his brother Harald, arrived at Ramsey demanding that Olaf hand over half the kingdom to them. As with the Orkneys, attempts to divide the kingdom among several ambitious adult male contenders were not uncommon – and nor was treachery. On this occasion, Olaf agreed to come to a parley with his nephews but was attacked and murdered by their leader, Ragnald, at this meeting on the feast of saints Peter and Paul in 1153. According to the *Manx Chronicle*, he treacherously pretended to be about to do homage to put Olaf off his guard, then hit him over the head with his battleaxe. Ragnald succeeded as king, being the senior of the three brothers, but when they went on to ravage Galloway they were heavily defeated and within weeks Godred returned from Norway to overthrow them. Either one brother was killed and two blinded or all three were killed. Godred now revived his grandfather Godred 'Crovan's ambitions in Ireland and attacked Dublin, driving out the forces of 'High King' (1150–66) Muirchertach McLochlainn, king of Ulster. He defeated an Ulster attack in which the king's brother was killed and was recognised as overlord of Dublin, but soon his lords were being alienated by his tyranny and some turned to his sister's husband, Somerled of the Isles/Argyll. One of his vassal Hebridean chieftains, Thorfinn, secured Somerled's agreement to transfer the local lords' allegiance to Somerled's son and Olaf's grandson, Dugald, but as Thorfinn was taking the boy around the Isles to receive pledges Godred was 'tipped off' and prepared his fleet for war. The two fleets met in battle off the north coast of Man on 3 January 1156, and despite Godred's being larger his captains (possibly alienated by his despotism) were less determined and he lost the battle. As a result he had to agree to a treaty, under which he lost much of the overseas Manx dominions (including most of the 'Sudreys', the islands around Arran, Bute, Islay, Jura, Colonsay and possibly parts of Galloway) to his brother-in-law Somerled. This marked the foundation of the new lordship of the Isles, at Man's expense; for the moment Godred retained the Outer Hebrides of Lewis and Harris. Somerled's fleet and powers of attracting warriors came to outmatch Godred's, and he invaded Man in a second war in 1158 to evict Godred. Man duly became part of Somerled's thalassocracy, dominated by his Hebridean-based fleet; Godred fled to Norway.

Godred II was able to return on Somerled's death for an invasion of mainland Scotland at Renfrew in 1164, bringing a Norwegian army, and defeated an attempt by his brother Ragnald to secure the kingdom for himself. But although the Manx kingdom thereafter avoided reconquest by the Islesmen and around 1182 the Manxmen fought off an attack by another Ragnald, an adventurer from the royal kindred, in Godred's absence Norway remained a more potent threat. On Godred's death on 10 November 1187, probably in his fifties or early sixties, his adult illegitimate son Ragnald seized power at the invitation of leading Manxmen sent to recall him from the Hebrides, denying the kingdom to Godred's legitimate son Olaf II 'the Black' despite Godred's express wishes. Olaf was declared too young to rule as he was only ten, and had to make do with Lewis in the Outer Hebrides once he was an adult. Even then he dared to complain to Ragnald in 1206/07 that he needed more territory than one infertile island to support himself and was seized and handed over to King William of Scots, who imprisoned him for seven years. He was released on the king's death in 1214. Meanwhile Ragnald had annoyed King John by aiding his sister Auffrica's husband, John de Courcy, the ex-lord of Ulster (founder of Carrickfergus and Dundrum castles), when he was driven out of that land by his Anglo-Norman rival Hugh de Lacey at John's request in 1204. Ragnald led an unsuccessful attempt to restore De Courcy to power in July 1205, but the walls of Dundrum Castle – ironically, built by De Courcy – proved too strong to take and Ragnald gave up and went home; his brother-in-law was later captured by King John and imprisoned for life. One Irish poem of this time written in Ragnald's praise even suggested that he might be made 'High King' of Ireland at Tara – so was this in his mind as an ultimate aim? In retaliation, during John's expedition to Ireland in 1210 he sent an army across to Man to ravage and punish it to warn Ragnald to obey the king's orders, but Ragnald was overseas and eluded capture. In May 1212 he signed up to peace with King John and became his vassal, and even received a grant of land at Carlingford in Ulster – a place with a useful harbour for his ships, so John clearly trusted him not to use it to invade again. He was later required to do homage by John's son and successor Henry III once the boy king had established his authority at the end of a civil war with his French challenger Prince Louis (1218).

Olaf arrived back on Man in 1214/15 after King William's death, having first gone on pilgrimage to the shrine of St James at Compostela in Spain to give thanks for his deliverance. Ragnald agreed to give him his land of Lewis back and added the hand of Lanon, daughter of a Kintyre nobleman and sister of his own wife, but this misfired. The new local bishop 'of the Isles' (Man and the Sudreys), Ragnald/Reginald, found out that Olaf had previously had his new wife's cousin as his mistress, and said that that meant his wife was within the prohibited degree of kinship to allow the marriage to be legal under Church law. Olaf obligingly separated from Lanon and married the daughter of Earl Ferchar of Ross instead – as he had backed Ragnald in the disputed election to the bishopric against his half-brother's candidate, Nicholas, it is possible that Bishop Ragnald was acting with his connivance to rid him of an unwanted wife. His new marriage gave him useful links at the Scots court as Ferchar was a close ally of King Alexander II and so could win him Scots military aid if needed. But his affronted sister-in-law, his half-brother Ragnald's queen, was furious and asked her son Godred, then living on Skye, to kill Olaf in a letter which she forged in her husband's name (1223?). Godred and his men landed on Lewis and attacked Olaf's residence, but he managed to escape to a boat and reach the mainland and the court of his father-in-law the Earl of Ross. The governor/royal sheriff of Skye, Paul Balkison, who had not agreed with Godred's plan but had been unable to stop it, joined Olaf there and helped him to return secretly to Skye, where they attacked Godred while he was on a small nearby island with a church (possibly Iona). Godred's men were killed, but he claimed sanctuary in a church and Paul seized and blinded him. Olaf thus regained Lewis and duly secured control of all the Outer Hebrides, which Ragnald temporarily recognised by treaty, but when he attempted to invade Man itself (1224?) he was driven back. It was then Ragnald's turn to be treacherous and attack his half-brother's lands without warning, with the aid of his new ally Alan, lord of Galloway, whose illegitimate son Thomas was to be married off to Ragnald's daughter; they also failed.

Eventually Olaf managed to muster enough Hebridean support to invade Man in 1226, after an appeal from the island's nobles to him following Ragnald's deceit in using a tax raised to 'pay tribute to King Henry of England' as a dowry for his daughter's marriage to Alan of Galloway's son. Logically, Ragnald was now offering Man as an effective vassal to the ambitious Alan, with the latter's son Thomas intended as its next ruler. Ragnald was driven out and the chronicle says that Olaf gained his inheritance after thirty-eight years, but the dispute was not over yet. In 1228 Olaf's temporary absence saw an invasion by Ragnald and his ally Alan, plus Alan's brother Earl Thomas of Atholl – the participation of so many mainland troops from beyond autonomous Galloway would suggest that King Alexander was backing the invasion. The Gallowegians and Athollmen ransacked and laid waste to the island; after Alan went home his officials remained on the island to collect taxes and emphasise its new role as his vassal. Olaf was able to return and drive the invaders out, and as the refugee islanders emerged from hiding it was Ragnald's turn to flee. The following winter he landed at St Patrick's island (Peel) with five ships and set up his base at Ronaldsway, gaining control of the southern half of Man, but the alarmed King Alexander II of Scots now turned on his 'over-mighty subject' Alan and was soon to invade Galloway so Ragnald had no Galloway aid. Olaf held onto the northern half of Man. In a final clash on the Tynwald Hill on Man, Olaf's army attacked and killed Ragnald on 14 February (St Valentine's Day) 1230 to end the civil war. Allegedly Olaf had not wanted his brother dead. The southern part of Man was devastated in this war and a subsequent pirate attack, and Olaf went to Norway to secure official recognition of his rule. But at this point the vigorous new king of Norway, Haakon 'the Good' (r. 1217–63), forced Olaf to become his vassal and share the kingdom with Ragnald's son Godred 'Donn', who had gone to his court claiming to be the legitimate ruler. Haakon tried to impose his own candidate, Uspak Osmundssen, as king of the 'Sudreys' and sent him to the Hebrides on the Norwegian fleet of eighty ships that had escorted Olaf and Godred back to Man from Bergen. Uspak was a relative of the House of Somerled according to the Norse sagas, and may have been intended as the Norwegian viceroy of all the Hebrides. Skye was attacked by half the fleet and local commander Thorkell was killed, and the two halves of the fleet then reunited. But when the fleet reached the Firth of Clyde Uspak was killed at a siege while invading the island of Bute, hit by a heavy stone fired from the walls according to the *Manx Chronicle*; the Norse sagas have him dying later on Kintyre. Olaf and Godred now divided the kingdom, with Godred taking the 'Sudreys' in Uspak's place, based on Lewis, but he was soon killed after disposing of the other Godred's killer Paul Balkison. Traditionally Lewis passed on Olaf's death to a son of his who is not in the Manx records, Leod or Ljot, ancestor of the MacLeods, but no documents earlier than the seventeenth century mentions him. Leod, whether or not Olaf's son, was the presumed ancestor of the MacLeod clan on the Isle of Skye and married the heiress of MacArailt, lord of Dunvegan. Leod's elder son Tormod founded the line of MacLeod of Dunvegan; the younger son married Dorothea, daughter of the Earl of Ross, ruled Lewis and Harris, and fought for King Robert Bruce in the 1310s.

Olaf was now forced to accept the authority of Henry III of England and loan ships to him; this annoyed Haakon and Olaf died on the eve of having to go to Norway and explain himself, on 21 May 1237 at St Patrick's Isle, aged sixty. His eldest son by Christina of Ross, Harald, aged fourteen, succeeded and in 1238 left Man to spend some months in the Isles, leaving his adviser Loughlin as regent. However, the latter's men got into a brawl at the Tynwald with the three sons of Nils, friends of Harald's but at feud with Loughlin, when the young men came to Man at Harald's invitation, and lives were lost including two of the sons of Nils and a friend of Harald's called Joseph. As a result Loughlin feared Harald's wrath, and as his sovereign returned he fled Man for Wales, taking Harald's younger brother, Godred; the ship was hit by a storm and both drowned, according to the *Manx Chronicle*. (However, a legal document from the court of the Welsh ruler Llewelyn 'Fawr' of Gwynedd dated *c.* 1240 refers to a Godred, son of the king of Man, as a witness.) Harald, now heirless, faced the suspicion of King Haakon for not coming to his court to do homage, and Haakon sent out two officials, Cospatrick and Gilchrist, who took control of Man in Harald's absence, levied taxes without reference to him and on his return refused to let him land. He had to go to Norway to do homage to get his lands back (1239?) and was forced to admit Norwegian suzerainty, staying for two years at Haakon's court. Having done this, he had to reassure King

Henry that he was not acting against English interests; he later accepted knighthood from him. Harald was drowned off Sumburgh Head in a storm while returning from a second summons to Norway, with his bride, Haakon's daughter Cecilia, and the new bishop Lawrence of Man (who had had to be consecrated by his superior the Archbishop of Nidaros) in April (?) 1248. His brother Ragnald succeeded but was murdered within weeks on 30 May, in a meadow near the church at Rushen by a certain Ivar, a 'knight', so a member of the elite. He was succeeded by Harald II, son of Godred Donn, who may have been connected to the killing. As a usurper Harald was denied recognition by King Haakon, summoned to Norway, and detained there. In his absence, Ewen/Eoghan MacDugald (MacDougall), head of the branch of the House of Somerled ruling in Lorne, landed with a military force at Ronaldsway to press his claims to Man but was disappointed of local support. According to the *Manx Chronicle* the citizens were irritated at his boasts about King Haakon of Norway making him 'king of the Isles', and they protested that that title only belonged to their own king. He had to pull his troops back to the offshore tidal island of St Michael as armed citizens rallied against him in the town, and when the tide went out the latter crossed the causeway to attack but he had by now embarked most of his men so they sailed off successfully. In 1252 Haakon imposed Ragnald's brother Magnus, youngest son of Olaf and lobbying for the crown in Norway in 1250, as king, and sent him home to Man to great rejoicing. He escaped Norwegian authority after Haakon died during the Norse expedition to Scotland in 1263 but was forced to cede part of his lands and the right of succession to the new power in the southern Hebrides, Alexander III of Scotland. He also obtained backing from Henry III of England, who knighted him on a visit to London in 1256, and probably commissioned the original version of the *Manx Chronicle*, written at the abbey of Rushen, which is our main source for his dynasty. (The extant version is fourteenth century.) When King Alexander III threatened to invade Man in autumn 1264, mustering a fleet at Dumfries, Magnus hastened there to pledge loyalty and secure a grant of his kingdom as the Scots king's vassal. Following the death of Haakon, the other great sea lord of the north-western seas, in December 1263, the kingdom of Man now had nobody to turn to against Scotland but England and the latter was now embroiled in civil war between Henry III and Simon de Montfort; Magnus had to surrender.

Man after the end of its independence

Alexander III secured the island on Magnus's death in November 1265, though the latter's son Godred launched an unsuccessful invasion in

1275. The Bishop of Man had recently died, and the English abbot of Furness Abbey, Lancastershire, turned up at Alexander III's court claiming the right of election for his abbey as it had founded Rushen Abbey on Man and hence the Manx Church. Meanwhile the local clergy on Man had elected the popular Abbot of Rushen, Gilbert, as bishop, but without waiting for them Alexander chose the brother of his 'bailiff' of Man and sent him off to the archbishop of Trondjheim in Norway to be consecrated. This insult led to anger on Man and substantial support for Godred's landing and claim to the throne, but Alexander sent in ninety shiploads of troops headed by John de Vesci and John Comyn, justiciar of Galloway. The *Lanercost Chronicle* says that the heavily armed troops massacred the lightly armed Manxmen in the resulting battle in October 1275, and the Scots king reoccupied the island and made his eldest son Alexander its titular ruler. (The prince, however, predeceased his father.) Magnus's widow Mary was said in Scots sources used by the later *Complete Peerage* to have married Ewen McDougall of Lorn (*q.v.*); a so-called 'heiress of King Magnus' called Auffrica of Connacht put in a claim to the kingdom of Man in England in 1293 but her pedigree is unknown. (She was called after her putative ancestor Auffrica, wife of Olaf 'the Red', which suggests a genuine family link.) From this point Man became a political pawn between Scotland and England during the Scottish Wars of Independence, falling to the currently stronger power; Edward I seized it as the price of his recognition of King John Balliol in 1290, Balliol regained it in 1293, Edward seized it when he deposed Balliol in 1296, and Robert Bruce recovered it in 1313. From 1296 to 1310 the English king's governor (at least nominally, as he had many other duties) was Anthony Bek, bishop of Durham and thus on the front line of warfare between Scotland and England as lord of the 'palatinate' of Durham. He was replaced in 1311 by Edward II's brash, bitchy and highly unpopular close companion and reputed lover, the Breton squire Piers Gaveston, whom angry English barons were to kidnap and murder in 1312. Bruce then landed on Man in May 1315 to recover Rushen Castle from rebels and secure it for Scotland again. Man was then temporarily seized by a mixed English and anti-Bruce Scottish fleet under Bruce's exiled enemy John MacDougall, dispossessed lord of Lorne/Argyll, who may have had a dynastic claim on it via his great-aunt's marriage to Man's last king. After a fairly stable period from 1319 under King Robert Bruce, whose rights to Man were recognised by Edward III of England in their peace treaty of 1328, it was finally secured by England as Edward III invaded Scotland in 1333. It was granted by Edward on 9 August 1333 to William de Montacute/Montague, Earl of Salisbury (1301–44) – as a full kingdom not a feudal fief, Edward thus abdicating his rights as its current king to 'King' William (I) Montacute. This senior royal 'trusty', son and heir of William, third Lord Montague/ Montacute (d. 1319), was an older contemporary of the king, trusted to help him arrest the hated regent Roger Mortimer at Nottingham Castle in 1330. He was given Man in full autonomous lordship as its 'king', but he was resisted by the islanders and their Scots garrison until he established his rule by force sometime after 1341 (and was crowned).

Name	Date of accession	Date of death/dep.	Years ruled
?Llywarch 'Hen'	560s?	Late 560s? (dep.)	
(Direct rule by Rheged in later sixth century)			
(Direct rule by Northumbria from *c.* 620)			
?Merfyn/Mermin	Mid-C7th	*c.* 680	20/30?
?Sandde	Mid-C8th		
?Elidyr	Late C8th		
?Gwriad	Early C9th		
(Viking settlement)			
Godred MacFergus	*c.* 836	*c.* 853	*c.* 17
Ketil 'Flatnose'	*c.* 853	*c.* 866	*c.* 13
Ragnald of York	*c.* 914	921	*c.* 7
Gebeachan	?	937 (k.)	<16
MacRagnall	?	*c.* 942	<5
Maccus Haraldsen	*c.* 960?	*c.* 980	*c.* 20?
Godred Haraldsen	970s?	*c.* 989	<20?
(co-ruler)			
Ragnald Godredson	*c.* 989?	1005	16?
Kenneth Godredson	?	1005	<16?
Sigurd of Orkney	1005	April 1014	9
Thorfinn of Orkney	1020s?	*c.* 1065	*c.* 30?
(overlord)			
Margad Ragnaldsen of	<1052	1061	>9?
Dublin (aka Echmarcach)			
Murchad of Leinster and	1061	1070	9
Dublin			
Godred Sihtricson (or	1070?	1070s	<9?
co-ruler earlier)			
Fingal Mc Godred	1070s	1079	< 9
Godred 'Crovan' ('White	1079	1095	16
Hands')			
Laghman (i)	1095	1097?	2?
Magnus 'Bareleg', King of	1098	1103	4
Norway (direct rule)			
Sigurd, King of Norway	1103	1103/4	Months?
(direct rule)			

Lords of the Isles

Name	Date of accession	Date of death/dep.	Years ruled
Laghman (ii)	*c.* 1104?	*c.* 1110?	6? (Total: 8?)
Donald MacTeige	?1110	1113/14	trad. 3
Olaf Godredson 'the Red' (claimant from 1103)	1113/14	1153	39/40
Godred II Olafson	1153	1158	dep. 5
Somerled of the Isles	1158	1164	k. 6
Godred II Olafson (ii)	1164	10 Nov. 1187	23 (Total: 28)
Ragnald Godredson	late 1187	14 Feb. 1230	42
Olaf II 'the Black' Godredson (b. 1177)	1226/1230	May 1237	7/11
Godred III 'Donn' Ragnaldson (Sudreys)	1230	1230	Months
Harald I Olafson	May 1237	April 1248?	<11
Ragnald II Haraldson	6 May 1248	30 May 1248	24 days
Harald II	1248	1250 (dep.)	2
Magnus Haraldson	1252	November 1265	13

(Scottish rule 1265–90)
(English rule 1290–1312)
(Scottish rule 1313–30)
(English rule from 1330: full possession granted to William de Montacute, Earl of Salisbury)

6

The Clans of the North-West and Hebrides to *c.* 1700

MacDonald of Clanranald

This was the genealogically senior line of the MacDonalds after the death of John 'of the Isles' in around 1386, but as referred to above it did not inherit the main MacDonald lordship in defiance of normal legal and genealogical tradition. Instead John passed on his lordship to Donald, his son by his second marriage – this marriage taking place in July 1350 to Margaret Stewart, daughter of Robert (1316–90), the 'High Steward' of Scotland and head of the Stewart family and later King Robert II of Scots. This arrangement disinherited his six sons by his first wife, whom he divorced to make way for Margaret – Amy MacRuadhri MacDonald, the heiress of the MacRuadhri branch of the dynasty, who were lords of Garmoran and the other lands of the west coast of Scotland south from Glenelg to Ardnamurchan and Morvern and inland to Glengarry. John's marriage to Amy (probably a decade or so earlier, *c.* 1335/40) had probably not been intended to bring him this bloc of lands as at the time of the arrangement she had at least one male kinsman ahead of her in the line of succession. But she became heiress when her brother Ranald MacRuadhri, head of the family and unmarried, was assassinated by his hostile neighbour the Earl of Ross at Elcho nunnery near Perth in spring 1346 as he led his levies south to join King David II's invasion of England. Hugh's ancestors, the main lords of the mainland east and north of the MacRuadhris' lands, had been granted Skye by King Robert I to cement their new loyalty to the Bruces, and he was also claiming Garmoran to be included in this grant but the MacRuadhris defied him; hence the attempt to solve the dispute by killing the clan's leader in a swift and unexpected coup. The usual follow-up to this would have been invasion of the disputed territory by the murderer, but Amy's husband John 'of the Isles' claimed Garmoran and the other family lands for his (six) sons by her and occupied the territory. Within four years he had divorced Amy and married Margaret Stewart, but their sons remained as heirs to the MacRuadhri territory. The eldest, John, died before his father (*c.* 1380) and his son Angus was left out of the division; it was decided some time before 'Lord' John died that the eldest survivor, Godfrey (the Norse 'Guthfrith'), would be disinherited from the main inheritance which he would normally have expected. The usual reasons for this would be either a family dispute – in this case, presumably with his father – or mental or physical incapacity which his subsequent fightback shows is unlikely; he merely inherited lands on Uist in the Outer Hebrides. This led to his descendants, the 'Clan Goffraith', claiming Garmoran by right of age from the heirs of his younger brother Ranald and fighting them over it sporadically for the next century or so; as we shall see below, sometime before 1388 Godfrey seized possession of Garmoran from Ranald's son and probably held it for his lifetime. Ranald, as the next eldest son of John and Amy, was supposed to have the main, coastal bloc of lands in Garmoran instead of Godfrey under John's plan; his next brother, Hugh/Aodh, would have Glentilt, Alexander/Alistair 'Carrach' would have the lands that later became Keppoch and Dalchoisnie, and Mark/Marcus would have Crocanduih. The boys' mother Amy appears according to tradition to have lived at Castle Tioram in Garmoran, the main residence of the MacRuadhri family, after her divorce and erected new buildings there, so she presumably acted as custodian of the inheritance for her sons until they were old enough to rule and transferred the loyalty of her tenants to her children. In 1373 her ex-husband John issued a charter to his chosen heir for the main MacRuadhri inheritance, Ranald, which gave him Garmoran, Moidart, Arisaig and Lochaber, as well as Castle Tioram; this may have followed his mother's death as he was probably already in his early thirties and had been old enough to rule for years.

Ranald did not have long to enjoy his inheritance, and died at around the same time as his father John in around 1386, aged probably around forty-five to fifty. He had five sons and his lands were divided as his father's had been, a perennial problem for a bloc of family territory in the Gaelic world. The necessity was always to keep a far larger bloc for the eldest son and make sure that the junior lines backed him up in case of war with the neighbours; the MacDonalds and the Campbells were usually both good at this and King James I was to find this out to his cost as he arrested 'Lord of the Isles' Alexander in 1428 and tried unsuccessfully to find an ambitious kinsman to replace him. Ranald's eldest son, Alan, inherited the main bloc of lands in coastal Garmoran, centred on Castle Tioram, and later led the clan forces to assist his cousin Donald 'Lord of the Isles' in the 1411 expedition that ended at the Battle of Harlaw in Aberdeenshire. He married a Stewart lady (possibly from one of the junior branches in Argyll) and died either in 1419 or 1430. His next brother was Donald, who was supposed to inherit the lands of Glengarry from his father in ?1386 and founded that branch of the family (*q.v.*). However, Donald was denied his lands by his uncle Godfrey, Ranald's elder brother, who seized them and is described as 'lord of Garmoran' in a charter of 1388. Alan was also denied most or all of his inheritance by Godfrey for an uncertain length of time, possibly all of Godfrey's lifetime. As of July 1389, when Godfrey issued a charter to Inchaffray Abbey as 'lord of Uist', he described himself as resident at 'Ylantirum' Castle, i.e. Castle Tioram, the centre of the later Clanranald lordship. Godfrey's son Alexander is also described in documents as lord of Garmoran, with 1,000 men at his call, and was clearly the principal lord of the MacDonalds in this area until he was summoned to Parliament (i.e. as a feudal lord and tenant-in-chief of the king) and arrested and executed by King James I on the latter's visit to Inverness in 1427. Alan may well only have recovered all his lands then, if he was still alive; logically 'Lord of the Isles' Alexander had backed Godfrey's kin against him, so Alexander's arrest by the king enabled him to regain his inheritance.

Alan was succeeded by his son Roderick or Ruadhri, who married Margaret Balloch of Islay and died in 1481. Little is known of him, but his younger brother Alan was given the 'sixty penny lands' of Knoydart by their father and founded the line of MacDonald of Knoydart. (His son was John/Ian, the second lord of Knoydart; then followed John's son Ranald.) Ruadhri's son Alan MacRuadhri of Clanranald was already leading the clan forces at the 'Battle of Bloody Bay' around 1480/82 (possibly as heir not as ruling lord) when the family and the other senior MacDonald lines joined the revolt against embattled 'Lord of the Isles' John MacDonald led by his illegitimate son, Angus. The latter seems to have led an 'autonomist' MacDonald revolt against his father in protest at the latter abandoning the usual policy of armed hostility to the kings of Scots and agreeing to become a royal 'lord of Parliament', created as such by and subject to the king's authority and removable at will rather than having an inalienable hereditary right to his lands. The MacDonalds of Keppoch, led by Donald MacAngus, and the MacDonalds of Sleat, led by Donald/Domnhall 'Gallach', also fought for Angus, and the MacIains and MacLeods fought for John in this naval clash near the Mull town of

Tobermory. Angus won the battle, with heavy losses on both sides, and John fled to Ireland, but the latter was restored after Angus was murdered in a private dispute by his piper around 1490. Alan clearly favoured the restricting of royal power and the continuation of the old ways of autonomy, and he also took part in a defiant raid on Inverness, the centre of royal power in the western Highlands, in 1491 with his neighbour Ewan Cameron, thirteenth chief of that clan, his own cousin (and neighbour) Alexander MacDonald of Lochalsh, his kinsman of Keppoch, and the 'Clan Chattan' federation of clans north-east of his territory, which was traditionally led by the Mackintoshes. Lacking a resident royal army to tackle these experienced guerrilla raiders, King James IV had to use loyalist rivals of the raiders to fight them off – in this case, the Camerons' and Mackintoshes' hereditary enemies the Mackenzies of Kintail, the descendants of the early to mid-fourteenth-century clan founder 'Coinneach MacCoinneach' (Kenneth son of Kenneth), whose Irish grandfather Colin Fitzgerald had been granted Kintail by Alexander III in January 1266. The Mackenzies were defeated and a Mackintosh garrison was installed in Inverness in defiance of the young king but later evicted. When James had the time and troops available to invade Argyll in 1493, however, Alan MacRuadhri was among the prudent local chiefs who hurried to come and do homage to avoid being attacked, and as such he followed his chief's abdication of the lordship of the Isles in the king's favour by recognising James as his chief and his overlord.

Under the new dispensation the king would exercise legal control of the western Highlands for the first time, but he was an absentee lord and in practice local feuds and sporadic 'tit-for-tat' clashes and cattle raids between rival clans continued on a low level. Meanwhile Alan succeeded in 1505 in acquiring a royal grant of lands in Uist and Benbecula that the late 'Lord of the Isles' John had granted to his half-brother Hugh of Sleat, who had since died, and thus 'cut out' the Sleat line by using the new royal overlord and his written authority. But local power and the ability to maintain loyalty by leadership and fear still rested on the use of military power, and such clashes could annoy the king. One of these incidents around 1507/08 involved Alan MacRuadhri capturing and imprisoning the Mackintosh clan chief in a private war, and in retaliation the Mackintoshes complained to the king. This was probably why Alan was summoned to the royal court at Blair Atholl (or less probably Inverness) to answer charges in 1509. To defy such an order usually meant being placed in contempt of royal authority and outlawed, with a powerful local magnate authorised to lay waste to the offender's lands with fire and the sword; and temporary or permanent confiscation of lands could follow. Alan had enough confidence in being able to clear himself to go to Inverness or else decided it was safer to sacrifice himself to having his lands ravaged and occupied (probably by the ever-ambitious Campbells or Gordons), and he was speedily arrested, tried and executed in the king's presence as a rebel and thus made an example of to his turbulent neighbours.

Alan's eldest son by his first wife, Florence MacIain, Ranald or Ragnald 'Ban' ('the Fair') succeeded him, and was killed in or before 1513, possibly as early as 1505. His son Dugald, sixth lord of the dynasty, was reputedly a despotic tyrant and was killed by rebellious clansmen in 1520, whereupon his uncle Alexander or Alisdair, younger son of Alan, seized power. He died sometime after 1530 and was succeeded by his son John 'Moydartach', that is, of Moidart. These chiefs kept to the prudent course of loyalty to the Stewarts as the new 'Lords of the Isles', whatever their hankerings after the ancient line of MacDonalds. The long minority of James V from 1513 to 1528 left the Highlands largely unsupervised and open to autonomist self-rule by the feuding local dynasts, subject to sporadic interference by the regency's usual local viceroys, the earls of Huntly. But once James V was adult he was as vigorous as his father and great-grandfather in insisting on recognition of royal power by armed force. By the mid-sixteenth century, the Clanranald chief was usually known by the name of 'Mac Mhic Ailean', that is, grandson of Alan (either the one executed in 1509 or his grandfather), distinguishing him from 'Mac Mhic Alisdair' of Glengarry. Alan's youngest son, by one of the Frasers of Lovat, was Ranald 'Gallda' ('the Foreigner', a reference to his youthful fostering with the Frasers), who took over control with Fraser help after his cousin John's arrest by the king during the latter's tour of the Isles in 1540. He had been fostered by his mother's kin, to the dismay of the Clanranald landholders as the Frasers were allied to the Gordons, earls of Huntly, their powerful neighbours and the greatest military-political grouping in Buchan. The Gordons, whose influence extended as far west as the Great Glen, were the traditional foes of the other MacDonald lines and had a hankering after their lands in Lochaber, with successive earls of Huntly holding royal office as enforcers of royal power and offering their services to the sovereign whenever there was a call to ravage 'rebel' MacDonald lands (and hopefully seize them too). But the clan chiefs of the north-west also faced a new threat. James V took a fleet loaded with up-to-date cannon round the northern seas to Orkney and the Outer Hebrides in 1540 to show that he would punish defiance in person, making him the first Scots king to venture so far north, and rounded up chiefs who he suspected of disloyalty like John 'Moydartach'. After this demonstration of royal power Ranald (who seems to have been one of those who obeyed a summons to visit the king to do homage) took the trouble to acquire a royal charter legalising his ownership of Moidart and Arisaig at the king's court, dated 14 December 1540, to make his new possession legally watertight. But as with similar actions by ambitious royal 'stooges' in Gaelic Ireland, a royal charter was useless in military reality without local backing.

There was now a revolt within the Clanranald elite against Ranald Gallda's accession and an attempt to prevent his election as clan chief, in the name of his cousin John 'Moydartach', son of Alexander, whom the king had deported. John had fought for the anti-royal rebel Donald 'Gorm' MacDonald of Sleat (genealogically close kin to the late 'Lord' John so with a right to these lands under local custom despite illegitimate blood) in his attack on Crown lands in the Inner Hebrides in 1539, so he had credentials as someone who could defy royal authority and/or the Gordons and Frasers. John was now imprisoned in the south, but the Scots government had passed from the interventionist James V, who died suddenly aged only thirty in December 1542, to a weak regency for his infant daughter Queen Mary. The new regent, the Earl of Arran (head of the Hamiltons), suspected the loyalty of Ranald 'Gallda' and his Fraser allies due to their links to his potential challengers in the regency council, particularly Archibald Campbell, fourth Earl of Argyll (d. 1558), head of the Campbells and nephew to the Frasers' patron the Earl of Huntly. Arran was threatened with overthrow by an army raised by a clique of nobles led by Argyll and Huntly, and so needed to distract them at home.

In 1543 the Arran regency released John Moydartach as a potential ally to take over the clan and attack the Gordon–Campbell alliance, and gave him a charter to the Clanranald lands. At the time Arran was preparing to seek the aid of Henry VIII of England by agreeing to betroth Queen Mary to Henry's son and heir Edward, and the MacDonalds had a useful history of being English allies; indeed Henry was now involved with the exiled bastard heir to the defunct lordship of the Isles, Donald 'Dubh'. The regency also released other chiefs arrested by James V in 1540 who could be of use against the Gordons and Campbells, such as James MacDonald of Dunivaig and Islay. John Moydartach was re-elected as clan chief of Clanranald as Ranald fled to the Frasers, but the Frasers helped Ranald to invade and took the principal chiefly residence of Castle Tioram while their chief Lord Lovat, Ranald's uncle, had the charter of the Clanranald lands held by John Moydartach cancelled. Ranald may now have been invested as chief instead by a pro-Fraser faction, but John fought back and brought in his kinsmen from Keppoch and Ardnamurchan plus the Camerons of

Lochiel to assist him. In 1544 Clanranald and their allies, MacDonald of Keppoch and Clan Cameron of Lochiel, attacked the Clan Fraser lands of Abertarf and Stratherrick in the Great Glen, east of the Clanranald lands, followed by an attack northwards on Glenmoriston (then occupied by the expansionist Gordons of Huntly) and Urquhart Castle. This campaign then led to a retaliatory invasion of Clanranald lands by the Earl of Huntly's Gordons and their Fraser allies, but John avoided battle and lurked in the hills around Loch Hourn, the 'Rough Bounds', and his clan troops could not be cornered by the invaders who were unfamiliar with the layout of the region and were exposed to ambush. The invaders split up to search for John but had to give up, and it was while the Frasers were withdrawing from his lands that John intercepted them in the famous inter-clan battle known as the 'Battle of the Shirts' after crossing Loch Lochy to its south bank in the lower Great Glen. This battle was fought in July 1544, possibly at 'Blar na Leana', the 'Field of the Swampy Meadow'. It was contested between the Clanranald/Keppoch/Cameron forces (numbering around 500) and the Frasers of Lovat (numbering around 300), with Ranald 'Gallda' among the latter. The battle was so called because it was a hot summer's day and the clansmen fought in their shirts after removing their heavy protective plaids and/or mail jerkins. It was one of the bloodiest battles in clan history, probably exacerbated by the warriors' lack of protection, and traditionally only eight MacDonalds and five Frasers survived; the losses inhibited both coalitions from major actions for decades. Lord Lovat (Fraser) and his heir were killed in the battle and were buried at Beauly priory; Ranald 'Gallda', who was with his Fraser patrons, was also killed.

John 'Moydartach' MacDonald survived as clan chief despite the subsequent armed intervention of the Scots regency to curb his power when he was short of men. In 1545 he raided up the Great Glen to Urquhart Castle to drive back the Gordons, and then sailed with his levies to Ulster to attend a gathering of Hebridean chiefs who had traditionally made up the 'Council of the Isles' and recognise Donald 'Dubh', now an English client, as 'Lord of the Isles'. The plan was for Donald to invade the Hebrides with English aid and attack the Scots regency in the rear, but Donald's death a few months later prevented this. John Moydartach and his clan backed the claims of James MacDonald of Dunivaig and Islay in 1545–46 to succeed Donald 'Dubh' as leader of the invasion and rightful 'Lord of the Isles', and their group sent an envoy to Henry VIII asking for a new treaty with him for aiding an attack on the mainland. The English do not appear to have replied. John, however, remained defiant towards the regency, and his failure to send troops as required to fight for them against the summer 1547 invasion by the new English regency (for Edward VI) showed his allegiance and boldness. He was accused of treason and summoned to court in Edinburgh for assorted raids on his neighbours, but contemptuously ignored all such demands. Indeed, there was a notable lack of a west Highlands turnout for this campaign – mostly from those who had warred on the Frasers in the Clanranald succession dispute of 1544, logically in fear of arrest on Fraser ally Huntly's orders if they turned up.

George Gordon, fourth Earl of Huntly (d. 1562), head of the Gordons and ally of the defeated Frasers, was one of the regency council for Queen Mary and was sent against Clanranald by the Scots regency with an army after John Moydartach failed to turn up to a gathering of Highland chiefs summoned to meet Queen-Mother Marie de Guise in Aberdeen in June 1552. Clearly wary of John's capacity to wage guerrilla war and mainly concerned to keep him occupied in the Great Glen, he only 'showed the flag' in the relatively safe lowlands of the Great Glen rather than invading his hilly dominions where the Gordons could be ambushed. He went no further west than Abertarff (the site of the later 'Fort Augustus') at the south end of Loch Ness and did not dare try to reconquer Glenmoriston; apparently his expected Mackintosh/Clan Chattan troops failed to show up in protest at his earlier execution of a Mackintosh chief. Instead his nephew and fellow councillor Archibald Campbell, fourth Earl of Argyll and head of the Campbells, was sent by sea up from Inveraray Castle to attack Castle Tioram in a continuation of James V's policy of overawing the Hebrides by naval power. Argyll was used to such potentially risky naval campaigns; he had fought against John Moydartach's kinsman Alexander/Alisdair 'Carrach' of Dunivaig in 1530 and the pro-English Earl Matthew of Lennox's naval attack on the Firth of Clyde in 1544. The naval expedition was timed to coincide with Huntly drawing John and his clansmen east into the Great Glen to confront him, and was calculated to catch the MacDonald stronghold when it was undermanned. This was a dangerous moment as the well-resourced Campbell chief had both men and cannon in plenty, but the cautious Argyll bombarded the castle from the sea rather than landing and risking an ambush. Soon John and his men were arriving back home, having taken the gamble that Huntly was not going to advance further, and Argyll gave up the siege and sailed home. John had survived the double-pronged attack, and from then on Huntly and Argyll were drawn back into the struggles of the great nobles over the regency for Queen Mary and then the English invasion after 1547. John continued to defy the new head of the regency who now took over, Queen Mother Marie of Guise, but eventually accepted a summons to meet her in Perth in 1555 to avoid another invasion. The talks were unsuccessful and Marie placed John under arrest, but he slipped out of Perth and made his way home; despite his defiance and his failure to turn up to her subsequent summons of Highland chiefs to Inverness in summer 1556 he was never attacked by the government. Most of his energies in the early to mid-1560s went on a private war over Tiree and Gigha with the MacDonalds of Dunivaig/Islay, in which the Macleans (rivals of the latter for Islay) were on John's side; both John and his foe James MacDonald of Dunivaig were bound over by the Privy Council to keep the peace in 1565 with huge 'sureties' of £10,000 each. The fifth Earl of Argyll acted as guarantor. Keeping out of politics and not annoying his powerful neighbours further, John survived as chief until his death in 1584 at Castle Tioram. His son Alan succeeded as ninth chief and died in 1593, to be succeeded by his son Donald. (A younger son of Alan, John, was the first lord of Glenaladale, a junior branch of the family.) Donald was among the recalcitrant Hebridean chiefs who had been defying the king's laws and not keeping the peace who James VI sought to rein in, and so was summoned to court on threat of forfeiture and arrested there in 1609. He was released in return for promises of good behaviour and recognising the king's authority, which probably also encompassed keeping his warlike clan from aiding local Hebridean resistance to the royal 'planting' of Lewis. He was granted his lands anew by royal charter in 1610 as part of the king's efforts to bring the isolated Hebridean chiefs under full royal legal authority, and died in 1619.

The Clanranald clan continued its low-level wars against its traditional enemies and sporadic acts of criminality are recorded in complaints to the government. Donald's son John, now chief (d. 1670), was complained of for alleged piracy against passing ships off his coast in 1627 and 1636, and as Catholics he and his clan were at risk of punishment as the Covenanters took over control of Scotland's government in 1637–38. He and his son by Moira MacLeod, Donald, led a contingent of troops that served in Montrose's largely Catholic army in 1644–45, joining up with their distant kin from Ulster under Alisdair 'MacColkitto', son of the exiled MacDonald laird of the island of Colonsay. If the Royalists had won then the local MacDonalds and the returning exiles would have been able to reclaim much of the lands they had lost to the pro-Covenanter Campbells over the past 150 years, and the Royalist ravaging of Argyll and sack of Inveraray Castle in winter 1644–45 no doubt gave them particular satisfaction. The 'high point' of the campaign in local west Highland terms was the Royalists' defeat of 'Mac Cailean Mór', the feared eighth Earl of Argyll, and his lieutenant Sir Duncan

Campbell of Auchinbreck at Inverlochy on 2 February 1645, when a
Highland charge broke the better-armed Covenanters' battle line. But
the Covenanters ultimately prevailed, not least due to the Highlanders'
inflexible tradition of taking their loot home after major victories and so
diminishing Montrose's army just when he needed all his troops to press
forward after a success. Most of the MacDonalds went home to the west
Highlands for a respite from war (and to deal with the harvest) after
Montrose's great victory at Kilsyth in July 1645 opened the Lowlands
to him and destroyed the last Covenanter army currently there, so they
were absent when the returning Covenanter army in England, under
David Leslie, ambushed and destroyed Montrose's under-strength army
at Philiphaugh in the Borders in September. Montrose escaped back to
the Highlands and the MacDonalds (and the Mackenzies of Seaforth
who had fought for the Campbells at Inverlochy) joined him to attack
Inverness in spring 1646, but the war was lost and, with the Royalists in
England overwhelmed, the king ordered Montrose to leave for exile. For
the moment the Covenanter regime had too much on its hands (including
the surrendered king) to bother with punishing the pro-Royalist clans,
whom the moderate Covenanter peers hoped could still be used to help
save the king's English throne as the affronted Campbells refused to
countenance an invasion of England. Argyll withdrew from government
to Inveraray in a sulk at this plan, and the ex-Royalist Duke of Hamilton
took command of the campaign. But following the defeat of the moderate
Covenanter/Royalist 'Engager' Scots invasion of England to rescue King
Charles in autumn 1648, Argyll and his 'hard-line' Covenanters regained
control in Edinburgh and set out to crush opposition. After King Charles'
execution they would only invite his son to Scotland as their puppet to
head a Presbyterian regime, and John MacDonald of Clanranald was
among the Catholic clan chiefs whose lands were declared forfeit in
1649 for their part in Montrose's 'rebellion'. Fortunately he managed to
have this reversed by a personal appeal and submission to Argyll, who
had too many foes in the north-west (and among the 'Engagers' in the
Lowlands) to afford the time and resources to evict all the recalcitrant
chiefs. The MacDonalds retained their lands and stayed out of 1650s
politics thereafter, but welcomed the Restoration in 1660 as ex-Royalists
like the Earl of Glencairn took over the government in Edinburgh and
backed the rights of loyal Catholic chiefs as a counterbalance to the
distrusted ex-Covenanter Lowlands lords.

John died in 1670 and was succeeded by his son Donald, a brave and
dashing if somewhat headstrong officer in the Montrose campaign who
appears to have been at a loose end in the quieter world of the post-war
Highlands. According to family tradition the bored and increasingly

mercurial chief, a hot-tempered autocrat, spent much of his time shooting game and in his old age declined into a trigger-happy eccentric who took 'pot-shots' at anything and anyone that took his fancy from the battlements of Castle Tioram. Married to Moira MacLeod, he died in 1685/86 and was succeeded by his son Alan, the thirteenth lord of Clanranald, who had been brought up with his cousins on the island of Benbecula in the Outer Hebrides and had no interest in the family castle. (Sir Donald, the tenth lord, son of Alan, had had a younger son named Ranald who was the first MacDonald lord of Benbecula; his grandson Donald, the third lord, was thus second cousin to his contemporary Alan's father Donald of Clanranald.) Alan, a Catholic and Jacobite, was among the west Highland chiefs who rallied to Montrose's kinsman John Graham of Claverhouse, 'Bonnie Dundee', in 1689 and fought at Killiecrankie. Some 500 clansmen and Alan's fifteen-year-old heir were said to have fallen at Killiecrankie, and after the defeat of the Jacobites in Moray in 1690 the Williamite government sent troops to occupy the main rebel areas. Alan fled abroad to France to join his king, and Castle Tioram was occupied by government troops and used as a garrison for the district. Fourteen soldiers were installed there at the time that Alan returned from exile in 1715 to rally his clansmen to the cause of James III, and he stormed and burnt his ancestral home before leading his men off to fight for their king. He was unfortunately killed at the Battle of Sheriffmuir, and was succeeded by his younger brother Ranald, the fourteenth lord. The latter also lived in exile in France as a Jacobite, and died childless in 1725; his sister Margaret was married to Donald, the third lord of Benbecula, who was now the nearest heir as the grandson of Sir Donald's younger son and so took over the clan. He remained loyal to the Hanoverian regime and kept out of trouble, dying in 1730, as did his son Ranald (1692–1753), the sixteenth lord; thus the family survived the vicissitudes of the 'Forty-Five' and after. But they never rebuilt Castle Tioram, and continued to live elsewhere.

MacDonald/MacDonell of Glengarry

A junior branch of Clanranald, the MacDonalds of Glengarry were founded by Donald, a younger son of the first lord Ranald of Clanranald and brother of the second lord, Allan. Donald is counted as the second lord of Glengarry by genealogical reckoning, with his father Ranald as the first, but he and his brothers – among them his elder brother Alan, lord of Clanranald – were denied their inheritance when their father Ranald died by the latter's elder brother, Godfrey of Uist (see article on Clanranald.) This situation continued through Donald's lifetime with

'Lord of the Isles' Donald, his father's half-brother and head of the dynasty, backing Godfrey, so he did not actually occupy the Glengarry estate; he died in 1420. His first wife was Laleve McIver, by whom he had John, the third lord; his second wife, mother of Alexander/Alisdair, the fourth lord, was one of the Frasers. Alexander was the first of the line to actually occupy Glengarry, which was carried out after Godfrey's son and successor Alexander of Uist was executed for treason by King James I in 1427. His nickname 'Na Collie' ('of the Woods') is presumably a reference to his having to live as a landless fugitive until his kin were evicted from Glengarry. The king required 'Lord of the Isles' Alexander (d. 1449) to accept his legal grant of Glengarry to its rightful heir Alexander, as a royal tenant, and the king's lieutenant Earl Alexander of Mar enforced it by threat of armed attack. However, Alexander cannot have felt entirely secure until his cousin the 'Lord of the Isles' was subsequently arrested by King James while attending a summons to Parliament at Inverness and imprisoned, curbing the independence of the 'Lord'. He married Mary Maclean of Duart and died in 1460; their son was John or Ian, the fifth lord (d. 1501), who defied the royal requirement for the vassals of the defunct lordship of the Isles to come and do homage to King James IV on his visits to the Hebrides in 1493 and 1495. John married a cousin, one of the Camerons of Lochiel, whose maternal grandfather was the powerful local chieftain Hector Maclean of Duart (*q.v.*). He may have been killed by treachery after being invited to an interview with the Fraser of Lovat chief at Abertarff, but an alternative version has him dying naturally at Invergarry.

John's son was Alexander or Alasdair the sixth lord, who married Margaret MacDonald of the line of Lochalsh – which marriage brought the family a claim to be the genealogically senior line of the MacDonald dynasty (in the female line) as she was the heiress to the Lochalsh family. She was descended from Celestine, the (probably legitimate) younger son of 'Lord of the Isles' Alexander (d. 1449) and half-brother of the last 'Lord', John (d. 1503). Celestine's family were the closest surviving MacDonald line to the last 'Lord', and probably the senior legitimate line – though Celestine is not called a legitimate brother in all his brother John's charters relating to him, and later scholars have disagreed as to whether his mother was the same as John's (Elizabeth Seton) or a lady from the family of the Earls of Ross, i.e. the same mother as Hugh of Sleat's (and if so whether she and Alexander were married). When their male line died out, Margaret transmitted their claim to her son by Alexander of Glengarry, Angus. She and Alexander inherited half of the Lochalsh lands (including Lochcarron and Strome Castle) when her father Sir Donald MacDonald of Lochalsh died in 1519, but the

Mackenzies of Kintail gained the other half and a famous feud followed. The then (ninth) Mackenzie chief of Kintail, John, was the son of chief Kenneth (d. 1491?), who had been married to a daughter of 'Lord of the Isles' John MacDonald but had been a foe of the Lochalsh line in a struggle to rule Strathpeffer, defeating Alexander of Lochalsh at the Battle of 'Blair-na-Pairc' around 1485/90. John Mackenzie was also at feud with his half-uncle Hector Mackenzie of Gairloch, a MacDonald ally as son of a lady of the MacDonald of Morar line. (Kenneth Mackenzie's father Alexander, sixth chief of Kintail, had been confirmed as lord of Kintail by 'Lord of the Isles' John by charter in 1463 but had defected to the Crown's side in the 1472–76 war, which added to hostility.) Mutual raiding between Glengarry and Kintail followed, with an apparent 'peak' in the later decades of the sixteenth century. Alexander, sixth lord of Glengarry, received a royal pardon for his and his father's refusal to do homage to James IV from the latter's son James V in 1531, and now became a Crown vassal. He acquired a royal charter confirming his rights to Glengarry, Morar, half of Lochalsh, Lochcarron, Loch Broom and Strome Castle on 6 March 1539. He joined the rebellion of his cousin Donald 'Gorm' of Sleat later that year and joined in the attack on Eilean Donan Castle, and after its defeat and Donald's death was tricked into obeying a summons to the king at Edinburgh and arrested there. He was released later, probably after the king's death in December 1542, and subsequently backed his cousin John 'Moydartach' of Clanranald and the Camerons against the Frasers of Lovat and their Clanranald chieftainship nominee Ranald 'Gallda' at the 'Battle of the Shirts' in July 1544. (See section on Clanranald.) He then joined in the rebellious meeting of the principal hereditary members of the revived 'Council of the Isles' as it met in defiance of the government on Islay in 1545 to pledge allegiance to Donald 'Dubh', pretender to the title of 'Lord of the Isles', and backed their recognition of Henry VIII of England as their overlord. He died in 1560; his son Angus, seventh lord, married firstly (c. 1542) Janet Maclean, daughter of the formidable clan chief Hector 'Og' Maclean of Duart (see section on the Macleans), by whom he had his eldest son and heir Donald, eighth chief. Angus then married Margaret MacLeod of Dunvegan as his second wife, and he finally married Mary Mackenzie of Kintail.

Sometime in the mid-sixteenth century the then MacDonald of Glengarry chief, probably Angus or his son, waged a local war against the Mathesons of Lochalsh for control of Lochcarron, which the MacDonalds won; the Matheson chief, Dugald, was left with about a third of his ancestral lands and was thrown into a MacDonald prison and died. Dugald's son Murdoch 'Buidhe' ('Yellow-Haired') Matheson, hopelessly outnumbered in case of conflict, transferred his remaining lands except for two farms to their powerful neighbours the Mackenzies of Kintail in return for their military support but the MacDonalds defeated them both. Angus' reign also seems to have seen the conflict with the Mackenzies of Kintail come to a head, with Colin, tenth chief of Kintail (d. 1594), being married to a Grant and having links to Queen Mary (in whose cause his father had been killed in 1568). Angus was ambushed and captured and his retainers slaughtered by the Mackenzies on one occasion and his uncles were killed on another (1580). Their sons subsequently raided and burnt the Mackenzie-held lands of Applecross in Wester Ross and burnt the murderer John 'Og' and his family to death in their house (1597), and Donald's own son Angus 'Og' carried out other merciless raids; in retaliation the Mackenzies ravaged Moidart. The Mackenzies secured a commission of 'fire and the sword' from the Privy Council to attack Angus's lands by dint of complaining about his breaking the peace, but after they managed to capture him the council ordered his release. Angus senior died in 1574; his eldest son and successor Donald, eighth lord, was born around 1545 and died in February 1645 (reputedly on the day of the great clan victory over the Campbells at Inverlochy), well into his nineties. He received a royal charter for his lands, transferring them to him from his father, from the regency government for James VI on 8 July 1574. He was originally meant to marry the daughter of Grant of Freuchie and an agreement for the transfer of lands contingent to this was drawn up with his father Angus in November 1571, but later documents show that the plan collapsed (possibly due to Donald) although he and the Grant daughter did temporarily cohabit for a year and a day according to the local custom of 'handfasting' and had a son, Angus (k. 1602, as below). Was their marital arrangement not recognised by the Church? Donald certainly legally married Margaret MacDonell of Moidart, his next or first wife, by whom he had four sons – Alasdair 'Dearg', the eldest, who predeceased him; Alasdair 'Mór' ('the Great'), who founded the line of Aberchalder and Culachie; John 'Og', who founded the line of Leck and Ardnabie and died in 1614; and Donald 'Gorm' of Scothouse, who married Margaret MacDonald of Sleat. John 'Og' was succeeded by his son (by a Grant of Glenmoriston) Angus of Ardnabie, and Donald was succeeded by his son Ranald of Scothouse, later tenth chief, who married Flora MacLeod.

In Donald's time the war with the Mackenzies over the lands of Lochcarron flared up again, according to tradition commencing with the murder of a MacDonald tenant suspected of poaching on his past record by an intercepting Mackenzie gamekeeper. The discovery of his hidden body two years later led to the retaliatory murder of the brother of the chief suspect by a MacDonald 'hit squad', the MacDonald chief (Donald of Glengarry) refusing to hand over the accused, and the victim's landlord Rory 'Mór' Mackenzie of Redcastle joining up with his kinsman Dugald Mackenzie of Applecross to 'target' Donald. The latter and his wife were visiting Dugald unawares when the latter tipped off Rory Mór and his men, and these lay in wait for Donald on his way home, slaughtered his escort, and carried him off for ransom with Strome/Lochcarron Castle being handed over to them. (Luckily he had sent his wife home by sea.) Donald used his influence in Edinburgh to make a complaint to the Privy Council about Mackenzie atrocities, but faced counter-charges about the Applecross burnings plus the Revd John Mackenzie of Dingwall accusing him of being an idolater (i.e. Catholic) and living in sin with a 'wife' whom he was not legally married to. This was apparently a reference to Donald having lived in a 'handfast union' with his fiancée/wife Helen Grant in 1571, without a ceremony recognised by the Church. (A record exists of their son, Angus, having been legitimated later on by the government.) Donald lost his nerve and fled Edinburgh, but the Privy Council ordered the Mackenzies to hand over Strome to the Earl of Argyll pending a settlement in March 1583. The feud escalated until Murdoch Matheson's son Ruadhri assisted the Mackenzie chief in sacking Strome Castle in 1602, securing Mackenzie control of Lochcarron, with a Privy Council decree endorsing the Mackenzies with a commission of 'fire and the sword' on their behalf. That year also saw a clan battle between the MacDonalds of Glengarry and the Mackenzies as the latter intercepted a MacDonald raid on Applecross, and Alexander MacGorrie, one of the MacDonald cousins involved in the killing of John 'Og' Mackenzie, was cornered and killed as the raiders were driven off (traditionally by having a rock dropped on his head from above as he backed against a rock face). Angus 'Og', Donald's eldest but 'illegitimate' son by Helen Grant, was drowned in November 1602 when he led a force of seventeen 'birlinns' to raid Applecross and on his way home was ambushed in the Strait of Kyleakin (between the mainland and Skye). The Mackenzie chief's wife apparently spotted his ship alone and vulnerable to attack from the battlements of Eilean Donan Castle and sent out a galley to attack it, and Angus' men did not see the attackers in the semi-dark until it was too late. The Mackenzies' cannon blasted their ship, causing panic, and it struck the 'Cailleach' rock and sank, drowning all sixty people aboard. In retaliation, the following year the MacDonalds surrounded the church of Kilchrist while the leading Mackenzies were inside attending a service, set it afire, and watched them all burn to death; the

MacDonald piper paraded round the building playing a tune which is still used by the clan. But despite these losses the Mackenzies gained and held most of the disputed Lochcarron lands; their twelfth chief Kenneth even secured a peerage from James VI. Donald MacDonell of Glengarry defied a royal order of 25 March 1609 to appear before the Privy Council in Edinburgh over more disturbances but was not punished. In 1627 Donald acquired a royal charter from Charles I turning his lands into a 'free barony', with only the king as his overlord. By this time Invergarry House, built on 'Raven's Rock', had superseded the sacked Strome Castle (now in Mackenzie hands) as the main family residence.

Having outlived his eldest son Alasdair 'Dearg', Donald was succeeded by the latter's son by Jean Cameron, Alexander Aeneas, the ninth lord (d. 6 December 1680). He fought for Montrose in 1644–45, along with his Clanranald kin, and served at the major local clash with the Campbells at Inverlochy in February 1645. After Montrose's flight from the Lowlands when his army was destroyed at Philiphaugh in September 1645 Aeneas put him up at Invergarry for some time. He then took a regiment of his clansmen to Ireland to fight for the Royalist commander, the Marquis of Ormonde, in 1647 but lost 400 men in a clash with Sir Thomas Esmond en route to Wexford. He was proclaimed a rebel by the Covenanter-controlled Privy Council in Edinburgh in 1649 for failing to produce some fugitives, presumably fellow Royalists who had fought for the king in 1645 or 1648, but managed to avoid punitive action. Unlike many local chiefs, he not only joined Charles II's army as it fought Cromwell in 1650–51 but accompanied his king on the risky march south into England. Thus he was present at the Battle of Worcester on 3 September 1651 when the king's small army was overwhelmed by Cromwell's troops, but managed to escape back to Scotland. There he fought for the Earl of Glencairn against Cromwell's army in 1653–54, retrieved some Campbell defectors under Lord Lorne (the Marquis of Argyll's heir) by force as they tried to desert at New Year 1654, and on the Royalists' defeat was forced into flight as General Monck occupied the lands of Lochaber and sacked his new mansion at Invergarry. His lands were forfeited though he received the honorary rank of major-general from the king, but he regained his estates at the Restoration in 1660. This well-connected Restoration landowner, married to Margaret MacDonald of Sleat, shrewdly made the most of his loyal service to the king in person at the nadir of the latter's fortunes in 1651. He thus succeeded in securing official recognition that he was the correct lineal heir of the line of the Lords of the Isles as the nearest in blood (legitimately) to the last 'Lord', John (d. 1503), and was duly granted the crucially named peerage of 'Lord MacDonald of Aros' as head of the MacDonald dynasty on 20 December 1660. A royal writ of 18 July 1672 required Lord MacDonald, as head of the MacDonald clan and heir to the late Celestine of Lochalsh (by female descent) under the usual inheritance laws – both of common law and of dynastic inheritance – to serve as guarantor for his clansmen's obedience to royal law and to produce any of them who were served legal notices as malefactors to appear in court. This was a major step forward in achieving the support of the Stuart legal system and the administration in Edinburgh for Aeneas MacDonell of Glengarry as head of the entire dynasty and heir to the Scots peerage created for John MacDonald 'of the Isles' by James III in 1476. It eclipsed the senior line of Clanranald, which was not descended from 'Lord' Alexander (d. 1449) but only from his grandfather John (d. 1386?), and made the most of the fact that in Scotland a peerage could be transmitted via a female unlike in England – as the Hamilton peerage had descended from the first duke (executed 1649), who had no son, via his daughter to the Douglas-Hamiltons. The one problem was that the new Lord MacDonald had no children, and the peerage had been created for him personally rather than revived so it must descend to the heirs of his body rather than to any brothers or cousins. Thus when he died in 1680 the peerage lapsed again; though his heir to Glengarry, his uncle Donald of Scothouse's son Ranald/Reginald (d. 1705), could have applied for it to be recreated for him.

Ranald, as tenth lord of Glengarry and chief from 1680, also had the genealogical benefit of his mother being Margaret MacDonald of Sleat so he could claim descent via her from Hugh of Sleat (d. 1494/95), illegitimate (?) son of 'Lord' Alexander (d. 1449) and nearest – though not legally unchallengeable – male kin to the last 'Lord', John. Ranald, however, did not make the effort to put in a new application for the peerage, possibly due to lack of anticipated support for it in Edinburgh. He married Flora MacLeod of Drynoch, and had two sons. The younger, Angus or Aeneas, inherited Scothouse and married Catherine MacLeod of Bernera; the elder, Alasdair 'Dubh' ('the Dark'), led the clan's troops in the army of James Graham of Claverhouse, 'Bonnie Dundee', for James VII and II in 1689 and fought at the Battle of Killiecrankie, reputedly carrying the king's standard. His elder son Donald 'Gorm' also fought there, and was killed. Alasdair succeeded as eleventh lord of Glengarry in 1705, and in August 1714 was first to sign the pledge of allegiance which assorted Highland chiefs were asked to sign by John Erskine, Earl of Mar, who presented it to George I as he landed at Greenwich. But in 1715 he joined the Jacobite rebellion by attending the 'hunting match' that the disillusioned Mar called at Braemar to have an excuse to call Jacobite enthusiasts and their followers (plus large numbers of horses) together without attracting government suspicion. He pledged 800 men to Mar, and led them to fight at the Battle of Sheriffmuir. After the battle he was created 'Lord MacDonald' by the 'Old Pretender', aka James III, in December 1716, but this restoration of the peerage was only titular as the rebellion had by then collapsed and the rightful king had fled back to the Continent. Alasdair then had his house burnt down by government troops and had to flee, aided the 1718 Jacobite rising, and finally submitted to the government in 1720 and was pardoned but secretly received a commission to act as James IIIs local agent. He died on 28 October 1721. He married firstly Anne Lovat, by whom he had no children, and secondly Mary Mackenzie (d. 1726), daughter of Kenneth Mackenzie, third Earl of Seaforth (d, 1678), by whom he had his heir Donald, who was killed in the Jacobite rising of 1719 (in which Aeneas also helped), and a younger son, John, who succeeded as twelfth lord. John or Ian, who died on 1 September 1754, married firstly Margaret MacDonald of Hilton, by whom he had his sons (his heir, Alexander/Alasdair, and Aeneas), and secondly Helen Gordon of Glenbucket. His second son, Aeneas, and his kinsman Colonel MacDonald of Lochgarry, led the clan troops for 'Bonnie Prince Charlie' in 1745–46 while John stayed out of the conflict apart from one moment of glory when the clan helped in the ambush of two regiments of the Royal Scots (en route from Fort Augustus to reinforce Fort William) at Highbridge on the Spean during the prince's rally at Glenfinnan. The Macleans (*q.v.*) had successfully fooled the British troops into thinking that their small ambush party at the bridge was larger and caused their party to flee back up the road towards Fort Augustus. The nervous British commander, Major Scott, proposed to take refuge in nearby Invergarry House, but John and his men emerged to attack them down a hillside and helped the other Jacobites to surround them and force their surrender. John's second son Aeneas was killed at the Battle of Falkirk, and the colonel led the clan at Culloden, where their prince controversially removed them from their usual position of honour on the right wing just before the battle (though that meant that they did not take part in the main charge and so casualties were lower). Clan tradition had it that Robert Bruce had given them the privilege of fighting on the right wing at Bannockburn, so this was an insult. Afterwards Colonel MacDonell escorted the fleeing Prince to Invergarry House, where he had his final indoor meal (traditionally said to be cooked salmon) before he took to the heather next day. Shortly after the prince had left, the 'redcoats' arrived to burn down Invergarry House. The colonel then escorted the prince on his wanderings around the west Highlands and was evacuated with him to France from Loch nan Uamh, while the family's homes and lands were pillaged and burnt by 'Butcher' Cumberland's troops.

Alasdair, nicknamed 'Ruadh' ('the Red'), born around 1725, was sent abroad by his Catholic and Jacobite father to be educated in France in 1738, and was a Jacobite cadet officer in Lord Drummond's regiment of Guards at Louis XV's court from 1743. He then served under the Jacobite exile commander George Keith, the Earl Marischal, from March 1744 and was part of his expeditionary force that was intended to sail to invade England on French ships in 1744. This was postponed, and in early spring 1745 he was sent on a secret mission to the west Highlands to sound out the local chiefs concerning their willingness to rise on behalf of their king, James III, if his son Prince Charles Edward Stuart invaded. The results were disappointing, and Alasdair MacDonell returned to France convinced that a revolt would fail unless it was strongly supported by French troops and determined to advise the prince not to sail without this. Unfortunately, by the time he arrived in France the prince had already sailed for Scotland. Alasdair sailed to join him later that year, but on 23 November his ship was intercepted en route by the British frigate HMS *Sheerness* and he was captured and put in the Tower of London. He was released in July 1747, returned to France where he continued to work for the prince, and in December 1749 arrived secretly in Scotland again. Apparently his mission was to retrieve a cache of money hidden by the prince's followers during the 1745–46 rebellion near Loch Arkaig and remove it to safety, but he took it for his own use or for the British government. It is at this point that legend and surmise take over from facts, as there was a dangerous British/Hanoverian spy nicknamed 'Pickle' operating in the prince's court at this time and passing on information to the British government, a man who had turned up at the Prime Minister Henry Pelham's house in Arlington Street near St James's Palace in London to offer his services. He is believed to have been the man who betrayed the senior Jacobite agent Dr Archibald Cameron, the younger brother of Cameron of Lochiel, to the government in 1751, resulting in Cameron's execution at Tyburn on an old charge of treason dating from his activities with the prince in Scotland in 1745–46. The identity of 'Pickle' was unclear at the time, but in 1897 the Scots author Andrew Lang (better known for fairy stories) identified him as Alasdair MacDonald of Glengarry. Alasdair, who inherited the family estates and revenues (what was left of them after plundering by British troops) when his father died in September 1754 but who had no money, may have turned against the prince after the clan troops were peremptorily moved from their usual position on the right wing of the Stuart army to the left wing at Culloden, a possible insult. He may have been annoyed that the prince did not wait for his report before invading Scotland in 1745 and felt that the latter bore the responsibility for the resulting bloodbath (and his own brother's death in battle at Falkirk) by taking too many risks. Alternatively, he may have been worked on and 'turned' in captivity in the Tower in 1745–47, being released in return for services in spying, and the 'spontaneous visit to Mr Pelham's house to offer his services' may have been a cover story for something that had been going on for longer. Certainly he was short of money, and he ended up dying in a hut on his estates (his house had been sacked by British troops and he could not afford to rebuild it) in 1761. His reputation remains controversial, but he achieved more fame in posterity as the main inspiration for the villain in the fictional account of the Jacobite rebellion and its aftermath by D. K. Broster in her trilogy in the 1920s. In *The Gleam in the North* (1927), the sequel to *The Flight of the Heron*, the hero Ewan Cameron's kinsman Dr Archibald Cameron, a historical figure, is betrayed to his death by an anonymous British government agent, 'Pickle', on whom Cameron swears vengeance. In the third and final book, *The Dark Mile* (1929), Cameron discovers to his horror that a family friend who has been of great service to him, 'Finlay MacPhair of Glenshian', is 'Pickle', and is unable to decide what to do about it but MacPhair is fatally injured in an accidental fire before he has to act. The character and family backstory of MacPhair, who is far from an unsympathetic figure and who does his best to convince himself and others that he acted to save lives in a futile revolt, is based clearly on Alasdair MacDonell of Glengarry.

MacDonald of Keppoch

The founder of this line was Alexander or Alisdair 'Carrach', a younger son of John, 'Lord of the Isles' (d. 1386?), and Amy MacRuadhri. Full brother to Ranald, the founding lord of Clanranald, he was an even more obscure figure but appears to have been rather younger than Ranald and also long-lived. Presumably born before his parents' divorce in 1350, he was still alive in 1431 when he was cited as a rebel in a document of King James IV – i.e. he was a supporter of his kinsman the arrested 'Lord of the Isles' Alexander and had taken part in (or sent his men to aid) the revolt of Domnhall 'Balloch' MacDonald against the royal army in 1431. The MacDonalds of Keppoch had thus participated in Domnhall's victory over the royal lieutenant in the Highlands, Alexander Stewart, Earl of Mar, at Inverlochy and had aided the subsequent guerrilla war when reinforcements enabled Mar to invade Lochaber, and as a punishment King James confiscated a large segment of Alisdair 'Carrach's estates and transferred them to the loyal Mackintoshes of Clan Chattan. Thereafter the MacDonalds of Keppoch played a much more minor role in west Highlands wars than their better-endowed kin of Clanranald and Glengarry (the latter a junior branch of, and so allied to, the former), and Alasdair and his heirs seem to have kept out of anti-government risings or at least avoided documentary condemnation. Alisdair was succeeded by his son Angus, the second lord of Keppoch, who married a McPhee and on the forfeiture of the lordship of the Isles to James IV in 1493 was made the king's local commander and lieutenant in Lochaber. This would indicate that his part of the clan had taken a consistent pro-government 'line' in the troubles of the 1460s–70s and the king felt he could rely on them, as he did on the MacIains of Ardnamurchan but not on the more genealogically senior MacDonald lines. Were the junior branches trusted as they had no hope of claiming the defunct 'Lordship' and so were less likely to rebel? Angus' son Donald, the third lord, was among those local lords who signed up in 1497 to a royal order to turn in any of their clansmen who were accused of crimes to appear in court, on pain of being accused of contempt of royal authority with them. He was killed in a local inter-clan battle later in 1497 as the end of the 'Lordship' brought a rise in disorder with the new lord, the king, far away and not acceptable to many clans; plausibly Donald was endeavouring to keep order for King James but was seen as a traitor by his rivals. These years of turbulence also saw the subsequent expulsion of his young son and successor John, the fourth lord, in 1497/98 and the installation of Donald's younger brother, Alasdair, as the new (fifth) lord. The excluded heirs of John MacDonald were to continue as minor local lairds in Lochaber, and a century and a half later included the famous Highlands poet Ian 'Lom' MacDonald (*c.* 1620–1715) who in his youth was supposed to have been one of the MacDonalds who guided Montrose and his army in an epic overnight trek round the flanks of Ben Nevis in February 1645 to take the Earl of Argyll's Covenanters by surprise at Inverlochy.

A cattle raid on the MacDonald of Keppoch lands of the Braes of Lochaber by the MacLarens in 1497/98 saw the MacDonalds pursuing and defeating the raiders at the Battle of Glenurchy and recapturing the cattle – all part of the normal activities of petty inter-clan rivalry and competition for prestige and resources, keeping the clans' warriors occupied. But in this case the MacLarens were unwilling to take their defeat lightly and called in their ally Dugald Stewart, first lord of Appin, head of a junior branch of the Stewarts descended from the marriage of his grandfather Robert Stewart of Innermeath to the daughter of the 'Governor'/regent Robert Stewart, Duke of Albany. Dugald was thus the great-nephew of Sir John Stewart the 'Black Knight of Lorn', second husband of Queen Joan Beaufort, the widow of James I, and was distant royal kin both via her link and via his paternal ancestor Alexander Stewart, hereditary 'High Steward' of Scotland (d. 1309). In a region open to Campbell encroachment, the Stewarts of Appin made up for what they lacked in landed and military power with their royal blood and links to their cousins the earls of Atholl. On this occasion the Stewarts aided the MacLarens in a second invasion of Lochaber, and in the subsequent battle in 1498 or 1499 both Alisdair MacDonald of Keppoch, the new lord, and his attacker Dugald Stewart were killed. Alisdair was succeeded by his son Donald 'Glas', the sixth lord of Keppoch, who died around 1513/17; his son and successor Ranald 'Mór' MacDonald, the seventh lord (married to a daughter of the Mackintosh chief), was involved in the Clanranald succession dispute war of 1544 and fought for John Moydartach against the Frasers at the 'Battle of the Shirts'. In retaliation, when the Mackintoshes captured him and his ally Ewan Cameron, that clan's chief, in 1547, the Earl of Huntly (a Fraser ally) executed them both for alleged brigandage. The lordship then passed to Ranald's son Alasdair, the eighth chief (killed in an inter-clan clash in 1549 or 1554), and then to his brother Ranald Og, the ninth lord (d. 1587), who fought a private war against the Mackintoshes until the regent Moray summoned the leading participants to Parliament and imposed peace in 1569. The next chief was Ranald Og's son Alasdair 'nan Cleach' ('of the tricks'), the tenth lord, who was born around 1570 and died before 1641, probably in 1635. Alasdair's elder son and successor by Janet MacDougall of Dunolly, Ranald 'Og', is named as the eleventh lord by the mainstream MacDonald genealogists, but not by some history books – hence some confusion over the numbering of the subsequent chiefs. Married to a Mackintosh, he died in 1641 and the clan chieftainship passed to his brother, Donald 'Glas', the eleventh lord. Donald led his clansmen to fight for Montrose and took a prominent part in the Battle of Inverlochy, on local territory on whose layout he was able to advise his commander, in February 1645. Donald, like his Clanranald kinsmen, submitted to the Earl/Marquis of Argyll after the Royalist collapse and avoided having his isolated lands confiscated; he died around 1657. His son and successor (by his second wife, a Forrester of Kilbeggie in Clackmannanshire), Alasdair, the twelfth lord, and the latter's brother and heir, Ranald, were both killed by seven discontented clansmen in a notorious ambush in 1663. 'Tobair-nan-Ceann', the 'Well of Heads' near Loch Oich and Invergarry, is linked to this; it is famed for an incident where the severed heads of seven executed captives were washed by their killers before being presented to the local clan chief,

MacDonell of Glengarry. The executed prisoners were the men who had killed Alisdair and Ranald in 1663 – led by Alan 'Dearg' and Donald, the sons of the murdered brothers' uncle Alasdair, younger brother of the late chief Donald, who now succeeded as thirteenth chief. No action was taken in the clan to apprehend the killers, indicating consensus to avoid a probably costly blood feud; nor did the government intervene, as the targets had been of no political value. But the murdered men's supporters did not give up and sometime later the bard Ian 'Lom' MacDonald, descended from a previous overthrown clan chief as mentioned above, took the case to the neighbouring MacDonald chiefs of Sleat and Glengarry. These two lords – the senior leaders of the clan – had the manpower and reputation to defy the cover-up that was going on within the Keppoch branch, and duly approached the Privy Council in Edinburgh. The latter had other priorities and probably saw the incident as of little moment as not affecting the king's peace. Only seven years later, when new ministers were in power in Edinburgh with no past connections to the west Highlands from old Royalist alliances, were warrants finally issued for the murderers' arrest. Sleat and Glengarry then aided the arrest and execution of the miscreants; their heads were washed at the nearby well and presented to the local chief, Glengarry.

A feud between the MacDonalds of Keppoch and the Mackintoshes (the usual foes of the Clanranald branch) over the rents that the Mackintoshes were failing to pay for leased MacDonald lands in Glenroy and Glenspean added to local disorder in the latter part of the reign of Charles II and into the reign of James II. By now Alisdair of Keppoch had been succeeded by his younger, surviving son by his second marriage, Archibald (d. 1682), who was in turn succeeded by his son by a MacMartin of Letterfinlay, Coll. The (Catholic) MacDonalds made themselves useful to King James, their co-religionist, in summer 1685 by assisting the suppression of the revolt by the exiled (Protestant) ninth Earl of Argyll. The latter, sentenced to death for defying the autocratic government over James's succession rights in 1681 and forced to flee to Holland after a dramatic escape from Edinburgh Castle, invaded his ancestral clan territory in the name of Charles II's eldest illegitimate son, the Duke of Monmouth. They claimed that the duke was the legitimate king and James was a fratricidal usurper. Argyll failed to achieve much support or take government-held Inveraray Castle, moved south to the Clyde and was quickly rounded up by government troops, but the prudent decision of most of his Campbell clansmen not to rise for him was at least in part due to the size of the – partly MacDonald – government force that faced him in Argyll and made an example of 'rebels'. But the help that Keppoch had given to the king was not sufficient to make his ministers overlook the blatant low-level warfare that was now going on between his clan and the Mackintoshes. The Mackintosh chief Lachlan secured the backing of James II's Privy Council by a complaint about his Keppoch neighbours, and as the latter failed to appear on the due date to answer charges Mackintosh had 'letters of fire and sword' issued to enable him to ravage their lands in retaliation in 1688. But the clan held out against his attack, and fought his invading Mackintosh clansmen in the Battle of Mulroy on 4 August 1688, the last inter-clan battle fought in the Highlands. They lost the battle, but retreated into the hills and harassed his plundering clansmen. The overthrow of King James in England then intervened. The government's authority collapsed, and Coll, who had recently succeeded as fifteenth or sixteenth chief, took his clansmen to assist 'Bonnie Dundee' in his campaign to restore the king to power in the Lowlands in spring 1689. The MacDonalds of Keppoch fought at the Battle of Killiecrankie, but were most notable in the 1689–90 campaigns for their ferocious reprisals against the Mackintoshes, who were now deprived of any government backer. Making the most of their opportunity, the MacDonalds of Keppoch carried out a thorough pillaging of their enemies' territory, where the damages were subsequently costed at £35,950 in Scots money (£2,995 in English money). In reprisal the Williamite general Hugh Mackay and his army carried out a campaign of repression in the region with several notorious atrocities, most famously on the island of Eigg, which was at that time in the possession of inhabitants paying allegiance to Keppoch so the MacDonalds were the main target.

The clan then submitted and its chief came to swear allegiance to King William by 1 January 1692, as required to avoid dispossession; it was the MacDonalds of Glencoe who failed to turn up to swear in time and were massacred in retaliation as an example, but it could easily have been those of Keppoch given their past record. In 1715 the clan again assisted the Jacobite cause at the Battle of Sheriffmuir. Coll MacDonald died before the 1745 rising, probably in 1729. The next (sixteenth or seventeenth) chief, Alisdair, his son by Barbara MacDonald of Sleat, joined the cause of Charles Edward Stuart in 1745, and gave him invaluable support in the opening clash of the campaign on the day of the rendezvous at Glenfinnan on 16 August. Clan Cameron of Lochiel and Clanranald had gathered at the meeting place to greet the prince, but as MacDonald of Keppoch was en route he heard that a party of two companies of the Royal Scots regiment had been sent from the main British Army base at Fort Augustus down the military road alongside Loch Lochy to reinforce Fort William. Led by a Captain Scott, these eighty-five men would have been able to rally the British garrison at the latter to resist a Jacobite attack if not to attack Glenfinnan, and the Highlanders' route east into the Great Glen en route to Edinburgh would probably have been blocked for longer. Accordingly the outnumbered but resolute MacDonalds, led by Alisdair, prepared an ambush for the advancing British column at the 'pinch-point' of Highbridge, the eponymous bridge where the military road crossed the River Spean en route to Fort William. The woods around the bridge enabled the defenders to hide their true numbers, and a small party of eleven men led by Major Donald MacDonald of Tir-na-Dris (with a piper) waited openly at the bridge to deny the British passage. Their confidence and the major's bold demands that the advancing 'redcoats' surrender persuaded the latter that there must be a much larger party of rebels hiding around the bridge, and thus the bluff worked and a headlong attack on the defence was avoided. The MacDonalds opened fire, more men appeared around the (now demolished) inn nearby to reinforce those on the bridge or showed themselves among the trees to either side of the road, and parties of Jacobites dashed to and fro in the woods to make it appear that there was a great deal of activity among a much larger force. The British duly panicked and retreated back up the road under fire, heading up the loch side towards the safety of MacDonell of Glengarry's residence at Invergarry, where they could hold out if needed. But as they reached the open ground between Loch Lochy and Loch Oich, short of their destination, with the MacDonalds in pursuit, the British troops saw a large party of the enemy gathered on a nearby hill ready to intercept them. They veered off the road to head for Invergarry House and make a stand there, but MacDonell of Glengarry and his men came to the Jacobites' aid, charging down a hillside. Fearing a rout and massacre, Major Scott halted his men and received an envoy from Alisdair MacDonald under a flag of truce. This time he agreed to surrender, and he and his men were marched off into captivity, unaware of the trick that had been played on them; his horse was then taken off by MacDonald to be presented to the prince at Glenfinnan a few hours later. The skirmish was a timely morale-booster for the clan gathering at Glenfinnan, encouraging the Jacobites (among whom even Cameron of Lochiel was dubious of their prospects and had nearly not turned up) to march boldly for the Lowlands. It was also used for a major scene in the aforementioned *The Flight of the Heron*, where the hero Ewen Cameron rather than MacDonald of Keppoch plays the trick at Highbridge and his English friend and nemesis is the British officer who surrenders.

MacDonald and his clansmen then took part in the Jacobite siege of Fort William in March 1746, aided by the Camerons. This commenced on 20 March, but the well-armed government troops held out behind strong ramparts and repelled the only serious attempt to storm the fortress. The Highlanders were needed by their prince at Inverness, and had to abandon the siege on 4 April and hurry north to the prince's main army to reach them in time before the battle with the Duke of Cumberland's army. The clan contingent was present at Culloden, where Alasdair the clan chief, and many of the clan were killed. Their lands were occupied and ravaged by Cumberland's soldiers, but Alasdair's illegitimate teenage son Angus took charge as Alasdair's son by Jessie Stewart of Appin, Ranald (d. 1797?), was underage. He became acting chief (though he is not recognised in some of the clan lists) and managed to save his inheritance from confiscation. He was duly recognised by the government as the seventeenth chief. He later abdicated as clan chief in favour of the legitimate claimant, Ranald, once the latter was adult.

MacDonald/MacIain of Ardnamurchan

This line was founded by Ian or John 'Sprangach', 'the Bold', the third and youngest son of Angus 'Mór', the ally of Robert Bruce. Younger brother of 'Lords of the Isles' Alexander and John (d. 1386?), he was thus uncle to the founders of the Clanranald and Keppoch dynasties. Little is known of him beyond his inheritance of the peninsula of Ardnamurchan and the surrounding lands on the mainland, running south of Knoydart to Morvern. The adjacent lands of Knoydart were mostly in the hands of the 'Slochd Alien Uc Alien' branch of the MacDonalds, the last of whom was killed shortly before this territory was given to MacDonell of Glengarry in 1611. Another, junior MacDonald dynasty held some lands in Knoydart – the clan of Ian 'Ruadh', the MacDonalds or MacAllisters 'of the Loup', who emigrated to Ontario, Canada in 1784. They were descended from an eponymous Alisdair or Alexander (*fl. c.* 1280–99), who was either a younger son of the MacDonald founding ancestor Donald, grandson of Somerled, or a younger brother of Angus 'Mór', the ally of Robert Bruce. His son Donald was alive around 1314; his descendant John was ruling the family lands in Kintyre by 1493 as a junior ally of Clanranald, and was succeeded by around 1515 by his son Angus.

The rule by Ian 'Sprangach' of Ardnamurchan appears to have been uneventful, but his clan were too small in terms of resources to make a major impact on politics or warfare at this date in the fourteenth century and were loyal allies of their more powerful neighbours of Clanranald and of the 'Lords of the Isles'. The third chief, Alexander or Alisdair, was killed at the Battle of Harlaw in 1411, fighting for 'Lord of the Isles' Donald – the first cousin of his father. His son and successor, John or Ian, was killed at the Battle of Inverlochy in 1431, fighting for Domnall 'Balloch' against the invasion of King James I's army under the Earl of Mar after the arrest of 'Lord of the Isles' Alexander. The most famous and powerful of the chiefs was John MacIain, ruler of the clan in the later fifteenth century, who cast his fortunes in with the aggressive King James IV after the latter forced the weak 'Lord of the Isles' John MacAlexander (d. 1503) to abdicate and suppressed the lordship of the Isles. The king was now the 'Lord' and thus the overlord of the local clan chiefs, but he could only visit the region occasionally though James IV was more interested in it than his predecessors (and was developing a fleet too) and arrived at Dunstaffnage Castle in August 1493, soon after deposing 'Lord' John, to summon the principal lords to do homage. But who was to act as the king's 'strongman' in his absence, and reap the rewards of lands and office that would bring? John MacIain was a weaker contender for the role of the new leading MacDonald dynast than his two main rivals, Alexander of Lochalsh (son of Celestine, the younger son of 'Lord' Alexander, and thus 'Lord' John's first cousin) and John of Dunivaig.

Both these men apparently did homage to James on his visit to Dunstaffnage to secure royal legal confirmation of their lands, and were certainly knighted. But John MacIain, who also offered his services to the king and did homage to him (probably in August 1493) in return for a legal document confirming his lands, thereafter pursued a strict line of adherence to centralising royal demands whereas his rivals had their own independent ambitions and showed a disregard for royal authority at times. John of Dunivaig notoriously showed his opposition to the king taking over Dunaverty Castle by taking it over himself and (according to a later story possibly based on oral memories) hanging its new royal custodian from the battlements as soon as the king had left by sea on this 1493 royal tour of the Argyll region. Alexander of Lochalsh was also prepared to continue his usual attacks on his neighbours and hereditary clan foes, such as the Mackenzies, without the king's permission and so to defy the concept of the 'king's peace'. John MacIain, by contrast, was eager to do the king's work and to aid James in suppressing disorder and defiance, and the seventeenth-century family historian surmised that he feared for his own safety if Alexander of Lochalsh ever took over the defunct lordship so he set out to destroy him. In 1494/95 he followed up a major attack by Alexander of Lochalsh on the Mackenzies (which they defeated) by ambushing and killing him in obscure circumstances on Oronsay. This violent death of the deposed 'Lord' John's nearest legitimate male kin and strongest clan sub-leader left a vacancy in local power, to MacIain's benefit as the man on the spot who could do the king's work for him; MacIain now secured in June 1494 the role of the king's bailiff on Islay, once centre of the MacDonald lordship and the most fertile and valuable of the islands of the Inner Hebrides and now mostly owned by John of Dunivaig. He was in dispute with his cousin Alan MacRuadhri of Clanranald for the control of Sunart, which he secured around 1495. He also secured a grant of local royal lands, giving him further legal security, income and prestige to hire armed retainers. As such he was the 'coming man' as the king's deputy, and in either 1494 or 1499 he struck again at the most dangerous of the king's defiers – and his own rivals. He arrested John of Dunivaig and his three sons in a 'swoop' at Finlaggan and sent them off in chains to Edinburgh, where they were tried, found guilty of brigandage and hanged from the same gallows as a warning to Highland lords of the reach of the king's justice. As required by a new royal law of April 1497, the chiefs were to be responsible for seeing that any of their clans named in legal suits turned up to face justice, on pain of being charged with them; MacIain led the local western Highland lords who 'signed up' to orders from the royal lieutenant, the Earl of Argyll, to obey this.

Thereafter John MacIain was the king's 'strongman' in the southern Hebrides at the cost of a blood feud with the line of MacDonald of Dunivaig, but the latter were at a disadvantage until James IV fell in battle in 1513 as they were 'rebels' and the early years of the sixteenth century saw their lands nibbled away from the south by encroachment by the Campbells, earls of Argyll and royal allies. John MacIain was seen as the king's local 'enforcer' and military recruiter, as in March 1507 it was John whom the king's Ulster ally Hugh O'Donnell named as his preferred commander if the king sent him a force of 4,000 Highlanders to fight his unnamed enemies. (James refused.) However, John MacIain's position weakened after the king fell at Flodden as he could no longer count on royal support and the regency was riven by factional feuds and English and French attempts to dominate it, and local inter-clan clashes resumed with no firm centralised control. The vicissitudes of politics in Edinburgh also distracted the nearest local great earl, Argyll, from imposing order or coming to the king's agents' rescue; it was now every man for himself. In 1515 the MacDonalds of Lochalsh took advantage of the unsettled situation to attack the royal-owned Mingary Castle, which John MacIain currently controlled, and they took it in a second attack in 1517. In 1518 John MacIain was killed in an ambush by the MacDonalds of Dunivaig in retaliation for his part in betraying their chief and his sons to James IV, and his dynasty went into eclipse as the military pre-eminence in the lands north of Mull passed back to Clanranald and Glengarry. John's son Alexander or Alisdair died in 1538; he was succeeded by his identically named son, who died around 1570. When James V achieved his majority this vigorous king showed more favour for the MacDonalds of Dunivaig and Islay than to the MacIains, presumably on the same basis as his father's favour for MacIain of Ardnamurchan as a 'controllable' junior line dependant on his favour. When James sought to keep his unreliable and aggressive uncle Henry VIII's regime embroiled in a war in Ulster in 1532 by sending a force of around 8,000 Hebridean mercenaries (mainly MacDonalds) there, he chose Alexander of Dunivaig to command – and took the latter's son south to Edinburgh to have a supervised education near court as his protégé. James of Dunivaig was not, however, entirely trusted by the king, as in 1540 he was one of the chiefs rounded up and taken south in the king's armed expedition round the Hebrides; Dunivaig Castle was given a new royal castellan, a Stewart from Bute. Meanwhile John MacIain's son Alisdair, the eighth chief, at feud with the line of Dunivaig over the killing of John, allied himself to Clanranald as the next senior genealogical heir to the defunct 'lordship' after Dunivaig/ Lochalsh, and in July 1544 he led his clansmen to support Clanranald at the famous 'Battle of the Shirts' (see section on Clanranald). This was a result of his decision that year to join his kinsmen of Keppoch and Glengarry to back up the claim of John 'Moydartach' (of Moidart) to Clanranald against the Fraser- and Gordon-supported claim of Ranald 'Gallda'. After the struggles of the regency years in the 1540s and 1550s, the clan of MacIain of Ardnamurchan went into eclipse.

Donald MacDonald of Clanranald and his son John were recognised as overlords of the MacIains, the line of MacDonald of Ardnamurchan, by the latter's clan in 1618 as its defenders against the pretensions of the encroaching Campbells. The latter's head (the fourth Earl of Argyll) had at some point acquired a deed of surrender of the family lands from an heiress, Mariota, though it does not appear to have been acted upon – possibly her male kin rejected it by force. The clan was in some turmoil, as the son of its 1560s chief John, John 'Og', had been assassinated in 1596, apparently by his ambitious uncle '(Alistair?) Mac Vic Ian', who was soon killed in a clash with the Camerons (his late nephew's fiancée's kin) and was buried at Kiell on Morvern. Argyll now induced the latter's son, chief John 'Mac Allister vic Ian' of Ardnamurchan, to resign his lands and hand their title deeds over in an agreement of 1602. John was supposed to stay on as the Campbells' tenant on payment of one 'mark' 'feu-duty' and receive the same protection as the earl's other tenants, but it appears that he and his kin were cheated by the

Campbells; after he died, between 1605 and 1611, the earl secured his lands, including Mingary Castle. The heir was the underage Alistair MacIain MacDonald, to whom a kinsman acted as 'tutor'. In 1612 the earl installed his own kinsman Donald Campbell of Barbreck-Lochow as Mingary's custodian to act as his agent and receive the due rents for the Ardnamurchan lands, and others of the clan gained various other lands. The 'tutor' of Ardnamurchan's son John went to Edinburgh in winter 1615/16 to complain about Donald Campbell's exactions to Argyll and his kinsman Campbell of Lundie, and although they were absent he secured an official letter to Donald advising him to treat the tenants less harshly – which appears to have been ignored. In retaliation the MacDonalds of Ardnamurchan turned to Clanranald (who had also secured a legal grant of the lands from Argyll by some means) for help, and in May 1618 the latter's son John expelled the Campbells by force. But the latter had the advantage of friends in Edinburgh (and had the title deeds) and knew how to 'work the system' of royal law. They appealed to the Privy Council, and in 1619 senior judges Sir George Hay and George Erskine ruled that Duncan Campbell had the law on his side but should compensate the MacDonalds. John MacDonald, now the eleventh lord of Clanranald (d. 1670), and his allies Maclean of Coll and MacLeod of Harris, were required by the council to act as sureties for young Alistair of Ardnamurchan's good behaviour and obedience to Donald Campbell and join him in swearing loyalty in 1620. (Alistair was referred to as 'of Ylandtirum', probably meaning Eilean Tioram.) The suspicious Campbell accused Alistair of gathering the 'Clan Iain' together to swear an oath to regain their lands by legal means and if that failed start a rebellion in 1622; this was never proved and Alistair appeared before the council to swear his innocence.

But complaints continued, including one from the Bishop of the Isles early in 1622 that Alistair had sent an armed messenger to interrupt the new local Kirk minister of Ardnamurchan at a service and hand him a letter ordering him to clear out of the area (as a Presbyterian enemy of the Catholic MacIains?). In autumn 1624 it appears that the feared revolt occurred. Clanranald, Maclean and MacLeod failed to produce Alistair to appear before the Privy Council by January as required and were duly listed as 'rebels' with him under the current government policy of collective punishment for chiefs who failed to rein in their clansmen or neighbours. Alistair and his men had seized an English ship and were using it to carry out acts of alleged piracy, capturing other ships, and this continued after King James's death in March 1625. In April the Bishop of Glasgow and Sir William Livingston of Kilsyth were authorised to despatch a ship from Ayr to combat the pirates, and a commission of 'fire and the sword' was issued to leading Campbells – the earl's son Lord Lorne (the later Covenanter leader), Duncan of Auchinbreck and the lord of Ardkinglas among them – to punish the MacIains. Ruadhri MacLeod of Harris, as a government 'trusty', drove the pirates off Skye that summer, and then Lord Lorne and his army arrived at Ardnamurchan to meet him while the MacIains took refuge in the woods of Moidart, part of the Clanranald lands. The rebellion was evidently suppressed thoroughly, with Lorne receiving the thanks of the government and no MacIains ever reappearing as owners of their hereditary lands (which Duncan Campbell now rented for 2,000 'marks'). But some of their kin still appear from time to time in the legal records, usually tenants cited as malefactors. For example, Alistair and his men were denounced to the Privy Council again by Duncan Campbell (now knighted) for interrupting and driving off a party of Campbells who were fishing in the River Shiel on 4 June 1630.

1. Castle Tioram. The main stronghold of the MacRuadhri descendants of Somerled, including Robert Bruce's ally Christina of Garmoran. Home of heiress Amy MacRuadhri, who transmitted it to her son's Clanranald descendants. (© Carolyn MacDonell)

2. Armadale Castle, Skye. An early MacDonald stronghold on Skye. The present neo-Gothic building was begun in 1790, extended in 1815 and partly rebuilt after an 1855 fire. (© Carolyn MacDonell)

3. Dunluce Castle, Ulster. Main stronghold of the MacDonalds of Dunivaig, lords of the Glynns, and after them the MacDonells, earls of Antrim. (© Carolyn MacDonell)

4. Glenarm Castle, Ulster. The other main home of the earls of Antrim, built in 1636 by Randall MacDonnell who supplied an Irish army to Montrose's campaigns. Posing are the clan chiefs of senior MacDonald lines: left to right, Sir Ian MacDonald of Sleat, Ranald MacDonnel of Glengarry, the earl of Antrim, Ranald MacDonald of Clanranald. (© Carolyn MacDonell)

5. Invergarry Castle. Centre of the lordship of the MacDonells of Glengarry, and their chiefs' residence in succession to Strome Castle. Charles Edward Stuart spent his last night under cover here after Culloden in 1746 and after his departure government troops burnt it. (© Carolyn MacDonell)

6. The Well of Heads, Invergarry. Monument marking the spot where the severed heads of seven executed murderers were washed by the MacDonells around 1670 before presentation to their chief. The accused had earlier killed the MacDonald of Keppoch chief on behalf of a rival. (© Carolyn MacDonell)

7. The Brough of Birsay, Orkney. (© Wayne Easton/Creative Commons)

7b. View south-east from the Brough of Birsay. The view over the site of Jarl Thorfinn's principal residence in the mid-eleventh century. (© Wayne Easton/ Creative Commons)

8. Deerness, Orkney. The site of a major naval battle around 1040, where Jarl Thorfinn 'Raven-Feeder' of Orkney routed king 'Karl Hundason' (probably Duncan) of Scots. (© Bill Boaden/Creative Commons)

9. Eilean Donan Castle. A major stronghold of the Lordship of the Isles, at the junction of Lochs Alsh, Duich and Long. Held by the Mathesons, then the Mackenzies of Kintail. Donald Gormsson MacDonald of Sleat died besieging it in the 1539 rebellion. Blown up by British troops after capture from a Jacobite/Spanish force in 1719. (© Carolyn MacDonell)

10. The church on Egilsay, Orkney. Built on the site of the martyrdom of Jarl/St Magnus in 1116(?) by the men of his cousin and rival, Jarl Haakon. (© Helen Baker/ Creative Commons)

11. Dunaverty Rock, Argyll. The site of a major MacDonald fortress, one of the key strongholds of their lordship seized by James IV in 1493. The king personally installed his own castellan, but once he sailed away the local chiefs hanged the man from the battlements. (© Becky Williamson/Creative Commons)

12. Loch Finlaggan, Islay. The site of the main residence of the early Lords of the Isles of Somerled's dynasty, where their rival family lines and other chiefs traditionally met. (© Brian Turner/Creative Commons)

13. Glenfinnan Monument. The statue of a Highlander erected to commemorate the gathering of the clans here to join Prince Charles Edward Stuart in 1745. The local MacDonalds of Clanranald and Keppoch, MacDonells of Glengarry and Camerons of Lochiel led the way. (© Tim Glover/Creative Commons)

14. The Sound of Sleat. Principal north–south waterway of the lordship, connecting its southern isles to the north and the Orkneys. Used by generations of Norse, Gaelic and mixed warlords for war and trade, and the site of occasional clashes. (© Carolyn MacDonell)

Right: 15. 'The Massacre Cave', Eigg. The site of a famous massacre of local MacDonalds by Alasdair 'Crotach' Macleod and his men in the early sixteenth century. (© Christian Jones/ Creative Commons)

Below: 16. Site of the Battle of Glenshiel, 1719. The location of the final appearance of foreign troops in a battle on British soil, as a Spanish regiment aided James Edward Stuart's Jacobite clansmen against General Wightman's British troops. (© Sylvia Duckworth/Creative Commons)

17. Inverlochy Castle, Argyll. The main stronghold in the southern part of the Great Glen, which frequently changed hands between the MacDonalds and Scots government nominees in the late medieval period. The site of one major battle between them in 1431, and a second where Montrose defeated the Campbells in 1645. (© Nigel Homer/Creative Commons)

18. Highbridge, Spean Bridge, Argyll. The site of the opening clash of the 'Forty-Five', where a Cameron-led force successfully ambushed a column of government troops. As the latter fled the MacDonells completed the victory. (© Sylvia Duckworth/Creative Commons)

19. Dunvegan Castle, Skye. The principal fortress of one of the two branches of the Macleods, and home of the famous 'Fairy Flag'. (© Andrew Hackney/Creative Commons)

20. Peel Castle, Isle of Man. The main stronghold of the early medieval kings of Man, the dynasty of Godred 'Crovan'. (© David Dixon/Creative Commons)

21. Tynwald Hill, Isle of Man. Meeting place of the British Isles' oldest legislative assembly, and a centre of Manx politics. The site of the final battle between the feuding royal brothers Ragnald and Olaf 'the Black' in 1230. (© David Dixon/ Creative Commons)

22. Rushen Abbey, Isle of Man. The main religious establishment on medieval Man founded by King Olaf 'the Red' (d. 1153) with monks from Furness Abbey. (© Chris Gunns/Creative Commons)

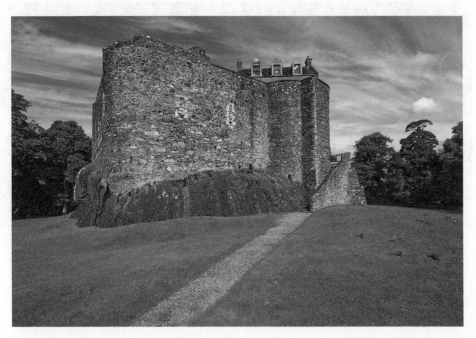

23. Dunstaffnage Castle, Argyll. Previously a royal fortress of the kings of Dalriada, it was the centre of Somerled's dynasty's power in Argyll. Held by the MacDougalls until Robert Bruce confiscated it in 1309. (© Mike Searle/Creative Commons)

24. Battlefield of Culloden, 1746. The view from the position held by the MacDonald regiments towards government lines before the final Highland charge of clan conflict. (© Bill Boaden/Creative Commons)

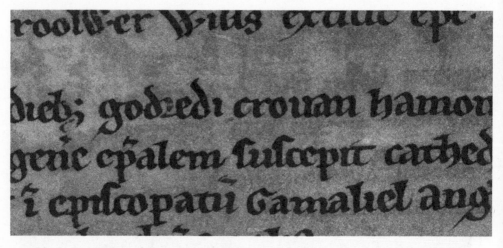

25. A manuscript reference to Godred 'Crovan' founding dynast of the medieval Manx kings. (Courtesy of the British Library)

26. St Magnus' Cathedral, Orkney. The site of St Magnus' burial and subsequent cult as patron saint of Orkney – forced on his reluctant successors by popular demand. (© Robert Scarth/Creative Commons)

27. A cartoon of the arrival of Prince Charles Edward Stuart at Holyrood, 1745. (Courtesy of the Rijksmuseum)

28. A composite image of the arms of the jarls/earls of Orkney. (© Tinynanorobots/
Creative Commons)

7

The Non-MacDonald Clans of the Region

Maclean of Kingairloch/Glenurquhart, and of Ardgour/Duart: 'Clan Gillean'

Clan Gillean were also descended from the early MacDonald 'Lords of the Isles', but in the female line. The first of the dynasty to make any impact, Charles Maclean or 'Tearlach Mac Eachainn', was lord of Glenurquhart and Kingairloch in the mid- to late fourteenth century. He married firstly one of the Mackintoshes, by whom he had two sons – Hector 'Buidhe', 'the Fair', lord of Glenurquhart, who lived from around 1380 to 1454 and became the royal constable of Urquhart Castle for the centralising King James I, and Farquhar, who lived from around 1382 to 1445 and succeeded his father as lord of Kingairloch. Hector was succeeded as (third) lord of Glenurquhart by his elder son, Hector; his younger son John Maclean or 'MacGilleon' was Bishop of the Isles from October 1441 and died in either 1470 or 1471. The younger Hector was succeeded by his son Ewen, fourth lord of Glenurquhart, who married a Mackay and succeeded to the lordship of Kingairloch too on the death of his cousin Donald, fourth lord of Kingairloch (d. 1505), who was son of Charles, the third lord (b. *c.* 1405), and grandson of Farquhar. Ewen Maclean, fourth lord of Glenurquhart and fifth of Kingairloch, was then succeeded around 1500–10 by his son Hector, fifth of Glenurquhart and sixth of Kingairloch, who was born around 1475 and married a MacDonald. He was succeeded by his son Donald (b. *c.* 1505), sixth of Glenurquhart and seventh of Kingairloch, who married Jean Mackintosh, daughter of the clan chief Lachlan 'Beg', fourteenth leader of Clan Mackintosh. Their son was Hector Maclean, seventh of Glenurquhart and eighth of Kingairloch, who lived from around 1545 to 1615 and married his distant cousin Marsali Maclean of Ardgour.

Their son was Donald, eighth of Glenurquhart and ninth of Kingairloch, who was born around 1580 and died around 1648; he married another cousin, Christian or Christina Maclean of Ardtornish, whose father Allan was the 'baillie' of Morvern. Their son Hector Maclean, ninth of Glenurquhart and tenth of Kingairloch, married his distant cousin Ewen Maclean of Ardgour's widow Sarah Maclean or MacLaine of Lochbuie (see also below). Hector was probably killed in the final Royalist campaign of 1654, when the earls of Glencairn and Middleton mounted a desperate campaign in the Highlands to stop the advance of the numerically superior, better-armed, and far more experienced English New Model Army regiments under General Monck and his deputy Thomas Morgan. Hector was succeeded by his son Donald, eleventh of Kingairloch, who lived from around 1640 to 1700; the latter was succeeded by the son of his second marriage (to Margaret Maclean of Coll), Donald the twelfth lord, who was born around 1665 and died in 1726. Donald's son by his first marriage (to Margaret Cameron), Lachlan, then succeeded as thirteenth lord; he was born around 1687 and died in 1756.

Charles or Tearlach Maclean, founder of the dynasty's fortunes, was known as 'Mac Mic Eachoinn', that is 'Grandson of Hugh'. The latter would appear to have been the first of the family to achieve distinction, among the leading rank of the vassals of the 'Lords of the Isles' in the mid-thirteenth century. Charles/Tearlach passed his main lands of Glenurquhart and Kingairloch to his sons by his first marriage. But he also married a second time, to the more prestigious Amy MacDonald, whose father John was one of the sons of John 'of the Isles' (d. 1386?) by his first marriage, to Amy MacRuadhri the heiress of Garmoran. John was the eldest son of the marriage but died around 1380, before his father, and probably only left daughters; Amy, named for her grandmother, was thus in a genealogically senior position as a MacDonald but in the hard reality of fourteenth-century Hebridean politics had been passed over as an heiress by her grandfather in his arrangements. Her equally passed-over uncle Godfrey of Uist, her grandfather's second son, had male heirs who could struggle against their kinsfolk for their 'rights', unsuccessfully; Amy and her descendants lacked any MacDonald support to do so. Amy was married off as second wife to Charles Maclean, whose Kingairloch lands lay to the south of her ancestors' Hebridean domains in Morvern; they only had a daughter, Margaret, who was lady of Kingairloch for her lifetime but with no rights to hand it on – the family entail then transferred it to her father's younger son by his first marriage, not to her own descendants. Margaret was married off to another ally and connection of the MacDonald dynasty who was a distant relative of her father – Lachlan Maclean, third lord of Duart Castle on the Isle of Mull. This senior line of the Macleans were substantial landholders and among the senior rank of supporting sub-chiefs of the 'Lords of the Isles' in the fourteenth century.

Lachlan's great-grandfather, Mael Coluim (i.e. Malcolm) MacGilliosa, was the third chief of the Clan Maclean and lord of Duart, which he held for the MacDonalds; he married Rioganach, another Gaelic name and apparently from distant Carrick, which was the hereditary lordship of the MacDonalds' patron and ally King Robert I. (Did MacGilliosa meet her kin and arrange the marriage while fighting for Robert in Carrick in the wars of independence?) Malcolm's grandfather Gillean 'na-Tuaighe', 'of the Battle-Axe', first clan chief of the Macleans, was said to have earned that nickname by his prowess fighting for King Alexander III against the Norse invaders at the Battle of Largs in 1263. Gillean's eponymous son, the second chief and Malcolm's father, did homage to Edward I in 1296 but fought for Robert Bruce in his Hebridean campaigns and at Bannockburn in 1314. Malcolm and Rioganach's son and heir was Ian or John 'Dubh', i.e. 'the Dark'; he married the daughter of Cumming, lord of the 'Braes of Lochaber', and was said in family tradition to have been a senior lieutenant of 'Lord of the Isles' John (d. 1386?). According to the story he and his brother, who served at John's court with him, had an ongoing feud with the Mackinnon chief, another lord at John's court who was jealous of their friendship with the 'Lord of the Isles' and despite their temporary rapprochement decided to ambush and murder them. The brothers were warned in advance and hot-headedly responded by killing Mackinnon, which act of bravado defied the customary requirements that the vassals of the 'Lord' keep the peace at his court whatever their private disputes. Fearing John's vengeance as Mackinnon was a favourite of his, they had to flee back home – or according to an alternative version they waited until he had left his then residence by sea before killing Mackinnon, then before he could find out pursued him in their own vessel, boarded his ship and carried him off as a hostage. He had to promise not to punish them before they would release him, and he kept his word.

Ian 'Dubh' Maclean was succeeded in his expanding domains around 1370 by his two sons, dividing his lands between them – the elder, Lachlan 'Lubanach' ('the Wily'), received Duart and the eastern part of Mull and the younger, Hector 'Regannach' ('the Stern'), received Lochbuie and the south and became the ancestor of the Macleans of Lochbuie. Lachlan is the first Maclean whom we can be certain held Duart Castle, as this was confirmed to him by charter in 1390. He married Mary MacDonald, a daughter of his father's friend and patron

John the 'Lord of the Isles', and as such was brother-in-law to 'Lord' Donald (d. 1420/23). The marriage took place in or soon after 1367, as a papal dispensation was granted to them to marry in that year; a story had it that John 'of the Isles' opposed the marriage and had to be coerced by Lachlan, who ambushed his future father-in-law's galley at sea, kidnapped him and held him captive on an isolated island (probably Inchcolmkill) until he agreed to the marriage. (This may be an echo of the story of the kidnapping of the 'Lord of the Isles' by Lachlan's father Ian cited above, as the story also refers to a Mackinnon chief being killed in the kidnapping; either one or the other probably kidnapped John, but not both.) Lachlan was succeeded by his son Hector or Eachinn 'Ruadh' ('the Red' or 'of the Battles'), who was in possession of Duart according to a charter which he witnessed on 28 January 1401, so his father had died by then. He was also hereditary keeper of Donconnell and Carnberg castles. A renowned swordsman, he is said to have slain a champion of the King of Norway in single combat on Mull, and to have commanded a maritime raid on Dublin (probably in 1400 as local sources record a Scots raid then). Hector was lieutenant to 'Lord of the Isles' Donald MacDonald at the Battle of Harlaw in 1411, and commanded a large contingent of clan troops there but was killed in the battle. It was Hector's son Lachlan 'Bronneach' ('the Swag-Bellied'), third owner of Duart Castle and seventh chief of Clan Maclean, who married firstly Margaret Maclean of Kingairloch, as above. Their son Donald 'the Hunter', was brought up by his mother's Maclean kin at Kingairloch, probably after his father died young, but was kept out of any chance of inheriting Kingairloch lands (probably due to doubts over the legitimacy of his parents' marriage). He became the first Maclean lord of Ardgour, in Ardnamurchan, which was transferred to the Maclean chief by his cousin 'Lord of the Isles' Donald around 1410. The incumbent MacMasters were dispossessed – according to family legend Donald's mother or his grandfather Charles Maclean of Kingairloch took him to the 'Lord of the Isles' at Ardtornish to ask him for some lands and the latter told him enigmatically to 'leap the dyke where it is lowest'. Donald took this as a hint to make his way by the easier means of helping out his lord and earning his gratitude rather than carving out his own estate by hard fighting, found out that the 'lord' was at odds with MacMaster of Ardgour, and ambushed and killed the latter; he was rewarded with his victim's estates. The grant was then confirmed by a charter which the king ratified.

Lachlan 'the Swag-Bellied' later married Margaret Stewart, probably daughter of Alexander, Earl of Mar (d. 1435), illegitimate son of the infamous 'Wolf of Badenoch' and cousin of King James I. Traditionally he met his wife after he was captured fighting for his father and the 'Lord of the Isles' against the Earl of Mar's army at the Battle of Harlaw in 1411 and was interned in the earl's custody. By her he had his successor as chief of the 'Clan Maclean', Lachlan 'Og', suggesting that his marriage to Margaret Maclean of Kingairloch was open to legal doubt and not accepted by the Church. Lachlan's third marriage was to Fionnuala, daughter of William MacLeod of Harris, by whom he had John Maclean, first lord of the island of Coll – which was apparently transferred to the Macleans in the early fifteenth century if not earlier by the 'Lords of the Isles', having been taken from a MacDonald owner by 'Lord of the Isles' Angus sometime around 1314. John's half-brother Lachlan 'Og', eighth chief of the Macleans, succeeded his father sometime after 1429, when the elder Lachlan was among those chiefs arrested with 'Lord of the Isles' Alexander and imprisoned by James I. The younger Lachlan married the daughter of Colin Campbell, first Earl of Argyll and chancellor to James III in the 1480s, who, as we have seen in the chapters on the 'Lords of the Isles', did his best to extend his power in the Inner Hebrides in this period at the expense of the last 'lord', John MacDonald (d. 1503). Argyll was also supposed by family tradition to have, unsuccessfully, tried to undermine his son-in-law Lachlan as a traitor and have his lands seized due to Lachlan's loyalty to the MacDonalds as they allied with King Edward IV of England in the Treaty of Ardtornish in 1462. Lachlan died in 1484 and was succeeded by his son Hector or Eachanan 'Odher' ('the Brown-Haired' or 'the Swarthy'), ninth chief, who acted as the (hereditary) lieutenant to the legitimate 'Lord of the Isles', John MacDonald, as the Macleans unsuccessfully helped him to tackle his rebellious illegitimate son Angus around 1480. The Macleans thus shared in John's defeat at the 'Battle of Bloody Bay', and Hector was among those captured by Angus.

Donald of Ardgour married Evere Cameron, daughter of Cameron of Lochiel, and died before 1463; his first son Ewen succeeded to Ardgour while his second son Niall 'Ban' succeeded to Borreray and founded that line. Ewen is recorded as steward of the household to 'Lord' John of the Isles in 1463. Ewen's son by a Chisholm lady, Lachlan Maclean, the third lord of Ardgour, was underage when his father died in battle fighting for the rebel MacDonald leader Angus 'Og' against the latter's father 'Lord' John at the 'Battle of Bloody Bay' near Tobermory in 1480/82. So Ewen's third brother John 'Ruadh' served as 'tutor' until his nephew's majority. Lachlan died without children, and was succeeded by his predeceasing next brother Charles' son John, the fourth lord. The same fate befell John, who was pardoned by James V for past acts of piracy in a charter granted at Solway in 1542 shortly before the king's

troops there suffered a disastrous defeat by the English king's Borders
warden Lord Dacre in the tidal marshes at the Solway Moss. Probably
John had brought his tenants to fight in the king's army there to show his
loyalty; however, he took the side of the rebel claimant to the lordship
of the Isles, Donald 'Dubh', in 1545 and joined the rebel 'Council of
the Isles' which assembled to recognise Donald as its lord and sign up
to alliance with Henry VIII of England. John was succeeded by his first
cousin's son Allan (b. 1520), son of John, son of Allan the third son of
Ewen. Allan, fifth lord of Ardgour, was succeeded by his elder son Ewan,
sixth lord, who married a Stewart and was killed in 1592 when he was
mistaken in an ambush for his kinsman Cameron of Lochiel. Ewan
left a son of around ten, Allan the seventh lord, so Ewan's youngest
brother Charles acted as 'tutor'; the middle brother, Lachlan, founded
the line of Maclean of Ballachan in Morvern. Allan was among the
most long-lived of contemporary Highland chiefs, and lived well into his
nineties and possibly to ninety-seven or -eight; he died in 1680 or 1681.
His two younger sons were killed in the Royalist army at the Battle of
Inverkeithing in Fife in 1651, fighting for Charles II as the king's troops
tried to stop Oliver Cromwell's troops landing on the north side of the
Firth of Forth and marching on Perth. To the dismay of the 'hard-line'
Presbyterian regime that held power in the Lowlands, the king had been
able to call on Catholic Royalists (in opposition to and loathed by the
Covenanter government) for military help to ward off the English New
Model Army after the Covenanters' own army was routed by Cromwell
at the Battle of Dunbar in September 1650; the Macleans were among
the Highland clans who duly signed up to help their king. Allan's elder
son by Catherine Cameron, John 'the Lame', the eighth chief of Ardgour,
also lived to over ninety, and died in 1695 aged probably ninety-two;
Allan's younger son Ewen was the first husband of his distant cousin
Sarah Maclean or MacLaine of Lochbuie (see above). John 'the Lame'
married firstly Anne Campbell of Dunstaffnage; their son was Captain
Ewen, ninth chief of Ardgour, who married Mary MacLaine (d. 1729)
and died in 1694. Captain Ewen and Mary's son was Allan, tenth chief
of Ardgour, who was born in 1668 and died in 1755.

The 1360s chieftain Lachlan of Duart's brother Hector or Eachain
'the Stern' founded the line of Lochbuie, and his lands were centred
on the south side of Mull. He built the family residence until 1752,
Moy Castle. His son Charles was the ancestor of the branch that
ruled Glen Urquhart and Dochgarroch. Charles, as lord of Urquhart
Castle in the Great Glen, joined the 'Clan Chattan' federation in 1390.
This was the one example of a 'collective' of several clans of distinct,
non-related families coming together as a political unit. The leadership

of this grouping was eventually settled in the Mackintosh family, and in 1609 Alexander Maclean of Dochgarroch, a cadet of the Glenurquhart family, joined Clan Chattan too. In both cases, this meant alignment with a formidable array of local clans against both the majority of the MacDonalds in Lochaber and the Camerons of Lochiel, who were long-term enemies of the Mackintoshes. By around 1500 the Lochbuie line had acquired Hebridean island lands on Mull, Tiree, Islay and Jura, along with Knapdale, Morvern and Lochaber on the mainland, and were also sporadically feuding with the Maclean line living at Duart. The Lochbuie line had received the title to some of the Clan Cameron lands, and also to Duror and Glencoe, from 'Lord of the Isles' Alexander sometime after he was released from the King of Scots' custody (i.e. 1437?), rewarding them for their loyalty, while the Macleans of Coll (led by John 'Garbh', a descendant of a younger son of Lachlan 'Lubanach') gained Lochiel from the Camerons. But it is unclear how long they held onto these lands against a Cameron fightback; the son of John 'Garbh', John of Coll, regained Lochiel at some point in the mid-fifteenth century and his son John 'Abrach' was born there, but was soon killed by the Camerons at Corpach, after which his clan fled again. Duart had a rival title to Duror, etc. given them by Alexander's son 'Lord' John, hence the inter-Maclean feud. Hector 'Odher' ('the Brown-Haired') Maclean of Duart, ninth chief of the Macleans, who was active in James IV's reign, followed the lead of John MacIain MacDonald of Ardnamurchan in making himself useful to the king in the aftermath of the dissolution of the lordship of the Isles, building up a bloc of lands and grants of royal offices. He submitted to James IV on his voyage to Dunstaffnage to receive homage from the local lords in summer 1493, and assisted him against the dissident lordship backers of the young contender Donald 'Dubh' in the 1500s, principally Torquil MacLeod of Lewis. He received confiscated 'rebel' lands as a reward. By contrast his kinsman Lachlan Maclean fought for Donald 'Dubh' in the rebellion and his lands and his castle were declared forfeited by the king in 1503, but this was as much a tactic to force his submission and his recognition of royal legal authority as a serious declaration of intent to evict him. He was pardoned and granted his lands (occupied by the Earl of Argyll) back by Parliament when he submitted in 1505. Hector also feuded with his cousin and rival John or Ian 'the Toothless' Maclean of Lochbuie, and was said by legend to have kidnapped him and imprisoned him on the remote island of Cairnburg after Ian's wife died and left him heirless, hoping to keep him childless so that he (Hector) would inherit Lochbuie. Ian's son by his first marriage, Eachuin/Ewan, had been killed during a feud with his father, who had disinherited him – he and his wife, the latter nicknamed the 'Black Swan', lived in a house on an artificial island on Loch Sghubhain north of Lochbuie and Eachuin's wife had been pressing him to demand more land from his father. The latter refused, and a clan battle ensued with the Macleans of Duart aiding Ian. Eachuin was defeated and killed, according to family tradition fighting on horseback; his head was cut off with a blow from a claymore, whereupon his horse galloped off the battlefield with his body still mounted. He was supposed to be the legendary ghostly 'Headless Horseman' who appeared to later generations to announce the imminent death of the current lord of Lochbuie. Another son of Ian's by this marriage was apparently killed by the Macleans of Lochbuie, possibly in this battle, and we can see an attempt by them to wipe the family out which would leave Hector of Duart as its heir on Ian's death. But Hector was foiled as his kidnap victim Ian had an affair with a maidservant working for the guards at the castle on Carinbeg, the result of which was Murdoch 'the Stunted', who was smuggled away to Ireland by his family's loyal supporters. Ian was then murdered by the Macleans of Duart and the acquisitive Hector took over Lochbuie, claiming that it was heirless, but Murdoch duly inherited Lochbuie on his return when he was adult, as the clan rejected the rule of the Duart branch and recognised him as chief.

Hector of Duart's son Lachlan 'MacGilleon', tenth chief of Clan Maclean of Duart, was illegitimate but was granted a royal charter of legitimisation in October 1496 and succeeded his father. Short of money, he sold off lands in Badenoch to the Earl of Huntly in 1508 and seems to have leased Duart Castle itself off for 45,000 'marks' to Stewart of Appin in April 1510 when he was given a royal safe conduct to visit the king. He or his son redeemed it later. He was killed fighting for James IV at Flodden in September 1513. He was succeeded by his son Lachlan 'Cattanach' (possibly 'the Shaggy', or else a reference to his fostering by the Clan Chattan), eleventh lord, another thuggish petty despot who in his case tangled fatally with the Campbells of Argyll. He had married the sister of Colin Campbell, third Earl of Argyll (d. 1530), Catherine Campbell, whom he and his Maclean of Lochbuie kinsmen (plus the MacLeods of Harris) assisted in repressing local disorder (i.e. by their foes) in the name of the Crown in the early years of James V. These clan chiefs, led by the Earl of Argyll, then unsuccessfully demanded a complete pardon for their own past misdeeds and control of all the region's Crown rents in return, in a petition to the Privy Council of 1517. But the Duart–Argyll alliance broke down; Lachlan 'Cattanach' found his wife to be infertile and had her stranded on a tidal rock off the nearby coast in order to drown her in an 'accident' rather than have to divorce and send her back to her brother and risk his rage. Unluckily for him some fishermen found and rescued his wife and delivered her safely to the Campbells, and as a result the earl put out a 'contract' on Maclean and sent out killers (led by his brother) who stabbed Lachlan in his bed in 1523. His son and successor by his wife after Catherine, Hector 'Mór' (the Great'), the twelfth chief of Duart, was renowned by tradition as the most accomplished, generous, heroic and popular of his family. He was the Maclean chief of Duart who submitted to and was arrested by King James V during his tour of the Hebrides in 1540; he and other chiefs were taken on board the king's fleet and deported to Dumbarton. Later at Stirling (May 1540) he formally did homage to the king to keep his lands as a royal vassal, and was kept in the south as a hostage for his men's submission for a year or two. He later persuaded various of his neighbours to submit to the king's authority too and so save their lands from confiscation. A formal charter was issued in 1542 confirming his claims to various estates – including part of Islay, home of the MacDonalds of Dunivaig, where Hector successfully claimed lands allegedly once held by now-lost charters (supposedly burnt by his family's 1480s foe Angus, son of the last 'Lord of the Isles'). This may have started, or exacerbated, the subsequent MacDonald of Dunivaig–Maclean feud over Islay, and the king had appointed a Stewart kinsman as castellan of Dunivaig so this man needed local support. Once the formidable and aggressive James V was dead and the regency in chaos loyalties were another matter, and in 1545 Hector joined his fellows in attending the meeting of the reconstituted 'Council of the Isles', which recognised the claim of Donald 'Dubh' to be their lord and which accepted the plan to do fealty to the Scots monarchy's foe Henry VIII. (Was this partly to save him from MacDonald attack as a 'traitor' to Donald?) This had to be abandoned when Donald then died and the Macleans refused to accept James MacDonald of Dunivaig as the rebellion's new leader in 1545–46, but the offending chiefs escaped punishment. Only Hector's younger brother Alan of Gigha was prepared to fight for the Dunivaig cause. Hector may have been influenced in his allegiance to the anti-Stuart cause by his marriage to Mary MacDonald, the daughter of the exiled chief Alexander of Dunivaig and brother of James – whose dynasty, his foes over Islay, had taken root in Ulster after the pro-Stuart Campbells, Hector's father's enemies, overran their lands.

Hector 'Mór', twelfth chief of Duart, spent a good deal of effort on punishing his cousins of Coll for trying to escape his authority and claiming that they held the island as a free barony of the Crown. His ravages of their land in the early 1560s were duly reported to the Privy Council and he was ordered to make reparation. His men fought as allies of the MacDonalds of Clanranald against their cousins of Dunivaig in a private war over Tiree in the years up to 1565. He was also involved in affairs in Ulster due to his family links with the MacDonalds of Dunivaig and the Glynns/Glens (via his mother) and with the Campbells. His daughter Catherine married Archibald Campbell, the fourth Earl of Argyll (d. 1558), some of whose Argyll tenants were recruited to the MacDonalds' army in Ulster, and either her or her sister Juliana subsequently married Calvagh (Charles) O'Donnell, lord of Tir Connaill/Tyrconnell and arch-foe of the O'Neill clan. Calvagh, who had overthrown his father Manus, fought a bitter war with his hereditary rival Shane O'Neill in the early 1560s, and he and his wife were kidnapped while visiting a monastery by Shane and held prisoner for years in Shane's castles. While Calvagh was tortured and exhibited in a cage and was eventually forced into promising to hand over disputed lands, Catherine/Juliana formed a relationship with her captor and on her husband's release (1564) stayed with Shane, whom she married. Hector journeyed to Ulster to give the union his blessing and arrange more military aid from the Hebrides for Shane, but the latter was killed by treachery by the MacDonells in 1567. The death in battle of James MacDonald of Dunivaig at Shane's hands in 1565 was a bonus for Hector, who used the clan's losses as an opportunity to ravage their lands on Gigha – for which Queen Mary issued a commission to the fifth Earl of Argyll to punish him in April 1567. Hector died in 1568 aged seventy-one, and was succeeded by his eldest son Hector or Eachainn 'Og' ('the Younger'). Another son, John 'Dubh', founded the line of Maclean of Kinlochaline, while Hector's daughter Catherine's marriage to the fourth Earl of Argyll, son of the man who had killed Hector's father, served to end the family feud. Catherine outlived the earl, and probably remarried to his and Hector's neighbour, John Stewart of Appin. Other daughters of Hector married Donald Maclean of Sleat (Mary) and Norman MacLeod of Lewis (Marjorie). The younger Hector married his sister Catherine's stepdaughter Janet Campbell, daughter of the fourth Earl of Argyll, and continued his father's realignment of the family as a Campbell ally in the struggles over power at the courts of Queen Mary and James VI. He died in 1573.

Hector's son and successor, Sir Lachlan 'Mór' ('the Great', 1558–98), fourteenth chief of Duart, sought a decisive advantage in the long-running dispute with the MacDonalds of Dunivaig over Islay by trickery. He invited their chief Angus to Duart with his leading kinsmen for a meeting (notably Angus's suspicious brothers refused to come), then seized them and held them hostage until Angus signed away the disputed 'Rhinns of Islay' to him. He kept Angus's son James and others as hostages for the surrender of the lands, but ended up being kidnapped by Angus and his men as he arrived to take over the lands and was invited to dinner at a house at Mullintrea. Some of the hostage Macleans were then executed by angry MacDonalds after a rumour that Lachlan's men were killing their prisoners. The dispute that had also involved his clansmen massacring a force of MacDonald of Dunivaig clansmen en route for the wars in Ulster when they were forced by bad weather to camp overnight on Maclean lands on Jura. The other branches of the MacDonalds backed the Dunivaig clan up while the MacLeods of Harris/Dunvegan backed Maclean, and in spring 1587 the government had to negotiate a mutual exchange of prisoners and order all involved to pay bonds for future good behaviour. The Macleans, backed up by the MacLeods, proceeded to ravage MacDonald lands on Islay and Gigha and besieged Dunivaig Castle, and their foes called in the other MacDonalds to help them; eventually the government imposed a truce in 1589. Sir Lachlan and his MacDonald foe were summoned to court in 1590, arrested and forced to pay up large financial bonds for their good behaviour, but Maclean later committed more raids and Lachlan later ignored a summons to Parliament on 14 July 1593 over this feud. In 1594 he was declared forfeit for this. Needing a powerful patron to save him from attack, he joined the army of his kinsman and Campbell clan chief Archibald Campbell, seventh Earl of Argyll (d. 1638), as the latter (a Protestant) fought on the king's behalf against a rebellion raised by George Gordon, sixth earl and first Marquis of Huntly (d. 1636). Huntly and his ally Francis Hay, ninth Earl of Erroll (d. 1631), were the kingdom's leading recalcitrant and pro-Spanish Catholics, and had been resisting the control of the king's government by Protestant lords and James's alignment with Elizabeth of England rather than her Spanish Catholic enemies. Notably James, who had more sympathies with the overbearing northern Catholic peers than with their arch-enemies the Presbyterian Church (who had excommunicated them in 1593 and were pressing him for drastic punishment of the rebels), was nervous about risking defeat by military action against their experienced Highland clan troops and had forgiven them past defiance. He was more concerned with a Protestant noble challenger, the reckless and violent Earl of Bothwell (nephew of his mother's last husband). But both Huntly and Erroll had been implicated in the recent plot known as the 'Spanish Blanks', when otherwise blank papers were found signed by them and others – apparently intended to be a 'bond' pledging treasonous rebellion on Spain's behalf to coerce the king. They were excommunicated by the Church and declared to be in rebellion for not handing themselves in, as James now required in return for their future pardon, and in summer 1594 their armed stand against the king in Buchan was joined by the defeated and refugee Bothwell. They assembled a force of around 2,000 men led by Huntly's Gordon clansmen to attack the royal forces, which Argyll was entrusted to lead north with the king following behind at a safe distance. The Argyll army included not only the earl's own Campbells and the Macleans but a large coalition of northern clans including the MacGillivrays, MacNeils and Grants, mostly hereditary rivals of the Gordons, and around 10,000 men duly confronted the advancing Huntly. The resulting Battle of Glenlivet on 3 October 1594 saw the outnumbered Huntly and his men treat it as a 'holy' campaign and say Mass beforehand, and a combination of religious zeal for their faith, desperation to avoid forfeiture, a more coherent Highland force used to fighting together compared to a motley coalition led by the young and inexperienced Argyll, and better cannons employed by the wealthy Huntly to bombard the royal forces won the day despite their lesser numbers. But the rebels failed to make anything of their victory, and frittered it away; Huntly refused to fight as the king advanced and withdrew into the hills, leaving his home to be burnt by the royal army. Negotiations followed, and in spring 1595 both Huntly and Erroll were allowed by the king to flee abroad.

Huntly was indeed pardoned and restored to his estates within a year, and the 1594 campaign was more of a trial of strength between the Protestant and Catholic factions of nobles than a major struggle. But the campaign had earned Maclean the king's pardon with Argyll no doubt putting in a word for him, and in 1596 he turned up at the king's court to submit and was pardoned and granted his lands. He may also have had help with his pardon from his wife Margaret Cunningham's brother, the seventh Earl of Glencairn. He was killed on 5 August 1598 in the Battle of 'Traigh Gruinart' ('Gruinart Strand/Beach') on Islay by Sir James MacDonald, later ninth of Dunivaig and at the time heir of the lord Angus, with whom he was still quarrelling over the ownership of Islay. Sir Lachlan was offered half of the island for his lifetime by his poorer-resourced foe after besieging him in Dunivaig Castle, but ignored it and tried to seize it all as the MacDonalds resumed the war. He landed a force of 800–1,000 men on Islay to seize it, but the MacDonalds sent help from Kintyre and Clan MacAlister of Arran aided Sir James too. The latter was still outnumbered, but cunningly retreated with his men inland at a suitable angle so that the setting sun shone in the eyes of the pursuing Macleans. When they were dazzled the Macleans and MacDonalds counter-attacked, and Sir Lachlan and around 280 of his men were killed. His son Sir Hector succeeded him; a younger son, Lachlan 'Og' ('the Younger'), inherited Torlisk. But James VI was closing in on his autonomous and disobedient western Highlands vassals, and was looking for excuses to impose his authority and make examples once he had gained the throne and resources of England in March 1603. He had already banned the name of MacGregor and confiscated that clan's lands east of Loch Lomond for alleged rampant brigandage. In 1604 he declared the lands of Lochbuie forfeit after discovering that the clan chief had been in touch illegally with Queen Elizabeth of England and had done fealty to her. But it was a different matter to actually enforce such a sequestration of lands in the remote western Highlands, and when the king sent out Lord Ochiltree to the Western Isles in 1608, to sort out various feuds among the local chiefs and their defiance of the king's laws, Maclean of Duart submitted peacefully and was pardoned. Meanwhile Hector 'Og' Maclean, fifteenth chief of Duart from 1598, kept out of trouble after his clan's losses on Islay, and died in 1623. His sons by his first wife (Jenette Mackenzie of Kintail) were Hector 'Mór', sixteenth chief, who died young without children in 1626, and Sir Lachlan of Morven, who was created a Baronet of Nova Scotia by Charles I in 1631 and subsequently led his clansmen to fight for Montrose against the Campbells at the Battle of Inverlochy in February 1645. Sir Lachlan escaped confiscation of his lands on Montrose's defeat by submission to his Campbell kinsman the eighth Earl of Argyll, head of the Covenanter regime, and died in 1649. He was succeeded by his half-brother Sir John, Bt, the elder son of Hector 'Og' by his second wife Isabella Acheson, who had emigrated to Sweden where a substantial Scots community lived at Gothenburg and Scots officers fought in the army of King Gustavus Adolphus (accession 1611, killed 1632) in the Thirty Years War. Sir John, who had gone by the name of 'Mackeleer' in Sweden, lived entirely in exile until the Restoration and rarely came near his estates thereafter, marrying a Swede (Anna Gubertz) and dying in 1666 aged sixty-six. His elder son and heir, Sir John Mackeleer/ Maclean (Bt), and his younger son Jacob both made their careers in Sweden; the senior member of the Duart family in Scotland was the elder Sir John's younger brother, Donald of Brolas. The line of Lochbuie however continued to be resident in the Highlands.

MacLeod of Lewis and Harris/MacLeod of Dunvegan

Traditionally descended from an eponymous 'Leod' (in Gaelic) or 'Liot' (in Norse), son of King Olaf 'the Black' of Man (d. 1230), according to MacLeod family histories and genealogies. The branch of the family that settled on Lewis and Harris in the Outer Hebrides were descended from Torquil, son of Leod, and were thus known as the 'Siol Torcaill' ('Seed of Torquil'); the branch of the family that lived on Skye, whose principal residence was Dunvegan, were descended from Leod's other son Tormod ('Norman' in Anglo-Scots) and so were the 'Siol Tormod' or 'Seed of Tormod'. However, Leod does not appear in any account of the royal house of Man, principally the *Manx Chronicle*, although at the time of Olaf's reign the Outer and possibly some of the Inner Hebrides were part of the Manx realm, and Olaf spent from the later 1180s to 1207 living on Skye and Lewis as lord of part of the Hebrides after his half-brother Ragnald excluded him from co-rule of Man (see chapter on Man). Modern doubts have been raised as to whether 'Leod' ever existed, or at least if he was really of the Manx royal house. The question has been examined by local genealogical and Norse experts, most pertinently by Andrew P. MacLeod in an online article, 'The Ancestry of Leod', in which he quotes an article by W. D. Sellar in *Transactions of the Gaelic Society of Inverness* volume XX, 'The Ancestry of the MacLeods Reconsidered'. This suggests that Leod was not a descendant of Olaf of Man, but the great-grandson of a similarly-named 'Olvir', that is 'Oliver' (or 'Olgar' in Gaelic). Eulogies for Sir Ruadhri of Dunvegan (d. 1626) and Ian 'Mór' of Dunvegan, who died in 1649, call the family the 'Cru Olbhuir', that is 'Seed of Olvir', and 'Sil Olbhuir', 'race of Olvir', while a genealogy of Christina MacLeod (sister of Torcall MacLeod of Lewis) appended to seventeenth-century Irish antiquarian MacFirbis's genealogy of the Macleans calls her the granddaughter of Tormod, son of Leod, and descended from Norwegian royalty via 'Ealga of the beautiful locks, daughter of Harald, son of Semmair king of Lochlainn (Norway)'. Another MacLeod historian, Matheson, believed that the 'Guillemuire' (a Gaelic name) cited as Leod's father in Christina's genealogy was a mistranslation of 'Olvir' not 'Olaf', and that the citation of this ancestor, i.e. the wrongly-named Olaf, as the king of Man was due to a late sixteenth-century MacLeod historian reading William Camden's history of England, where Olaf was named as the king of Man around 1220, and assuming this ancestor must be him. Matheson assumed that the reference to a mysterious 'Paice' as ancestor of Olvir/ Olaf means that this man was the 'Balki' in Orkney records, whose son Paul Balkison was the jarl's steward of Skye in the mid-twelfth century; thus 'Olaf or Olvir' must be the 'Olvir the Turbulent' who appears in the *Orkneyinga Saga* account of the 1140s–1150s and fought Jarl Paul in 1135/36. (See chapter on Orkney.) This Olvir's grandfather was indeed a 'Liot' or 'Leod'. But both Alick Morrison, in his 1986 book on the MacLeods, and Andrew P. MacLeod doubt that 'Olaf or Olvir' was this Olvir, and it is safer to assume that the identity of the father of Leod remains muddled.

MacLeods of Lewis *versus* the Mackenzies of Kintail

Tradition had it that the MacLeods inherited their Lewis lands via a marriage with an heiress of the Nicolson family, and both Sellar and Matheson think that the appearance of a 'burning mountain' in the MacLeod coat of arms may refer to them acting as local watchmen against raiders for their original landlords and chiefs, the Nicolsons. This would have been in the thirteenth century, with the troubled history of the Hebrides at a time of clan feuds, piracy and Norse invasion making the threat of attack constant. The first mention of the MacLeods is in a charter from David II's reign, where Torcall or Torquil MacLeod was granted 'four penny land' in Assynt on the mainland – an area where the MacLeods later built the castle of Ardvreck, a major residence of theirs. There is no mention of him as already holding land on the Isles. Later on they acquired Lewis, the smaller island of Raasay off Skye, Waternish on Skye, and Coigach and Gairloch on the mainland, and at the end of the fourteenth century became involved in a feud with the far more powerful mainland clan of Mackay of Reay, 'Clan Mac Aoidh' ('Sons of Hugh'), lords of Strathnaver. The Mackays were allegedly descended from the MacHeths, earls of Ross and of the ancient family of the kings of Moray, and in particular from Malcolm MacHeth, Earl of Ross (d. c. 1168), and certainly the MacHeths' expulsion from Moray by the kings of Scots had led to them retreating to the safety of Sutherland in the far north, whence they launched a major revolt against Alexander II in 1215, which ended with defeat and the death of Kenneth/Cinaed MacHeth. According to the *Blackcastle Manuscript* and other sources the first Mackay clan chief was Iye, born around 1210, whose son was Iye 'Mór' (married 1263) and grandson was Donald, third chief, who fought at Bannockburn for Robert Bruce and died in 1330 aged around sixty-five. His son was the fourth chief (seventh according to other sources), Angus, who married a MacLeod of Lewis, the then chief Roderick's sister Sidheag. After Angus's death, the 'Tutor of Mackay' Hucheon/Hugh 'the Black' (i.e. the regent for the underage successor, Angus's son Angus) mistreated her, and in revenge the MacLeod chiefs and her brother Gillecallum Beg (Malcolm 'the Little') invaded Mackay lands and attacked a party of Mackays in Strathnaver. This was either in 1403 or 1406, and the MacLeods were defeated. The MacLeod chief, Roderick, attacked Strathnaver himself in reprisal, but was ambushed at the Battle of 'Tuiteam Tarbhach' ('Plentiful Slaughter') on the banks of the River Oykel three miles from its junction with the River Cassley with Robert, Earl of Sutherland and greatest chief of the region, sending some of his men under Alexander Murray of Cubin to assist the Mackays.

The MacLeods were routed, and Roderick and reputedly all but one of his men were killed; 'Black Hugh' Mackay died in 1408 and his nephew Angus went on to lead a force of Mackays to assist Donald, 'Lord of the Isles', at the Battle of Harlaw in 1411. Angus Mackay subsequently married Donald's sister, and as a close MacDonald ally claimed the Earldom of Ross but was blocked by his enemies at the court of the Scots regent Duke Robert of Albany. As 'Aeneas in-Impress', Angus the 'Absolute', he went on to dominate the region until the unimpressed King James I, regarding him as an arrogant loose cannon, summoned him and arrested him at Inverness in 1427, held him prisoner for some time to teach him a lesson and deported his eldest son Neil to the Bass Rock in the Firth of Forth as a hostage for his good behaviour. The Mackays thus hemmed in the MacLeods on the mainland, and even after his arrest and subsequent pledge of loyalty to the king in 1427 Angus managed to reassert his power by sending his second son John /Ian to smash the Sutherlands' clan army and his rebellious cousins Morgan and Neil Neilson Mackay at the Battle of Drumnacoub sometime between 1427 and 1433.

The MacLeods restricted their pretensions to local dominance to the Outer Hebrides where they had military predominance and less risk of royal challenge, and ended up feuding with their own cousins the MacLeods of Dunvegan (who owned lands in Harris, the southern part of the island of Lewis) over the ownership of lands at Trotternish on Skye. To add to the confusion, James IV's government had granted these lands to both MacLeod branches at different times in the 1490s. Roderick or Ruadhri, the seventh chief of Lewis, lost his eldest son Roderick in the Battle of 'Bloody Bay' in 1480/82, and was succeeded by his younger son John as chief. The latter, married firstly to Catherine Campbell, the daughter of Colin, first Earl of Argyll, was involved in the Campbells' plans to use Donald 'Dubh' as a pawn in a revival of the lordship of the Isles. He later backed the rebellion in the young Donald's name in 1503–05, and was forfeited for that by the angry James IV in 1506. His brother Malcolm replaced him as a 'loyalist' clan chief, disinheriting John's son (by his second marriage). But the latter seized power on Malcolm's death around 1515. In 1528 this man, tenth clan chief John/Iain MacLeod of Lewis, supported his half-brother Donald 'Gruamach' Gorm MacDonald in a private war with the Dunvegan branch over Trotternish, and in 1539 he joined in his friend's attack on Eilean Donan Castle in a bid to restore the lordship of the Isles. In 1540 he was forced to attend on the arriving King James V when the latter landed on Lewis with a naval expedition to enforce the vassalage of the local chiefs. His son Ruadhri was taken along as a hostage on the king's expedition round the Hebrides to enforce his good behaviour, but was later released. John also joined the reconstituted 'Council of the Isles' to pledge allegiance to the anti-Stuart pretender to the lordship of the Isles, Donald 'Dubh', in 1545. While he backed Donald and pledged allegiance to Henry VIII of England and his son Ruadhri MacLeod led the clan troops to Ireland to aid Donald, his Dunvegan kin and the MacIains of Ardnamurchan were loyal to the regency for Queen Mary. He was pardoned after Donald's death and the end of the revolt, but in 1554 letters of 'fire and the sword' were issued against Ruadhri, as clan chief, and his allies John 'Moydartach' MacDonald of Clanranald and Donald MacDonald of Sleat for failing to turn up at Parliament at Inverness. The threatened attack was not carried out, and the MacLeods survived on their remote island until a disputed inheritance hit the next generation. Ruadhri had married the daughter of John or Ian Mackenzie of Kintail, ninth chief of that branch of the Mackenzies, who had been captured at Flodden by the English but escaped and had been captured again and ransomed at the Battle of Pinkie Cleugh against English 'Lord Protector' Somerset's invaders in 1547. Ruadhri was thus an ally of his brother-in-law Colin Mackenzie, tenth clan chief of Kintail (a Marian, killed at the Battle of Langside in 1568), and to complicate matters John/Ian Mackenzie's kinsman and 'tutor' in his teens, Hector 'Roy' Mackenzie, had secured a grant of MacLeod-owned Gairloch from James IV in 1494, evicted its MacLeod owners and subsequently fought over it with the latter's MacLeod of Lewis kin. The Mackenzies were thus not usual allies for a MacLeod, and trouble escalated after Ruadhri came to believe that his Mackenzie wife had been unfaithful and he was not the father of his son, Torquil. The latter came to be nicknamed 'Connanach' as he was brought up by his mother's kin in Strathconnan after she abandoned his father and ran off with his cousin John MacGillechallum of Raasay and Torquil was disinherited by his presumed father. Ruadhri divorced her and in 1541 married Barbara Stewart, daughter of the king's kinsman Andrew Stewart Lord Avandale; their son was Torquil 'Oighre' ('the Heir'). However, around 1566 the latter and around sixty others were drowned when their ship was sunk during a crossing from Lewis to Skye, and with the succession 'open' again, Torquil 'Connanach', now adult, and a Mackenzie army invaded Lewis; they kidnapped Ruadhri, held him prisoner in Stornoway Castle for two years, and forced him to accept Torquil publicly as his heir. Ruadhri was also involved in the notorious murder of his cousin John MacGillechallum of Raasay, with whom his wife had run off, and the latter's kin; he summoned them to a meeting at Waternish and called them one by one into his presence to be killed. The indignant Raasay survivors managed to hold out against him with the aid of the Mackenzies, the late John's wife's kin. In 1572 Ruadhri was forced to appear before the regency Privy Council and abdicate his lands of Lewis, Assynt, Coigach and Waternish, which were granted to Torquil 'Connanach' but only on 'life-rent' as a royal tenant. Once he returned home, on 2 July 1572, Ruadhri renounced his abdication as forced and thus illegal, and defied the fortunately embattled regency; in 1576 the regent, the Earl of Morton, brought Ruadhri and Torquil to agree to a settlement whereby Torquil would succeed his father.

The situation was now complicated by Ruadhri marrying again, to the daughter of Hector 'Og' Maclean of Duart and sister of Sir Lachlan 'Mór' Maclean (*q.v.*). He had two more sons, Torquil 'Dubh' and Tormod (plus several bastards). Ruadhri now made Torquil 'Dubh' his heir, but within a few years Torquil 'Connachach' and the Mackenzies had revolted against this arrangement and attacked Lewis again. Aided by Ruadhri's also-excluded bastards, they captured Ruadhri, locked him up in Stornoway Castle again and confiscated all his legal documents, of which the Mackenzies took custody. Torquil 'Connanach's son John held his grandfather prisoner, but he was killed and Ruadhri rescued by another of the latter's bastards, Ruadhri 'Og', and Ruadhri was restored to control of Lewis. He died in 1596 and was succeeded by Torquil 'Dubh', who then attacked his excluded half-brother Torquil 'Connanach' (who had inherited only Coigach) and the latter's Mackenzie allies and ravaged Lochbroom. For this Torquil 'Dubh' was successfully complained of to the Privy Council as a brigand by his victims, and after he refused a summons to the Privy Council the 'brieve' of Lewis and his Morrison kin were authorised to arrest him, which they did. Deported to Coigach on the mainland by the triumphant Torquil 'Connachach', he was executed by the latter in July 1597, but his three young sons and his illegitimate half-brother Niall held onto their Lewis lands and a civil war proceeded, with Torquil 'Connanach' unable to take over Lewis. Donald 'Gorm' of Sleat also laid claim to Lewis and attacked, but as the Mackenzies now had the title deeds they could present all the current claimants as being illegal, which the Privy Council agreed was the case; the 'Act of Estates' in 1597 proclaimed Lewis forfeit and announced that it would be settled by loyal mainlanders as royal tenants. The resultant attempt at colonisation, led by a group of Fife lairds as royal nominees, was assisted by the Mackenzies militarily but defied by Niall MacLeod and his nephews, the sons of Ruadhri 'Og', and the latter held out for around three years on the island of Bearasay off the west coast of Lewis. Eventually Niall surrendered to his kinsman Ruadhri 'Mór' MacLeod of Dunvegan and was deported, being executed in 1613, and two of his nephews were captured and executed by the Mackenzies, but the unrest on Lewis continued for years and one of Ruadhri 'Og's sons, Malcolm, joined in a rebellion on the island in 1615 and then escaped to Spain. The legal title passed to the MacLeods of Raasay, descendants of Malcolm (second son of the then lord of Lewis) in the mid-fifteenth century; their clan chief around 1600 was Callum 'Og', whose brother John MacGillechallum was killed at the Battle of Logiebride (or 'Logie Niach'), a skirmish at the annual Ross market at Conan Bridge at Candlemas 1597, by Clan Brayne and the Munros of Tulloch.

A younger son of Roderick MacLeod of Lewis (k. 1406), Tormod, had inherited Assynt in Ross and this remained with his descendants. They fought for the rebel Mackays of Aberach against the predatory senior Mackay line's 'tutor' 'Blach Hugh' ('Huisdean Dhu') in the 1500s, and fought against Clan Gunn at the Battle of Leckmelm in 1586. The only one of them to make a mark on history was the infamous Neil of Assynt, who gave hospitality to the fleeing Marquis of Montrose after the Battle of Carbisidale in 1650 then betrayed him to the pursuing Covenanter officer General Strachan. It did his reputation no good, and at the Restoration he was treated with hostility by his victim's triumphant Royalist allies and was finally dispossessed in 1672. The Mackenzies of Kintail, now earls of Seaforth, took his lands. They had gone on from strength to strength through a mixture of luck, shrewdness and the right connections, building on the foundations of the marital links to the MacDonalds of Islay and the Huntly-allied Frasers, plus their 1509 royal charter confirming their ownership of Kintail. As we have seen in the MacDonald chapter, they had abandoned 'Lord of the Isles' John for the Crown in the mid-1470s. Colin Mackenzie of Kintail (d. 1594), the eleventh chief and son of the chief killed fighting for Queen Mary at Langside in 1568, feuded with the Munros over the 'chanonry' of Ross and with Glengarry over Lochalsh, but he made a valuable marriage into the Grants. His son Kenneth (d. 1611) acquired a peerage from James VI as 'Lord Mackenzie of Kintail', cementing his landed rights with royal legal recognition and an entrée to the Scots peerage as his Glengarry rivals were to do from Charles II seventy years later. From this basis the family moved on to an earldom (Seaforth) under his elder son Colin (d. 1633), a royal 'trusty' in the newly pacified west Highlands and the builder of Brahan Castle, who not coincidentally for his success married Margaret Seton, daughter of the first Earl of Dunfermline, a royal minister. Colin's half-brother and successor George, second earl (d. 1651), was the lord of Eilean Donan, Lochalsh, Lochcarron, Strome and Carronach – all former MacDonald territories and a testimony to how well the Mackenzies had judged the means and timing of their ambitions to make themselves useful to James VI and then Charles I. As we shall see in the chapter on the clans in the seventeenth- and eighteenth-century wars, the second Earl of Seaforth was to attempt to navigate the choppy waters of the 'Scottish Revolution' and Royalist *versus* Covenanter wars in the 1640s by switching sides with the tides of war, not altogether successfully.

MacLeods of Dunvegan/Skye

The legendary founder of this line was Tormod or Norman, the son of the eponymous 'Leod', the clan founder (see previous section). Leod was supposed to have married a daughter of the seneschal of Skye, MacArailt or MacRailt (i.e. 'Son of Harald'), lord of Dunvegan, which duly passed to the MacLeods, and to have died around 1280. The clan's DNA shows similarities with the inhabitants of Man, which may come from the legendary link to the royal house of Man (see previous section) or from either Leod or Harald being Norse in origin. It is now thought that there may have been two, not one, Tormods, father and son, in the thirteenth century. One or other of them (from the timescale, the younger, if there were two) fought for Robert Bruce at Bannockburn, but at this stage the family were only junior landholders on Skye as its lordship was given by King Robert to the earls of Ross. The second or third lord, the son of the younger or the only Tormod, was Malcolm (*c.* 1296–1370), known in his old age from his weight problem as 'the Thick-Legged', who was the first owner of the famous clan relic known as 'Sir Rory's Horn'. This was apparently the horn of a fierce bull which he encountered one night in the wilderness near Glenelg and killed with his dirk before sawing off its horn as a trophy. The impressed locals recognised him as their lord, and Glenelg stayed in his family for centuries. He was the first of the clan to appear in Scots records, being named in a charter of David II around 1343 as 'Malcolm son to Tormode M' Cloyde', and is variously said to have married the daughter of Sir Neil Campbell of Lochow or of the Earl of Mar. He was buried on Iona. His eldest son was John or Ian 'Ciarr' (1320–92), probably the fourth lord, and his younger sons were Tormod of Bernerg, Murdo of Glenelg and Malcolm 'Og', the ancestor of the 'MacCallums' sub-dynasty.

John acquired a charter for Trotternish and other lands on Skye from King Robert II according to the *Bannatyne Manuscript* and was the father of William 'the Cleric' ('Cleireach'), who was so called as he was a younger son who had originally been destined for the Church. His father was a thug and domestic tyrant, whose equally violent wife (one of the Irish O'Neills) reputedly murdered two of their daughters in a medieval 'honour killing' for trying to flee with their lovers (who were then flogged to death). John was then killed by the MacGhittiches ('Clan of the Children of the Wolf') on Harris, where he had lands in the Outer Hebrides, after he executed their chief for pre-empting him by allegedly killing a rare white stag he was hoping to hunt. (The chief may have been set up by his enemies for this crime.) The younger MacGhittiches avenged their father by ambushing John and his family and followers on a visit to Harris at Rodel in 1392, and while William evacuated the survivors to safety his homicidal mother and illegitimate half-sisters were drowned when their ship hit a rock. William's elder brother Malcolm had died in a brawl at his wedding feast on Lewis as he married a MacLeod of Lewis girl, from which the enmity of the two lines of MacLeod was traced, and so William became clan chief in his mid-twenties, acquiring the lands of the Frasers of Aird before dying around 1402 or 1409 at Castle Camus on Skye. By now possession of Lewis and Harris, as the overlord of the two branches of MacLeod (the Dunvegan branch on Harris), had been confirmed by the Scots kings as belonging to the MacDonald 'Lords of the Isles', contradicting earlier grants of Skye to the earls of Ross. But later in the fourteenth century the lordship of Skye reverted to the earls of Ross, and thus the MacLeods of Dunvegan ended up holding half of their lands (Skye) from the Rosses and the other half (Harris) from their MacDonald rivals. Thus in the 1390s or early 1400s Donald 'Lord of the Isles' sent his brother Alexander of Lochalsh to invade and take over Ross, claiming that his marriage to the late, heirless Earl of Ross's daughter meant that he should have inherited it, but the MacLeods drove him out.

When William died he was succeeded by his underage son John 'Borb', 'the Turbulent', who had his cousin John 'the Unlucky' as his 'tutor' for six years, although some of the clan would have preferred his distant cousin Tormod from the Lewis branch and the offended Tormod then overran part of Glenelg. The MacDonalds took advantage of the minority to invade Skye and seize Dunscaith and Camus Castles, while a separate MacDonald expedition overran North Uist, and were besieging William's widow in Dunvegan Castle when the MacLeods of Lewis came to their kin's aid and drove them off. On his majority, John and his allies the MacLeods of Lewis had the military strength to force Donald, 'Lord of the Isles', to negotiate and to return all the disputed lands except North Uist, and John and his clan fought for Donald's army at the Battle of Harlaw in 1411. But John was at some point, possibly at Harlaw, badly wounded in the head and thereafter was a semi-invalid, living at Pabbay Castle and leaving most activities that required travel to others. He died in 1442, according to tradition after his head wound reopened when he overexerted himself taking part in a fencing match with his foster brother Somerled MacConn. He was succeeded by his son William 'Long-Sword' (1415–80/83), whose mother was traditionally the daughter of an Earl of Douglas. There was another son, Tormod or Norman, with the sources disagreeing over whether the latter was a younger son or (the *Bannatyne Manuscript*) was an older son who died before his father and so had his infant son set aside from the succession in William's favour. Norman may have been an older but illegitimate son, as he led the clan in a battle in 1428 (he died in 1429) and so would have been in his mid-teens at least by then. Norman's son founded the family of MacLeod of Waternish. One of William's two daughters, Fiongall/Fionnuala, may have married Lachlan Maclean, chief of Duart, but there is some dispute over whether her father William MacLeod was 'of Dunvegan' or 'of Harris'; the other daughter married Ruadhri, eighth chief of the MacLeods of Lewis (*q.v.*). William and his ally Ruadhri were witnesses to a charter granted by John, the new and last 'Lord of the Isles', in favour of John's half-brother Hugh MacDonald of Sleat on 28 June 1449. He was supposed to have accompanied his ally Hugh on a raid to Orkney and killed its earl in combat around 1460, but the latter fact is not verified by any written source or genealogy. William was killed at the Battle of 'Bloody Bay' near Tobermory in 1480/83, fighting for John, the last 'Lord of the Isles' (*q.v.*), who had been criticised for meekly surrendering to King James III, against his rebel son Angus 'Mór' MacDonald. Also in this army were the Macleans and MacNeils, and the skirmishes before the battle traditionally saw William's son Alexander/Alisdair 'Crotach' ('the Hump-Backed', possibly from a battle injury received in this war) lead the defeat of an invasion of Skye by the Clanranald chief which had landed at Aird Bay.

At the Battle of 'Bloody Bay' William's death led to his clan and their allies wavering, and traditionally Callum 'Clerich', the priestly standard bearer, unfurled the family's famous 'Fairy Flag' to make an appeal to their MacLeod of Lewis kinsmen to desert the cause of Angus 'Mór'. The other branch of MacLeods did so rather than attack their kin and the family flag, but Angus still won. William's son Alisdair (b. *c.* 1455), whose Maclean mother was a daughter of either the second clan chef Murdoch or the third chief John/Ian, succeeded him but had to cope with his foe Angus's rule of the lordship of the Isles from around 1480/83 to 1490. Angus punished the MacLeods by taking Duntulm Castle from them in a surprise attack, and it was possibly during the resulting war (or else as late as 1520, dates being vague) that the MacDonalds of Sleat, Angus's allies, invaded Skye and fought a major battle at Glendale. The

MacLeods had their greatest victory, but losses of manpower were so severe that they never recovered their former strength. More certainly, Alisdair 'Crotach' was involved in a war with Angus's Clanranald allies over the islands of the Minch, between Skye and the mainland, that saw the MacDonald inhabitants of Eigg refusing sustenance to the crew of a MacLeod 'birlinn' that was shipwrecked on Eigg; they instead killed and ate MacDonald livestock and were attacked and massacred. Three survivors were set adrift in an open boat but managed to get back to Skye and reported to Alisdair, who ravaged Eigg in a fury and, when the inhabitants hid in a cave, tracked them down and butchered them. The piles of bones were still pointed out to visitors three centuries later. This incident was variously dated by historians at any time from around 1510 to 1535, with tradition having it that the religious Alisdair prayed for six hours for divine guidance in whether or not to kill the refugees and decided not to do so unless the wind changed course to blow into the mouth of the cave within a time limit – which it then did with minutes to spare. In 1498 Alisdair did homage to James IV on one of the latter's visits to Argyll to secure the allegiance of the Hebridean chiefs, and he was awarded lands at Duirinish that had been confiscated from the defunct lordship of the Isles – one possible source of MacDonald grievance against him. In the early years of the regency after 1513 he and the Macleans were allies of the royal lieutenant, the Earl of Argyll, in repressing 'disorder' (i.e. by their foes) and sought control of all royal rents in the Inner Hebrides as a reward from the Privy Council in a petition of 1517; in effect Alisdair got away with his excesses because he was an ally of the earl against the MacDonalds who could be painted as treasonously hankering after the defunct 'lordship'. Another conflict in the third decade of the sixteenth century, probably in 1528, saw Donald 'Gruamach' MacDonald of Sleat invading Skye while Alisdair 'Crotach' was away in his lands on Harris, and the MacLeods of Lewis helped their kinsman to hurry back and tackle him; fortunately Dunvegan Castle resisted attack successfully in the meantime. The raiders were then driven out by the MacLeods in a battle where the undermanned Alisdair 'Crotach' did not dare to tackle the invaders and had to hold out on a hill near Loch Poolteil for ten days until Donald 'Mór' of Meidle arrived with reinforcements. The latter was killed in the resulting victory – though in fact he lived until at least 1530, so if this story is accurate the dates are wrong.

The overall picture is of extreme conflict following the end of the centralising lordship of the Isles and ongoing petty disputes that no overall authority was available to control, plus continuing hostility between the MacLeods of Dunvegan and the two local MacDonald lines of Sleat and Clanranald over dominance of the waterways south of the Kyle of Lochalsh. The king's expedition to the Hebrides with a large naval force in 1540 saw Alasdair 'Crotach' forced to attend on his sovereign and swear allegiance, in return for which he was pardoned for past aid to rebels. Increasingly hampered by his physical disability, Alasdair eventually abdicated from leadership of his clan and retired to the monastery of Rodel, which he had endowed. This abdication may be timed by the documentary evidence that he received royal approval for handing over his lands of eastern and western Lyndale in Duirinish lordship (part of the lands granted him as a royal tenant by the late king in 1498) to his eldest son William in 1541. Alisdair and his heir were also granted a charter of 'life rent' of the lands of Trotternish and Sleat in Skye and of North Uist by James V, on 30 November 1542 – one of the king's last actions. (The MacLeods of Lewis had a rival claim to Trotternish and the MacDonalds to Sleat, so this did not make for comfortable neighbourly relationships.) Alisdair was buried near Rodel monastery at his foundation of St Clement's church in 1547; he is also said to have founded a college of pipers on Skye. He was succeeded by the eldest of his three sons by a Cameron of Lochiel, William, the ninth chief (1505–51/53), but unfortunately William and his wife Agnes Fraser had only a daughter, Mary. Traditionally clan leadership passed via the male line, which made his brother Donald his heir – but lands held by Scots royal law could pass via a female, so those of his lands held by charter from the monarch could be claimed by her and the chances were that the Scots government would support her rights. At the time of William's death his brother Donald was in Ireland, probably fighting for Ulster allies of the Hebridean lords, so it was his cousin Ian/John 'a Chual Bain' who was chief mourner at the funeral and is said to have been acclaimed by the clan elders as chief; when Donald returned he was unable to overturn this. Mary MacLeod, as the underage owner of those clan lands held by royal grant and thus a 'tenant-in-chief', was a royal ward under medieval feudal law, and Queen Mary's regent, the Earl of Arran (head of the Hamiltons), granted her wardship and the right to select her husband to his ally the Earl of Huntly. But later Huntly fell out with the next regent, Queen Mother Marie de Guise (partly over his failure in 1552–55 to deal with John Moydartach MacDonald of Clanranald), and she granted Mary's wardship to his brother-in-law James MacDonald of Islay, head of the Dunivaig clan, instead on 27 June 1559. The MacDonalds had also seized Trotternish and North Uist in 1552/53 although they were meant to go to William's brother, Mary's uncle, Donald MacLeod, and as Donald could not achieve any support at court for his rights to Mary's lands or the title of head of the clan he resorted to force majeure and took over both with the support of the majority of the clan around 1554.

But the succession dispute now took a new and bloody turn, as the superseded John 'a Chual Bain', Donald's cousin, had a more forceful son, John 'Og' of Minginish, who was by now next heir in the male line after Donald, his brother Tormod, and John senior. Tormod was a prisoner in France from 1557, probably deported by order of the French queen mother or one of her French military commanders for disloyalty, and with him out of the way John 'Og' murdered Donald in 1557 at Kingsburgh and seized control of the clan. According to family tradition the scheming John 'Og' used the opportunity of a belated MacLeod clan gathering at Lyndale which was due to decide definitively on a new chief, and invited Donald to his residence to celebrate what he announced as Donald's election as chief. In fact the meeting had elected John Og's father John, and the unawares Donald and his six companions were speedily massacred by John 'Og' at the 'celebration', so the two Johns were rid of their rival. The elder John was disgusted at his son and banished him, but when the elder John died soon afterwards John 'Og' returned and became chief. He also killed Tormod's sons and when Tormod was ransomed and returned to Scotland in 1559 refused to admit him to the family lands, ruling as a tyrant, but although he survived an armed incursion by his cousin Mary's Campbell allies (he invited them to a feast at Dunvegan, got them drunk and massacred them too) he was eventually driven out by a larger Campbell force and fled to Ireland to be killed there. Thus the Earl of Argyll, head of the Campbells and brother-in-law of Queen Mary's half-brother and senior adviser Earl James of Moray, finally installed Tormod, William's younger brother and Mary's uncle, as clan chief in the early to mid-1560s.

Tormod MacLeod (*c.* 1509–85?), an ally of Queen Mary, now ruled the clan, and married the daughter of Hector 'Og' Maclean. His niece Mary continued to claim the family lands, but eventually sold her rights in them to her uncle Tormod; the money was of more use to her, and she married in 1573 Duncan Campbell of Castleswynie, kinsman of her earlier guardian the Earl of Argyll and heir to the line of Campbell of Auchinbreck. Tormod married a daughter of Argyll as his second wife. He died probably in early spring 1585, as he was dead by the time that a summons was issued to him to appear at Holyrood Palace in a legal case on 23 April 1585; his eldest son William (1560?–90) was served as heir to him on 31 July. William was required by King James VI that autumn to assist his neighbour Lachlan Maclean of Duart against an attack by Angus MacDonald of Dunivaig and Islay, and on 30 November 1586 was one of the local clan chiefs whom the Earl of Huntly was ordered to punish for interfering with the rights of royally nominated holders of fisheries. He married Janet Mackintosh, daughter of their sixteenth clan chief Lachlan; he died in October 1590 and his younger brother Ruadhri/Roderick acted as 'tutor' for his underage son John (1580–95). When John died Roderick succeeded as fifteenth clan chief, subsequently marrying Isabella MacDonell the daughter of the eighth chief of Glengarry. In 1594 Roderick assisted his ally Hugh MacDonald of Sleat in a campaign to aid the Catholic rebel Hugh O'Donnell in Ulster, each taking along 500 clansmen; Queen Elizabeth complained about this to James VI and the Privy Council summoned him to explain and to agree to desist from annoying the king's cousin and neighbour (whom he would soon succeed in England). In 1596 Roderick surrendered to his sovereign's demands and was pardoned, but he was soon in trouble with the legalistic, centralising king, who sought to end the informal ways of governance in the Hebrides and was requiring all landholders to produce or obtain documentary proof of ownership of their lands on pain of confiscation. Roderick MacLeod could not produce his written proofs of ownership when required in 1597, so, like the obstreperous MacLeods of Lewis, he was declared forfeit with his lands opened for colonisation, and the king's cousin Duke Ludovick of Lennox and his party of Fife lairdly 'adventurers' put in a successful bid for them.

Skye could have ended up going the same way as Lewis into a Scots royal colony, but in 1598 Roderick was able to satisfy the Privy Council that he was the legal owner of his estates at a meeting and the grant was cancelled. Unfortunately his visit to Edinburgh ended in disaster thanks to his lordly temper, as he struck a Privy Councillor, Sir Roderick Mackenzie of Coigach, in a private dispute in the Privy Council chamber at Holyrood Palace and, threatened with arrest for a breach of the king's peace, hastily fled back to Skye in secret. The row with Mackenzie was probably over the conduct of Mackenzie's friend Donald 'Gorm' MacDonald of Sleat, who had married Mackenzie's sister after divorcing Roderick MacLeod's sister for failing to get pregnant within a year of the wedding (as laid down in the marriage agreement), despite his written request to give her another chance. The resulting conflict was known as the 'War of the One-Eyed Woman', as allegedly Roderick's sister had lost an eye during her turbulent marriage and her husband rudely sent her back to her brother on a one-eyed horse with a one-eyed dog as a black 'joke'. This dispute escalated into tit-for-tat attacks by Roderick on Donald's lands in Trotternish, by Donald on Roderick's lands on Harris, by Roderick on Donald's lands on North Uist, and in 1601 by Donald and a large MacDonald army on Skye while Roderick was absent. This latter attack ended in the Battle of 'Cloire na-Creiche', the final inter-clan battle on Skye. The king was endeavouring to force his Hebridean vassals to keep the peace and sort out disputes in his courts rather than on the battlefield, and came down heavily on the rivals to order them to keep the peace and disband their armies by 10 August 1601 or be cited as rebels. MacLeod was to report to his ally the Earl of Argyll, and Donald 'Gorm' was to report to his ally the Earl of Huntly; these two well-armed peers would then supervise the ceasefire. MacLeod ignored the ultimatum, failed to appear before the Privy Council on time (a common reaction from Hebridean chiefs to summonses in this era), and was proclaimed a rebel, but his pardon was duly negotiated and both sides agreed to peace. The latter was celebrated by a banquet at Dunvegan Castle for the two rivals, at which the MacLeod piper traditionally played his new composition 'The MacDonald's Salute'. The era of private wars in the region were passing, and the Stuart monarchs hoped to govern by pen rather than by sword. In July 1606 the Earl of Argyll was granted the barony of Glenelg and re-granted it to Roderick Mackenzie as his tenant. Roderick, now knighted and re-granted his lands definitively as a royal barony by charter on 4 May 1610, died in 1626; he was succeeded by his elder son John or Ian 'Mór' (1595–1649), who married Sybil Mackenzie of Kintail in a MacLeod–Mackenzie reconciliation. John was in turn succeeded by his sons, firstly Ruadhri 'the Wily' (1635–64) and then John 'the Speckled' (1637–93).

Cameron of Lochiel

This is another west Highlands clan of uncertain lineage, of whom little is known in its early centuries beyond a basic chiefly genealogy of shaky accuracy. It emerged in Lochaber in the years around the time of the wars of independence, with the presumed seventh chief, John de Cameron, recorded as fighting for Robert Bruce at Bannockburn in June 1314. As with other leading clans that emerged out of the chaos of the wars of independence and the fall of the MacDougalls of Lorn, taking the right side in the wars was a crucial factor, with confiscated lands of English and Balliol/Comyn supporters opened to settlement and legal acquisition in a power vacuum. The Camerons were, however, closer to the centres of power and to rival 'power blocs' than the Mackenzies and Mackays and so were less able to expand easily in an absence of strong rivals and major wars, their territory of Lochiel being close to the major route down the Great Glen, and they lacked the MacDonalds' advantages of ancient lineage linked to the traditional lords of the region or an extensive network of allied kinsmen. John 'MacOchtery' (i.e. son of Uhtred), the eighth chief of Clan Cameron, may have fought for David II at Halidon Hill in 1333, and he was succeeded by the shadowy figures of his son Allan (mid- to late fourteenth century) and the latter's elder son Ewan. Allan was clan chief under King Robert II (r. 1371–90), and possibly also at the time that their feud against the 'Clan Chattan' federation seems to have led to a famous inter-clan duel of thirty champions from clans 'Kay' and 'Quele' (as Lowlands writers identified them), which took place on the 'North Inch' outside Perth in September 1396 under the presidency of King Robert III. This made a major impression on Lowlands chroniclers such as Walter Bower, who were unused to the semi-ritualised Highland battle 'barbarism', which they deplored, though it is still disputed exactly which clans fought in the battle. Ewan had no children, and his younger brother and successor Donald 'Dubh' ('the Dark' or 'the Black'), who fought in the MacDonald army at Harlaw in 1411, was the first prominent chief of the clan. The head of a group of probably interrelated families in the clan, he achieved the distinction of having the traditional title of the clan chief named after him – 'MacDomnhaill Dubh', 'Son of Dark-Haired Donald'. This suggests that he was the first of the family to set up a coherent and long-lasting group of connected families as a political and military unit, and was treated as the founding ancestor of the unit in clan memory. But he was still only one of a number of rival leaders of groupings in Lochaber around 1400, his main rivals being the MacDonald 'Clan Donald' (i.e. Clanranald/Glengarry/Keppoch/Ardnamurchan), the 'Clan Chattan' confederation led by the Mackintoshes, and the soon-to-be-obscured 'Mael-anfaidh' coalition of the MacMartins of Letterfinlay, the MacGillonies and the MacSorleys of Glen Nevis. The Camerons had the most success in overtaking this latter coalition in prominence and acquiring its lands and its tenants' allegiance, as Donald 'Dubh' Cameron married the heiress of the MacMartins.

Donald 'Dubh' also participated in the MacDonald attack led by his overlord, 'Lord of the Isles' Alexander, on Inverness in early summer 1429, possibly in the aftermath of a substantial loss of men in an inter-clan battle against the Mackintoshes (his uncomfortable allies on this expedition) if this is dateable to Palm Sunday 1429 as presumed. Inverness Castle held out and royal troops were approaching so Alexander had to retreat back down the Great Glen with the vigorous Continental war veteran King James I in pursuit, and Donald 'Dubh' and his allies duly faced the wrath of the king and the arrival of a large royal army in Lochaber to pursue the retreating MacDonalds. In the 'Battle of Split Allegiances' on 23 or 26 June, somewhere around the site of the later Fort William, the king's army unfurled the royal banner so that anyone who fought in the rebel army against it could be accused of treason against their sovereign; most of the Camerons and the Mackintoshes promptly changed sides but tradition has it that Donald 'Dubh' remained loyal to Alexander. The loyal Islesmen were defeated, but the royal expedition's supply links were too extended and the countryside was too unfamiliar to make possible a hunt for the elusive rebels in the hills of Lochaber, and the area escaped prolonged occupation or much damage. Having learnt his lesson about the relative power of the MacDonalds and the king at a time of interventionist royal governance, Donald submitted to James I, was pardoned as a valuable west Highlands ally in a district far from the centre of power of the king's cousin and local lieutenant Earl Alexander of Mar (in Moray and Buchan), and in 1431 aided the king's army against the MacDonald rebel Donald 'Balloch'. Unfortunately, on this occasion Mar's army, including the Camerons, was ambushed while in camp at Inverlochy and routed by a sudden attack by Donald 'Balloch'; Mar fled back to Moray, and Donald ravaged Lochiel and the lands of other loyalists. When 'Lord' Alexander was released from prison after James I's death in 1437 and returned home he targeted Lochiel too, and Donald 'Dubh' had to flee to Ireland. Alexander gave his lands to his local rival John 'Garbh' Maclean of Coll, but the MacDonalds were no more able to enforce the confiscation of 'rebel' lands than the king was and once Alexander had taken his clansmen home and dispersed his army Donald was able to return from Ireland, rally his clan, and evict the usurper. After this the MacDonalds grudgingly accepted the Camerons as their neighbours in Lochaber, and when John 'Garbh's son John of Coll temporarily seized Lochiel again (*c.* 1450–70) he was killed at Corpach by the Camerons. His infant son was rescued by the MacGillonies as the Macleans fled to safety. But their rival Maclean lords of Lochbuie, given other Cameron lands by Alexander and soon evicted, seem to have continued the struggle to regain their lost territory for decades.

Donald died some time before 1461 and was succeeded by his son Allan 'MacIlchy', the twelfth lord, who was known as 'Allan of the Forays' ('Nan Creach') from his constant warfare. Allan married a MacDonald to help reconcile the two power blocs, and in 1472 was duly appointed as their castellan of Castle Strome on Lochcarron. He is said to have made thirty-two expeditions in as many years, and clearly built up a war-ready and well-motivated clan fighting machine. But he also made enemies, and in 1480 his marital kin the MacDonalds of Keppoch, supposedly coming to aid him, treacherously attacked him in the rear while he was fighting a battle with his Mackenzie neighbours and killed him. He was succeeded by his son Ewen, the thirteenth chief, who married the Mackintosh chief Duncan's daughter Marjorie to end their family feud (without much success). Ewen built a new chiefly residence at Torcastle to replace the earlier family base at Eilean nan Craobh, an islet in Loch Eil near Corpach – the abandonment of the secure but cramped location of the latter suggests greater pretensions and confidence. Ewen helped John 'Moydartach' of Clanranald against the rival claimant Ranald 'Gallda' in the MacDonald early 1540s succession dispute, fighting for him at the 'Blar na Leine', the 'Battle of the Shirts', on a hot day in July 1544. The Frasers' and Grants' manpower were nearly wiped out in this encounter. (See section on Clanranald.) But the defeated parties complained to the regency government of the Earl of Arran and portrayed their attackers as rebel brigands, and in 1546 Arran granted the Mackintosh chief, as royal steward of Lochaber, the right to punish the enemy with 'fire and the sword' with outside assistance from the fourth Earl of Huntly. As chief lord of Buchan, with a large clan to call upon, Huntly easily outmatched his victims and resistance was futile. The Camerons in the nearer part of Lochaber were easier to reach from the Great Glen than the Clanranald dynasts, and Lochiel was ravaged and Ewen and his ally Donald, son of Donald 'Glas' MacDonald of Keppoch, were captured and taken off as prisoners. They were subsequently executed as rebels by Huntly at his administrative headquarters as Lieutenant of the North, Elgin, and their heads were nailed up on the town gate as a warning to others.

Lochiel, Glenloy and Loch Arkaig were confiscated by the earl, who was expanding his power down the Great Glen as local 'strongman' while the regency was preoccupied fighting off the English in 1547, and Lochalsh and Lochcarron were given by him to his allies Grant of Culcabock and Grant of Freuchie in lieu of compensation for losses suffered earlier at the hands of Cameron raiders and in the 1544 inter-clan war. Ewen's son (or possibly grandson as he was called 'M'Conill McEwen) Ewen 'Beag', fourteenth chief, and the latter's illegitimate son Donald were deprived of all their estates as a punishment, and Ewen was either captured later and executed by Huntly (1554?) or according to one story was captured by the Laird of MacDougall for getting his daughter pregnant and refusing to marry her, locked up in a castle on the islet of Inchconnell, and killed by his guards during an attempt by his clansmen to rescue him. His illegitimate son Donald was known as 'Taillear Dubh Na Tuaighe', the 'Black Tailor of the Axe', as he was brought up by the wife of a tailor near Lundrava and was later educated by his kin, the MacLachlans of Coruanan, and became an expert fighter with the axe. His uncle, Ewen 'Beg's brother Donald 'Dubh', also known as 'M'Connill' (i.e. son of Connill), later managed to get his ancestral lands back after joining the army of Queen Mary and taking part in her victory over his foe Huntly at the Battle of Corrichie in 1562. Huntly had overreached himself by not only acting as lord of the entire north but trying to be a major policy maker in Scotland by intimidating the recently returned queen's shaky new regime. His arrogant castellan even shut the gates of Inverness on the queen's entourage during her first tour of the Highlands to emphasise Gordon power while his son Sir John Gordon rose in rebellion, and Huntly may have planned to kidnap Mary when she visited his castle but if so was prevented as she kept away. He dithered about joining the revolt until the queen was safely back in Aberdeen, then changed his mind and marched on the town to be intercepted and routed by the royal army. Forced to surrender and hauled before the queen, he dropped dead on the spot and although his family were able to survive as the principal lords in Buchan (not least as they were usefully Catholic) their extra gains of recent years were confiscated. Donald 'Dubh' Cameron got his lands back, and in 1564 was granted Huntly's lands of Letterfinlay, Stronnabow and Lyndale (which he did have rights to as his grandfather had been Huntly's tenant there under a 1535 charter).

Having backed the right 'horse' in the war between the queen and Huntly, Donald 'Dubh' restored the family fortunes and married the daughter of his new local ally, Hector 'Mór' Maclean of Duart. He was killed in 1565 or 1569, possibly by rebellious clansmen, and as his son Allan, the sixteenth lord, was an infant (he was to observe the Battle of Inverlochy in 1645 aged eighty-three) Donald's uncles Ewen Cameron of Erracht and John/Ian Cameron of Lochiel were 'tutors'. Allan was sent off to Mull to be brought up by his maternal grandfather Hector Maclean as his great-uncles' ambitions were feared by the clan, and Ewen of Erracht claimed the chieftaincy and won Mackintosh backing by promising to hand over disputed lands but was forced to repudiate this promise after objections from the clan. The angry Mackintoshes attacked him, and the embattled clan called in the 'Black Tailor of the Axe' (see above), his cousin and son of the executed chieftain Ewen, who rallied the clan as a better leader. The treacherous Ewen of Erracht's son Donald was killed by the 'Tailor' at a meeting at Inverlochy Castle, and the latter took over the clan and held the family lands secure until Allan was able to return and take over as chief in 1577/78. Clashes with Allan's ambitious great-uncles and their men, however, continued until 1585, while the 'Tailor' retired to Cowal once his work in preserving the clan was done. Other clashes continued with the Huntlys' allies the Grants, who had kept some of the confiscated lands they had received in 1547 and who now gave these to the Mackintoshes, reviving the latter's feud with the Camerons. Allan fought for the rebel Catholic leader the

fifth Earl of Huntly, son of his family's late foe, against the royal army
(and its local Campbell forces) at the Battle of Glenlivet in 1594, but this
had its problems as Huntly did not pursue his victory and was keener
to influence (by intimidation if necessary) rather than annoy the king.
The royal army under the seventh Earl of Argyll, principal Protestant
magnate of Argyll, recovered from the defeat as the king came to its
aid, and Huntly retreated and in 1595 negotiated permission from the
king to go into exile unmolested. With him abroad Allan had no patron
and faced Argyll's wrath plus a Campbell attack on his lands, and the
king gave Allan's lands to loyalist courtier Sir Alexander Hay. Physical
possession of the lands was another matter, but Allan had lost his
legal rights to his lands and the Loch Eil estate was sold by Hay (more
interested in the cash than occupying them against local resistance) to
a local, Hector Maclean of Lochbuie. Allan had to face this greater
challenge as, unlike Hay, Maclean had the local 'presence' and men to
enforce his legal rights, and Allan ended up negotiating to sell his lands
to the Earl of Argyll and rent them back from him, thus continuing to
live there as a Campbell ally.

In 1598 the pardoned and restored Huntly did not need Allan's help
any longer and did not like the idea of his rival Argyll as the new lord
of Lochiel either. He thus took his revenge for the continuing land
dispute with Allan's clan and their attacks on his allies, and formed
an alliance with his unruly kinsman Alister Cameron of Glenneur.
According to family tradition, Allan, warned of an imminent revolt
by Glenneur, invited the latter to a meeting in an isolated spot, with
each bringing a few men, but kept a force of 120 men 'on hand' in a
nearby wood. Glenneur attacked him as he had expected, but he was
ready to run and as he made his retreat his men charged out of the
wood and killed his pursuer; Huntly was thus left without a Cameron
'puppet' to aid him. Presenting Allan and his clan as unruly brigands
to the law-enforcing King James VI, he secured a royal commission
for himself and his allies the Mackintoshes and Grants to punish the
Camerons and arrest Allan for unspecified crimes. Possibly another
confiscation of Cameron lands was hoped for, but the expected invasion
never occurred and Huntly, who as a Catholic and ex-rebel was loathed
by the powerful Presbyterian Church and its lordly allies and had been
balancing the power of the Scots king and the meddling King of Spain
against each other for a decade by promises to both, lost influence at
court again. Huntly and the Mackintosh–Grant coalition quarrelled,
and Allan shrewdly and successfully offered an alliance to the embattled
Huntly, which was accepted (1600); apparently he had to sell his lands
to Huntly's son Lord Gordon and rent them from him as the price of

peace. With Huntly as an ally, in 1601 he attacked the Mackintoshes and Grants and looted and seized land from them. Thanks to Huntly's backing he was able to avoid confiscation of his lands by the king but a Mackintosh complaint about his attacks led to the king requiring him to hand over his son John, tenant of Mamore for Lord Gordon, to be held prisoner in the Tolbooth at Edinburgh for his future good behaviour. John's lands were later sold to the underage Mackintosh chief's agent, Sir John Grant of Freuchie, as the terms for Grant using his influence in Edinburgh to secure John's release. Allan, meanwhile, finally secured a royal pardon for all past offences in 1624.

The way that the clan chiefs were being 'tied down' in a web of legal documentation, and the way land disputes were being created or settled in court or by sales rather than on the battlefield, reflected the greater centralisation and modernising carried out by James VI, who sought to govern by the pen not the sword. Even in remote Lochaber clan conflict now eased, though grudges remained over generations, and local peace was increasingly apparent. Allan Cameron outlived his son John, whose health had been affected by years locked up in the Tolbooth and who died around 1635. John had married Margaret Campbell of Glenorchy as part of a putative Cameron–Campbell reconciliation, and their son Ewen (born in 1629 at his mother's family home of Kilchurn Castle, Loch Awe) was brought up by his foster father Duncan MacMartin of Letterfinlay and later by his maternal kinsman Archibald Campbell, eighth Earl of Argyll. 'King Campbell', the predominant figure in the Covenanter governance of Scotland from 1638 to 1651 and arch-foe of the Royalists, was a major influence on Ewen Cameron, but his aged grandfather Allan was still the clan chief during the Royalist revolt of 1644–45 and so sent his clansmen to back Montrose. He helped the latter in the crucial local Inverlochy campaign in February 1645, with 500 men joining the Royalist army for the battle, and allegedly told Montrose of Argyll's presence at Inverlochy and sent scouts to guide his army round Ben Nevis so the Royalists could outflank the Campbells' guards and attack by surprise. As such he played a major role in the resulting victory, but Montrose was eventually defeated and Allan Cameron died in 1647, leaving his clan to his nominally Covenanter grandson, Argyll's ward. However, the young Ewen had developed equivocal feelings about his patron and the Covenanter cause, traditionally after having to witness the vengeful Covenanters executing Royalist prisoners after the Battle of Philiphaugh, and in 1650 he offered his clan's services to the army of Charles II at Stirling in return for a written request from the newly arrived king. His patron and landlord Argyll and the other local landowner with Cameron tenants, the Earl of Huntly, however, did what they could to hinder his recruitment of troops. Later on Ewen fought in the last-ditch Royalist defence of the Highlands from General Monck under the Earl of Glencairn in 1654, and had the honour of holding a crucial outpost at Tullich near Braemar as the English Parliamentarian New Model Army troops were advancing on the Royalist base. He held back the advancing Colonel Robert Lilburne and his men on a hillside for several hours, for which he received a letter of congratulations from the exiled king in France. After the Royalist defeat Monck occupied the Highlands and began to construct a network of fortresses and roads for a long-term military occupation, anticipating the better-known post-1715 work of General Wade, and Ewen and his men engaged in a guerrilla war against the construction of a local fort at Inverlochy. The enemies they harassed included Colonel William Brayne, whom Monck's commander Cromwell was later to send out to take over control of English-occupied Jamaica in the West Indies.

At the Restoration the Camerons and other ex-Royalists returned to favour with a sympathetic government, including at first Ewen's ex-commander Glencairn. The Camerons' Royalist activities in the 1640s and 1650s proved useful in gaining support where it mattered in Edinburgh and London, as did Ewen's kinship to the Campbells – with Argyll executed by Charles II and his son in disgrace the Glenorchy and Breadalbane sub-dynasties now moved into prominence. This helped when the Mackintoshes tried to regain disputed lands by force in September 1665 and a force of 1,500 men of Clan Chattan invaded them, setting up camp at the Fords of Arkaig. Ewen and around 1,000 Camerons, backed by the MacIains of Glencoe and the MacGregors, arrived on the opposite side of the River Arkaig to confront them, but neither would risk being the first to cross the river under fire and mediator John Campbell of Glenorchy then arrived with his own army to announce that he would attack the first to make a move. He thus forced Mackintosh to accept the solution which he had been offered in 1663 but rejected, and under a settlement signed on 19 September Mackintosh had to sell the lands of Glenloy/Glenluie and Arkaig to Ewen Cameron. Next day, under Campbell's watchful eye, Ewen crossed the river to meet Mackintosh, each with twenty-four men, and they agreed to drink to peace and exchange their swords, ending the dispute. Ewen continued in good favour at the Stuart court and in 1681/82 went to Edinburgh to meet the king's brother and temporary viceroy, his fellow Catholic the Duke of York (later James II and VII), but inter-clan battles were not entirely over yet and on 4 August 1688 Ewen was present with his clan troops at the Battle of Mulroy, aiding the MacDonalds of Keppoch against an attack by the Mackintoshes. As was appropriate for the Camerons' record, they aided a clan under penalty of State displeasure and an order for the ravaging of their lands with fire and the sword in favour of the invaders, with royal troops aiding the Mackintosh attackers to no avail. As a result of this Ewen faced an order for his arrest which was inconveniently issued while he was in Edinburgh later that year, but he was warned in time and cunningly hid with a sympathiser on the premises of the Tolbooth prison, which he rightly reckoned was the last place where anyone would look for him. He then escaped back to the Highlands safely as his clansmen smuggled him out of the city.

Sir Ewen Cameron backed the Jacobites in 1689 despite King James's regime having tried to arrest him in 1688, and accepted the appeal of refugee royal general Graham of Claverhouse ('Bonnie Dundee') for help in raising an army. He duly fought with a large contingent of his clan at Killiecrankie, where his experience as a guerrilla commander was invaluable to 'Bonnie' Dundee. Effectively deputy commander to the latter as commanding one of the largest clan contingents in the campaign (despite his son John and 500 of his men not arriving until after the battle), he expected to be asked to take over the army after Dundee was killed by a stray shot in the hour of victory. This was not done, presumably as he was not a regular soldier, and the Jacobites were soon halted in their advance on the Lowlands by the successful defence of Dunkeld. As Williamite reinforcements arrived and (Highlander) General Hugh Mackay pressed the Jacobites back, Cameron and his clan faced the threat of another invasion and confiscation if they held out, and he duly submitted and swore allegiance to King William and Queen Mary by 1 January 1692 as required. His allies the MacIains of Glencoe failed to do so on time, more due to the bad weather and the distance involved than to truculence, and were slaughtered by regime troops who were billeted on them – destroying another west Highland bastion against Campbell encroachment. Ewen kept his distance from the Jacobite cause thereafter, but kept in secret touch with the exiled Stuarts and handed over his estates to his son John (b. 1663?) in 1696 so that if he was discovered and indicted for treason he would not face the loss of the clan lands. He was indeed attainted in 1716 for his part in backing the 1715 rebellion, which he was too old to fight in, but was never captured and died in 1719, aged around ninety. John then succeeded him but had actually left for France in 1717, having been given a Jacobite peerage as 'Lord Lochiel' by James 'III and VIII' while the latter was briefly in Scotland during the rebellion. Living in France in exile while his clansmen smuggled his rents overseas to support him, he died in Flanders in 1747 in his early eighties. His son Donald (b. *c.*

1700), the nineteenth lord and the famous 'Gentle Lochiel', represented him in Scotland from 1719 and in 1745 reluctantly accepted the call of loyalty to rally to Prince Charles Edward Stuart despite serious misgivings over whether the rebellion would succeed or his clan would end up massacred.

The ultimate 'moderate Jacobite man of honour' and a subsequent figure in romantic historical fiction, Lochiel was not enthusiastic to risk all on rebellion when the prince landed and sent his brother Dr Archibald Cameron to tell him to go home. The prince ignored him and appealed for help, so Lochiel led 800 Camerons to the Glenfinnan gathering on 19 August 1745 and did his best to see the Stuart cause to victory despite lacking either military experience or zeal for the cause. He was wounded in the foot at the Battle of Falkirk on 17 January 1746, and then in March carried out his master's instructions to endeavour to take Fort William with his clan levies and their neighbours but lacked the artillery to do so. The well-armed Hanoverian troops held out behind strong walls, and Lochiel and his men had to give up after a fortnight of frustration as the prince summoned them to help him at Inverness against the main enemy army under the Duke of Cumberland. They only arrived just in time for the Battle of Culloden, where the clan were cut to pieces but Lochiel managed to escape with the survivors. He then had the honour of arranging the last hostile action in the campaign as he called a summons of his clan for 15 May (postponed to the 22nd in the vain hope of a larger turnout) to aid the fugitive prince and resist the advancing British army, but only around 200 Camerons, 120 MacDonalds and a few Macleans turned up. Accepting the inevitable, Lochiel dispersed his men and made for the hills; his home, Achnacarry House, was burnt by the 'redcoats' on 28 May and he ended up in hiding in an isolated area of Lochaber by Loch Sunart and thence at the house of Stewart of Ardshiel in Appin across the Great Glen. He then joined his fellow loyalist chief Cluny Macpherson in the remote mountainside hideout of 'Cluny's Cage' at the foot of Ben Alder, and in August moved on to Lochaber en route to a rendezvous with a French ship. On 19 September he and the prince's party were evacuated from Loch nan Uamh, leaving Scotland on a French ship; he died in exile in France in 1748. His sixteen-year-old son John was to return home in 1759. Meanwhile Lochiel's equally heroic younger brother Dr Archibald Cameron (1707–53), who had been in his party in hiding and had the important task of bringing the prince to safety at 'Cluny's Cage', did his best to revive Jacobite fortunes after 1747 by acting as a travelling messenger and co-ordinator. Having accompanied the prince to Madrid in the vain hope of Spanish aid in 1748 and visited Scotland in 1749, he was arrested on a second visit home at Brenachyle near Loch Katrine in 1753 while en route to try to recover a Jacobite cache of money hidden at Loch Arkaig. (See also the section on the MacDonalds of Glengarry.) He was then famously executed for treason as an example to other Jacobites despite not posing a serious threat to the government, and was later the central focus of the action as the doomed leader of a futile conspiracy in D. K. Broster's 1929 novel *The Gleam in the North*.

8

The Clans in the Major Wars for Scotland, 1642 to 1746

(i) MacDonalds rampant? The Montrose campaigns

The overthrow of the Episcopalian and increasingly Anglicanised administrative system of the Scottish Church by a popular Presbyterian rebellion (led and orchestrated by 'godly' peers as well as preachers) in 1637 saw the post-1603 system of Stuart monarchs in London 'governing by pen' (as James VI and I put it) removed by force. King Charles's government in Edinburgh, divided and short of troops as the latter still depended on loyal peers raising their tenants, was neutralised and later taken over by a resurgent, Presbyterian-dominated Parliament and its allied militant Scots Church Assembly. The incomplete work of the Reformation in 1560 in destroying all papist, medieval elements in the Church was now completed in defiance of the king, with the militants ruling by intimidation (though with apparent mass support in the Protestant Lowlands) and the furious king reduced to a figurehead. His attempts to reverse this by armed invasion were hampered by lack of money, arising from his ruling without Parliament in England since 1629, and active subversion by concerned pro-Presbyterian Calvinist peers in England who saw the Scots cause of defying popery as their own, and the king's armies were defeated in the two so-called 'Bishops' Wars' on the Borders in summer 1639 and 1640. With experienced Scots Presbyterian officers who had fought for the Protestant cause in the Thirty Years War commanding it, a Scots army won the Battle of Newburn in August 1640, marched into Northumberland and forced the king to call an English Parliament – thus giving his critics a forum for demanding religious and political change as the price of financial aid. The rolling crises that led to civil war followed – though it should be remembered that this successful 'Scots Revolution' was a Lowlands and Protestant affair that left the Catholic Highlands isolated and indeed alarmed. The political autonomy of the Highlands peers and chiefs had been drastically reduced under the administrative centralism of James VI – would religious persecution of the Catholics be next? The king's attempts to reverse the events in the Lowlands in 1637–40 thus gave him natural allies in the Highlands, such as the powerful Catholic clan of Gordon in Buchan (led by the dithering George Gordon, second Marquis of Huntly) who could march on Aberdeen. They could be used as a military force against the new regime in Edinburgh, as could the triumphant Catholic rebels in Ireland who had risen in November 1641 against the threat of land confiscations by the militantly Protestant Parliament in London and had inflamed Protestant opinion further with their massacres (which an expanding and lurid printed media played up).

The treaty between the rebellious Parliament in London and the triumphant Scots Covenanter regime in Edinburgh in 1643 provided for the latter to send an army into England despite its formal agreement of peace with the king in return for effective autonomy, reducing him to a political cipher, in 1641. This invasion duly materialised in early spring 1644 and a large Scots army (mostly Lowlanders recruited by the Presbyterian clergy and landlords) invaded Northumberland to take the king's local commander, William Cavendish, Duke of Newcastle, in the rear and force him to retreat to York and send to Charles for help. The king duly sent his nephew, Prince Rupert, to relieve York, but the resulting battle was a disaster as the Parliamentarian besiegers of the city were joined by both the Earl of Leven's Scots and the East Anglian Parliamentarian army (with Oliver Cromwell commanding its cavalry). As Charles I faced stalemate turning to defeat in England with the destruction of his northern English armies by the Parliamentarians and Leven's Scots Covenanter army at Marston Moor in July 1644, he belatedly turned to the plan put forward in 1643 by a Royalist but ex-Covenanter commander, James Graham, Earl/Marquis of Montrose (b. 1612). This was to raise the mainly Catholic Highland and Island clans to take the Covenanters in the rear, playing on the locals' fear of persecution by the militantly Protestant, centralising and evangelising Covenanters. The fact that the latter's main political leader was Archibald Campbell (b. 1607), eighth earl of Argyll and head of the Campbell clan (nicknamed 'King Campbell'), would also be useful in bringing in the MacDonalds to attack their hereditary foes. The ruthless Argyll, the ultimate 'political fixer' and a master tactician, had been a leading – background – figure in the first anti-papist revolt in Edinburgh in 1637 and the creation of the 'National Covenant' to rally resistance to the king and his bishops, despite being a Privy Councillor; coincidentally or not, his father, the seventh earl (d. 1638), had converted to Catholicism, which he spent his life fighting. Argyll, cannily allying himself to the militant Presbyterian clergy in the 'rebel' Church Assembly in 1638–39 as they voted to abolish the bishops and abandon the king's religious reforms, had elbowed more senior leaders like the Earl of Rothes aside with the help of the force majeure provided by a private army of Campbell clansmen. His religious sincerity and opposition to royal power coincided with his own political advancement to be the real master of Scotland for much of the 1640s. Long regarded as the ultimate villain by romantic Royalists as the man who opposed and killed their hero Montrose, he was in one sense the final Highlands chief to use his military might to achieve national prominence. But he did so as a Calvinist Presbyterian and a semi-republican, and when he later helped Charles II to pose as a Calvinist king in 1650–51 this was on his own terms as 'kingmaker'. At the height of his power 'King Campbell' was to crown Charles II at the final Stuart coronation in Scotland in 1651 – but after the Restoration the king had him executed as a traitor.

Argyll had already carried out a notable campaign of atrocities in Menteith and Atholl in 1640 to discourage a Royalist rising and famously burnt down the 'Bonnie Hoose of Airlie' (Airlie Castle) as recalled in a ballad. His combination of political ruthlessness and chicanery earned him many enemies – not least his distant cousin Montrose, who as a staunch Presbyterian had been one of the lords to rally to the Covenanter cause against the king's 'Popish' Church innovations and sign up to the Covenant in 1638. Montrose, a Graham from Menteith in southern Atholl and famously snubbed as uncouth by King Charles on his return from the Continent in the 1630s, was not a natural choice to lead Catholic Highlanders in a guerrilla campaign. The personal enmity between Argyll and Montrose had led to the latter, concerned at the Covenanter leadership insisting on emasculating royal powers in the 'King/Covenanter' treaty of Edinburgh in autumn 1641, plotting to overthrow Argyll by a coup. Unfortunately Argyll had found out his plans as a result of a messenger being arrested and imprisoned him before Charles arrived to sign the treaty.

In addition to the Scots clans, the king had been seeking since 1638–39 to use ex-Highland (and thus non-Covenanter) settlers in Ulster, many of them Catholic MacDonalds, as an army to invade mainland Scotland led by their principal aristocratic leader, the veteran courtier Randall

MacDonnell, Marquis of Antrim (b. 1609). He was related by blood to the MacDonalds and was a foe of the Campbells, with many of his men exiles driven out of Argyll by the Campbells. To add to the complexities of the situation, the Ulster-settled but Scots-descended Catholic warlord Antrim was the second husband of Catherine (*née* Manners), the widow of the king's murdered chief minister of 1625–28, George Villiers, Duke of Buckingham and a court veteran with experience of the French court and army too. Son of the first Earl of Antrim (d. 1636), a former rebel in the great Irish Catholic rebellion against Elizabeth I of 1598–1603, and maternal grandson of the rebellion's leader the Earl of Tyrone, MacDonnell had inherited massive estates in County Antrim where his MacDonnell (ex-MacDonald) kinsmen had settled since the early sixteenth century, when the Campbells had driven them out of Argyll. (His principal seat was the coastal stronghold of Dunluce Castle, thought to be the inspiration for local author C. S. Lewis's 'Cair Paravel' in the *Narnia* books.) MacDonnell's ancestor Alexander MacDonald, fifth lord of Dunivaig, had had to flee to Ulster after his father and brothers were executed as rebels by James IV in 1499, and he and his kin were eager to settle old scores with the Campbells – a major bonus to Montrose in 1644. A MacDonnell-sponsored and trained army had been intended to invade rebellious Scotland in 1639 to link up with a Highland rebellion by the Catholic Gordons and the king's own invasion from England, but had never taken place; its intended landing place, Dumbarton, had been secured by the Covenanters. The somnolent George Gordon, second Marquis of Huntly (b. 1592), head of the Gordon clan and descended via his Hamilton mother from King James II but also married to Argyll's sister Jane Campbell and intimidated by his brother-in-law, had failed to raise his clansmen in the north-east quickly or formulate a competent plan of action. Admittedly Hamilton, his cousin, had failed to send him promised help. Nominally a Protestant but at the head of a Catholic clan, antagonistic to the Covenanters, and educated at court so he knew the king well, Huntly's military service at court in France was put to little use; he was a pale shadow of his father, leader of the anti-Presbyterian and pro-Spanish Catholic nobles at James VI's court, who had several times raised rebellions and tried to coerce the king (or his grandfather, who died after losing a battle against Mary Stuart in 1562). He prudently or timorously refused to attack a gathering of armed Covenant volunteers, raised to fight the king, and their visitor Montrose near his lands at Turiff in February 1639, claiming that he had no orders from the king to start a war. Indecisive or fence-sitting, he was then taken by surprise by the Covenanter army's advance on his lands, and obeyed a summons to report to the Scots rebel government's envoy

Montrose to end up arrested. His troops under his second son Lewis Gordon, later Lord Aboyne, were then routed by a Covenanter army led by Montrose at the 'Brig O'Dee' on 17–18 June. His eldest son, Lord Gordon, was a more competent soldier but more pro-Covenanter and too cautious to risk ruin by rushing to back a distant king in 1639–43 (or his undermanned local army in 1644).

The king's opponents now had to resolve their differences or face being worn down by a more unified and determined enemy, with the added problem that Montrose had remarkable success in the Highlands. The latter had had no success in his first foray into the south-west earlier that year, and when he decided to try his luck in the Highlands and went to York it was just after Marston Moor so no troops could be spared. Lacking enough men to force his way across the Border, he had to cross it with two companions, disguised as a groom and hiding his royal standard in their luggage (August 1644). Luckily for Montrose the Marquis of Antrim had managed to send a force of around 1,600 men under Alistair MacDonald, 'MacColkitto' (son of the 'left-handed', that is ambidextrous, ex-lord of Colonsay, Colla or 'Coll Ciatach'), across from Ulster during June, so he had a suitably battle-hardened and manoeuvrable force to add to his local levies. These were experienced in fighting from Ulster, with Alistair a master of the art of the terrifying charge by claymore-wielding infantry. Alistair, whose father (a claimant to the lordship of the southern MacDonalds) had lost his Scottish lands to the Campbells in Alistair's youth, had had to relocate to Ulster with his warlike sons, who had joined the loyalist Catholic part of Charles I's army against the Irish rebels there in 1641 but, treated with suspicion by the Protestants, had later defected. Alistair, a Royalist uneasy at the Catholic rebel plans to coerce the king into acting as a figurehead, had later temporarily returned to the allegiance of the Scots Covenanter general in Ulster, Lord Leven, but was now acting for the Royalist commander Antrim. The MacDonalds were initially intended to operate in the lands of Lochaber which the MacDonalds of Islay and Coll had long disputed with Argyll's Campbell clansmen; Alistair's father had been the clan's leader in resistance to the Campbells in earlier decades and Alistair's men were mostly expatriate mercenaries who had taken service with their MacDonell kin in Ulster. But the MacDonald army that landed in Ardnamurchan in June 1644 had to move on east into the Highlands when the Campbells captured or burnt their ships. Heading for Badenoch en route to join an anti-Covenanter revolt by the Gordons, their route was cut off by the pro-Covenanter Grants so they had to move south into Atholl. The Gordons' leader Huntly, as useless a commander as in 1639, had been pushed into seizing Aberdeen

by his more active cousin Sir George Gordon of Haddo (supposedly
to coordinate with Montrose's arrival in Galloway in April) but had
fled into the mountains as Argyll arrived. Thus the Irish levies were
conveniently close to Montrose in Atholl as he arrived in the area to
meet his Graham kinsmen in mid-August, and he arranged a rendezvous
with them at Blair Atholl where both they and the local Stuarts and
Robertsons – who were initially braced to attack these Irish intruders –
accepted his leadership.

With his mixed Scots–Irish force assembled and a combination of
local Catholic resentment of the Covenant and MacDonald hatred
of the Campbells acting in his favour, Montrose was able to launch a
highly successful guerrilla war on the forces of the Edinburgh regime.
His own genius for strategy would have been useless against the far
more numerous and better-armed armies of the Covenant but for his
having a highly mobile force of Highlanders and Ulstermen, used to
long marches and quick retreats as well as being feared in battle for
their ferocity in the charge by their Lowland victims. The long-standing
antagonism between Highlanders and Lowlanders and the popular
conception of the former as bloodthirsty papist savages acted as a
psychological weapon in Montrose's favour, and was magnified by
his seemingly incredible successes, which masked his army's lack of
numbers or heavy weapons. Luckily some moderate and well-armed
Covenanters en route to join their army against the MacDonalds, led
by Lord Kilpont, deserted to the latter's old friend Montrose when they
ran into his small force. The 5,000 or so Royalists then moved down the
Tay towards Perth, and made short work of around 7,000 well-armed
Covenanter troops under Lord Elcho at Tippermuir (or Tibbermore)
outside Perth on 1 September. The Covenanters used 'Jesus and No
Quarter' as their watchword, without any irony at its incongruity; for
them the godly cause was equated with slaughtering Catholic Irishmen
and Highlanders. The ferocity and speed of the Royalist charge unnerved
their largely untested Lowlander militia opponents who turned tail and
fled after a brief encounter, with around 2,000 being slaughtered. But
Montrose had had to string out his army on a broad front only three
deep to pretend that he had more men than in reality, also restricting
their shooting to one volley (which luckily did the trick) and telling men
who had no ammunition to throw stones.

From then on the swift-moving Royalist force proceeded to dart
across the length and breadth of eastern Scotland, keeping ahead of its
better-equipped but nervous pursuers. The multiple but inexperienced
Covenanter forces in Scotland initially underestimated the challenge,
and were unable to catch the small army, besides lacking Montrose's

genius for using the terrain. The Covenanters were reduced to placing a price on Montrose's head 'dead or alive' on 12 September, regarding him as having put himself beyond the normal courtesies of war by his using 'barbarian' Catholic Highlanders and Irishmen, who had allegedly joined the 1641 massacres, and it seems that Argyll tried to have him assassinated by suborning his officers. This is the probable explanation for a murky incident after Tippermuir involving the murder of his lieutenant Lord Kilpont, whose killer fled to Argyll. But the Royalists were on more of a knife-edge than their enemies, given that many of the local Highlanders – used to quick raids to steal cattle and plunder, not to a long campaign – returned home after Tippermuir and could not be ordered to obey military discipline and stay. Some Angus tenants under pro-Royalist gentry came in to replace them, but as long as Huntly and his more dynamic sons, maternal kin to Argyll, remained aloof the Gordons' manpower (the main source of warriors in Buchan) would follow suit.

The well-armed Covenanter army defending Aberdeen, some 2,500 men to Montrose's 1,500, was defeated outside the walls on 13 September. Its superior armaments and cavalry were not used to their best effect due to poor generalship by the inexperienced Lord Balfour of Burleigh, and a chance to overrun the Royalists was missed by a cavalry brigade that had outflanked them. They stood still rather than pressing on, and Montrose had time to react. Unlike Rupert or Cromwell Montrose did not have enough cavalry to launch a disciplined and effective charge, and had to rely on the effect of a devastating infantry charge by MacDonald's Ulstermen followed by his men's superior ability in hand-to-hand combat. This could be countered by either cavalry or cannon, but the enemy command lacked the quick thinking to notice Montrose's dispositions and do that; when Sir William Forbes's Covenanter cavalry wing charged into MacDonald's massed ranks the latter dispersed to let them sweep past without effect. The Royalist cavalry were interspersed with musketeers so that the latter could shoot down their opponents, thus demoralising the larger cavalry force that faced – but did not charge – Nathaniel Gordon's small cavalry unit and softening them up ahead of an attack. The hundred or so Covenanter cavalry missed a crucial chance to overwhelm Gordon's thirty men whom they caught by surprise by rounding a hill suddenly, and Montrose sent reinforcements to help. The other wing of Covenanter cavalry charged Alistair's musketeers, who coolly opened their ranks to let them charge through then shot them from behind before they could turn. Once the Covenanter cavalry had been driven back, the MacDonalds could deal with their infantry in close combat. The Covenanters were outgeneralled by ingenious tactics,

and their precipitous retreat into Aberdeen was followed by the sack
of the city – where the numerous atrocities committed by the excited
Highlanders added to Lowland terror of Montrose. The sack was the
first major massacre of the Civil War in either England or Scotland, and
was hardly an act of deliberate policy as Montrose was unable to control
his undisciplined levies, who were not used to military discipline (though
he made no effort to do so either). The defenders' shooting of a Royalist
drummer boy sent with a message was the official pretext.

In military terms, Tippermuir and Aberdeen were sufficient reason
for Argyll and his lay and clerical allies to recall a substantial force
from England (where Leven's main army was besieging the port of
Newcastle). It would not have been easy for Leven or one of his more
effective lieutenants to track down and catch Montrose's mobile force in
the Highlands, but at least the Covenanters would have had adequate
commanders and troops used to battle. That this was not done argues
for a mixture of superior Lowlander and Covenanter contempt for
the quality of their 'barbarian' opponents, written off as cattle-lifting
clansmen, and Argyll's personal underestimation of Montrose. The
Campbell chief made a personal effort with his clan troops to catch
Montrose after the sack of Aberdeen, taking advantage of Alistair
MacDonald's return to the west in search of reinforcements, and
caught up with him at Fyvie Castle in October. Short of ammunition,
Montrose had to melt down the castle's pewter plates to make bullets.
But Argyll's force lacked adequate military skill (as opposed to numbers)
to storm the defensive bank that protected the eastern approach to the
castle, which was surrounded on its other three sides by marshes, and
Montrose and his Ulster MacDonald commander Magnus O'Cahan
beat the Campbells back and then slipped away. Argyll lost another
chance as Montrose outmarched him in the wilderness in heavy rain and
was then rejoined by Alistair MacDonald with a large new contingent
of men from the MacDonald clans of Lochaber, keen to settle old scores
with the Campbells. From now on the armies were better-matched and
each successive Royalist success added to Montrose's reputation.

The key to defeating the highly motivated and manoeuvrable Royalist
force lay in a mixture of firepower, cavalry and generalship, and even
then any Lowland army with a large artillery train or cavalry force was
at a disadvantage lumbering around the Highlands after fast-moving
clansmen. Lacking a force of experienced troops to pursue him, the
mission was delegated to those poor-quality local Lowland militia – and
their inexperienced but politically reliable generals – who had been left
in Scotland as the main army marched into England in January 1644.
One by one they were to be defeated in their increasingly desperate

attempts to deal with Montrose. Each Royalist victory improved morale, inspired recruits to join up and acquired extra plundered weaponry and ammunition. For the moment, the campaign turned into a 'clan war' between Campbell and MacDonald, with the added usefulness for Montrose of personally humiliating his arch-enemy. In midwinter 1644/45 Argyll's own Campbell lands in Argyll were being ravaged in a swift assault that saw his family residence of Inveraray Castle sacked, a major humiliation. The threat thus arose that Leven's army would have to return home to deal with Montrose in 1645 and Parliament would be fighting without its main ally.

The 'Presbyterian Cavalier' Montrose (as John Buchan aptly called him), with a mixed army of Protestant Royalist Lowlanders, Highland Catholics based on the MacDonald clan and Irish mercenaries brought in by his lieutenant Alastair, evaded the divided armies of the Covenant in an exhausting chase around eastern Scotland and making sporadic descents on the Lowlands. Wearing his militarily less skilled opponents out in unfamiliar territory and outsmarting their advantages of superior numbers and weaponry, his fit and ferocious Highlanders defeated the Covenanter armies one by one. Argyll had suffered the humiliation of having his home territory pillaged and his residence at Inveraray Castle sacked, and on 2 February 1645 Montrose wiped out his Campbell private army at Inverlochy after a daring march round the flanks of Ben Nevis – a thirty-six-hour trek, partly in the dark – to take his opponents by surprise. Having intended to trap Montrose at Kilcumein (the later Fort Augustus) between the Campbell army to the south and the advancing Earl of Seaforth's Caithness (Mackenzie) clansmen to the north, Argyll was caught by surprise to see the enemy descending on him from the hills on the flanks of his forces. According to tradition, the later bard Iain 'Lom' MacDonald, a local clansman from the Keppoch family who lived until 1715, acted as Montrose's guide. The Campbell infantry was commanded by a military veteran who had fought in Ulster, Sir Duncan Campbell of Auchinbreck, and was in a better shape than the townsmen of Perth at Tippermuir or the Aberdonians so their decision to fight and not withstand a siege was logical. (They probably also assumed that the Royalists were tired out from their long march across the Ben Nevis range.) Around 2,000 Campbells and 1,500 of General Baillie's men, aided by a couple of cannon, faced the disparate mixture of Highland clansmen and Irish mercenaries, but it was still no match for the Royalists at close quarters. A charge by the Royalists apparently caused panic. While his men were butchered and Inverlochy was sacked, 'Mac Cailean Mór' (who had been unable to fight due to a dislocated shoulder) abandoned his clansmen and sailed off down Loch

Linnhe in his galley. Back in Edinburgh he sought to minimise the effects of this alleged minor skirmish, and secured a vote by the Estates to have Montrose hanged, drawn and quartered, which he was finally able to implement in 1650.

As yet most senior nobles in Lowland and Highlands alike stood aside from the mainly Catholic royal army under its ex-Covenanter leader, with even the king's loyal Lieutenant of the North, Huntly, only furnishing a small contingent under his son Lord Aboyne. But Montrose seemed to be invincible, and the destruction of Campbell power removed a major element of the Covenanter military coalition. The possibility arose of a Royalist victory in both England and Scotland in 1645 – or at least of the Scots having to abandon their allies to save the Lowlands and thus losing all that they had gained in northern England in 1644. The king would have been in an even stronger position had Montrose been able to achieve this success earlier, as his campaign had only opened in early September 1644 with the Battle of Tippermuir. As in 1638–39, a large portion of the blame for slow Royalist military action must lie with Huntly, who had fallen victim to a Covenanter attack in 1639 when he should have been leading his tenants to assist Charles and Hamilton in Edinburgh (or at least been on his guard against attack). Much was probably down to the marquis's pride of social rank in his failure to back Montrose with his full military might in 1644 – the latter was socially his junior and had previously been fighting for the Covenant. The equally equivocating Earl of Seaforth (George Mackenzie), having fought against Montrose at Inverlochy, came to meet him at Elgin as he advanced across the north-east after Inverlochy, and so saved his estates from plunder – but he was never a committed and reliable ally. Nor were the Highlanders disciplined and patient enough to deal with the delaying tactics of the skilful and unflappable Baillie, who now understood that he was safer avoiding battle and so used the terrain to manoeuvre and delay the Royalist advance. Montrose's attempts to lure him into battle with chivalric challenges were ignored, and the slow progress made by the Royalist advance led to many of Montrose's clan levies abandoning his army when it halted at Dunkeld in April and going home. Reduced to around 1,500 men temporarily, Montrose made a bold dash for Dundee and succeeded in briefly occupying the town but had to retreat with minutes to spare as a larger and better-armed Covenanter army forced an entry.

Montrose now destroyed another of the Covenanter armies, this time led by Baillie, at Alford. The latter, joined by Colonel Hurry's remnants, initially had the advantage of numbers (*c.* 2,000) and equipment over Montrose and was too cautious to risk being tempted into combat on the Royalist general's chosen ground. But as Montrose gave up his careful circling and pulled back into the difficult terrain of the central Highlands, Baillie, more cautious than Hurry, had to move down the Spey for supplies and Hurry left him. He was further weakened by orders from the Edinburgh regime to hand part of his force over to his colleague Lord Lindsay, whom they trusted more but who stayed clear of Montrose down in Atholl, though Montrose was weakened too by the withdrawal in June of Alistair MacDonald (temporarily, to collect more clan troops) and most of the Gordons (on Huntly's orders). Eventually Montrose, rejoined by Lord Gordon, who was defying his father Huntly, managed to tempt Baillie out of a strong defensive position near Keith with a move towards the defenceless eastern Lowlands, forcing his enemy to hasten after him. On the banks of the River Don at Alford on 2 July Montrose lured Baillie into an attack over the river and up a hill, positioning most of his men out of sight behind the ridge so that the overconfident Covenanters attacked and could be intercepted by his cavalry. Apparently it was Lord Balcarres rather than Baillie who insisted on an attack and fell into the trap, but the result in any case was a complete rout of the Lowlander infantry. The only setback was the death in battle of Lord Gordon, Montrose's principal ally among that clan and the man able to defy his father's temporising.

Once again Montrose's success had shown that superior skill and élan could outwit the greater numbers and superior regular training of the Lowland Covenanters, and each success reduced his foes' morale. If his run of success continued, he might be able to win over the war-weary majority of the Scots leadership and their restive subjects to his side – provided that he could do so before Leven returned, thus gaining the numbers and Lowland infantry to meet him on equal terms. The main problem remained the fissiparous nature of his undisciplined army, where the Gordon contingent supplied reluctantly by Huntly had temporarily deserted before Alford and some angry officers recommended Montrose make an example of them after the battle. The earl avoided doing this and giving the Gordons an excuse to defect permanently, but the death at Alford of Lord Gordon, one of his closest and ablest officers, added to his potential problem with that clan. The enthusiastic courtier George Digby claimed on 28 July that Alford meant that Montrose now had no major obstacle left in Scotland, though this was an exaggeration.

Baillie's army having been destroyed by Montrose on 2 July, the Scots Parliament now had only a small force under Lindsay left to oppose the Royalists until Leslie returned home. They duly ordered the raising of a new, and thus untested, army of volunteers to meet the threat, and moved themselves to Perth to join the levies and halt Montrose's advance south. But Montrose slipped past them and headed towards Glasgow, forcing Baillie to march after him; by dint of his usual skill and some Covenanter blunders he drew the latter's army into combat at Kilsyth on 15 July before Lord Lanark and his Clydesdale levies could join them and make their numerical advantage overwhelming. Even so the Covenanters had around 6,000 infantry and 800 cavalry to his poorer-armed 4,400 infantry and 500 cavalry, but his mainly Highland troops had greater fighting skills. The committee of Scots Parliament figures assisting – and ultimately controlling – Baillie, a Covenanter equivalent of Soviet commissars, had the authority to countermand his orders and duly voted to move their position in order to seize a strategic hill and cut off Montrose's line of retreat. (This political interference with the generals' decisions would be equally apparent and equally disastrous at the Battle of Dunbar in 1650.) They ignored Baillie's warnings that Montrose might attack the army as it marched, and their army lost its one chance – of escaping Montrose's notice behind the brow of a hill – when some troops broke ranks to attack a Royalist outpost and drew the MacDonalds on them. Montrose was alerted, and when a horde of ferocious Highlanders intercepted the marching Covenanter infantry the latter were cut to pieces. Most of the 6,000 Covenanter infantry were slaughtered, and the cavalry had to flee. The result left the Lowlands defenceless against Montrose, and on 16 August he entered Glasgow. Edinburgh, unprotected with Leslie still in England, surrendered and he was able to summon a parliament for October. But his military success was deceptive – due to the need to conciliate the Lowlanders and the moderate Covenanter opinion he could not extort funds to pay his clan-based army, and the Highlanders were inclined to regard his success as the conclusion of their campaign. Their usual method of fighting was to go home with their loot after victory, and he had no means of compelling them to stay. Alistair MacDonald and his clansmen departed to attack the unprotected Campbells, their ancient foes, in Argyll, and Lord Aboyne took most of the Gordons home to Buchan. Montrose was left without more than 1,000 men at most, mainly Irish from Antrim and so disliked by the Lowlanders, and the extent of losses his army had inflicted on the successive Lowland armies over the past year was a cause of resentment among the people from whom he would need to recruit a new force to meet Leven. Despite some support from the southern Scots peers, led by Charles's ex-treasurer Lord Traquair, his position in August 1645 was more perilous than it looked. The fact that the Lowlanders would not pay for his Highland troops gave the latter no incentive to stay in his service, though the loyal Alistair MacDonald and some other clan commanders could be expected to return as promised in a few months.

Montrose was also hopelessly outnumbered; he arrived in Kelso to confront the returning Covenanter forces from England with at most 500 Irish infantry and around 1,200 cavalry, the latter mostly southern Scottish gentry. The latter were not used to fighting in his army, and MacDonald's Ulstermen were absent. Lord Aboyne had left with the Gordons, losing Montrose the most experienced of his remaining cavalry commanders, and the inexperienced Earl of Crawford had insisted on being given command of the cavalry. A socially important victim of Argyll, he could not be denied. David Leslie, arriving back from England ahead of his cousin Leven with the Covenanter advance force on 6 September, had around 4,000 experienced cavalry, who were used to combat at professionally fought encounters like Marston Moor. The earls of Home and Roxburgh, intending to defect to Montrose, were lured to Leslie's camp and arrested; they would have done better to hurry to the Royalists with local scouts to help Montrose to evade attack. Initially heading along the main road towards Edinburgh to await Montrose's expected retreat to the Highlands, Leslie was told that the Royalists were encamped nearby outside Selkirk and launched a surprise attack on their rendezvous at Philiphaugh in thick mist on the morning of 13 September. (One story blamed Charles's ex-minister Traquair for betraying Montrose's location to save himself from punishment in a Covenanter victory which he saw as inevitable.) The Royalist cavalry and recent recruits were cut to pieces in their camp, and in any case lacked the well-armed infantry or superior position that might have negated an overwhelming cavalry attack. The disaster was totally avoidable had Montrose sent out proper scouts – a rare lapse on his part. Nor was the mist unexpected for someone who had campaigned in the Highlands.

Montrose fought his best with 150 horsemen to save his army at Philiphaugh until they were overwhelmed and he and a dozen or so survivors had to flee the battlefield. He had to flee to the Highlands while the Covenanter army slaughtered his captured Irish Catholic followers in cold blood, and the king's cause was lost. Exemplary executions at Glasgow included his lieutenants Nathaniel Gordon and Magnus O'Cahan, with all treated like barbarous Irishmen. The executions extended to civilians such as Sir Robert Spottiswood, technically the king's Secretary of State so not under Covenanter jurisdiction, for taking the king's commission to act as lieutenant governor to Montrose, and the meeting of the Estates at St Andrews that winter was implacably anti-Royalist. But in any case the comparative numbers, training, and equipment of Montrose's small army – without his best Highland clansmen – after August 1645 meant that the disaster at Philiphaugh only anticipated an inevitable retreat in the face of the two Leslies and their large and well-armed forces. Even if the Royalists had managed to retire intact to the Highlands – as would have been possible had David Leslie missed his chance and marched on to Edinburgh – Montrose would have been back where he was in spring 1645, evading and attempting to wear out Leslie as he had done to Baillie. The Scots Covenanters would have been back in full control of the Lowlands, and the king would have been unable to call on Montrose for support for the rest of the 1645 campaign. The Royalist cause would have collapsed in England as it eventually did, if not yet in Scotland. Instead, Montrose was reduced to a local attack on Inverness with the temporary allegiance of Seaforth and his Mackenzies in spring 1646 but could not take on any major Covenanter armies. Charles had to flee from Oxford as the New Model Army closed in and chose to hand himself in to the Scots army at Newark, hoping to enlist the moderate Calvinist peers there to neuter Argyll's influence by promising support for a Presbyterian Church in both realms and then use the Scots to attack the Parliamentarians. As part of his negotiations Montrose was required to disarm and leave Scotland for Scandinavia. Meanwhile Alisdair 'MacColla' returned with his men to Ulster and went on to southern Ireland, where he took service with the Royalist commander Lord Taaffe but was captured after their defeat by Lord Inchiquin at Knocknanuss on 13 November 1647 and was apparently shot in cold blood.

Montrose had a second chance – albeit a slim one – to raise a Highland rebellion against the Covenanters in 1649, following Charles I's execution. The shocked Covenanters recognised his son as their king 'Charles II'. But he was in exile in Holland, and the Covenanters would only allow him to come to Scotland if he ruled as their puppet (as envisaged for his father in 1641); he turned to the Catholic Royalists in Ireland for help instead. Cromwell's invasion of Ireland duly neutralised Charles's Irish support later in 1649, forcing Charles back into negotiations – though many of his advisers, led by Sir Edward Hyde, opposed any link to the Covenanters, who had been the first to rebel against his father in 1637. Ironically, there was an 'Auld Alliance' element to the Royalist–Covenanter schemes as the new king's French mother Henrietta Maria and her countrymen sought hard-headedly to revive the old Scots–French alliance to counter the threat of Cromwell's menacing army and the regicide republican regime in London to France and Catholicism. The Argyll faction would not pardon the 'Engager' leaders as Charles wished, fearing another political coup, and Charles duly gave cautious backing to the exiled Montrose's actions as the late king's most brilliant general, now with the Scots community in

Gothenburg, raised men and money in Sweden for a Royalist invasion of Scotland. A favourite of the maverick Queen Christina (reigned 1632–54, abd.), the charismatic Montrose was unable to collect as many men as he wished or much weaponry and had to rely on Scots expatriates plus a few mercenaries, but on 12 January 1650 Charles sent him his unequivocal backing for an invasion plus the Order of the Garter.

As the king's chosen commander, Montrose sailed to the Orkneys with around 1,200 men in March and a month later landed in Caithness. But by this time Charles had opened negotiations with the Argyll faction's second embassy to him, at Breda in Holland – which the hard-line Presbyterian preacher Johnston of Warriston joined to ensure that there was no compromise. The terms required him to sign the Covenant, have a Presbyterian household, ban all those proscribed by the regime from his presence, accept all post-1641 Scots legislation to which his father had not agreed (including the proscription of assorted Catholics and Royalists), and submit all political decisions to Parliament and all religious decisions to the Church. In effect, he was to be reduced to a cipher. In effect the devious new king was following two contradictory lines of policy for his restoration, one backing Montrose's invasion for achieving power on his own terms and the second signing up to whatever the hard-line Covenanters required. Montrose had the advantages of many Covenanter troops being in Ulster, the Covenanter general David Leslie (Leven's cousin and deputy in England in 1644–46) being far to his south which gave him time, and the multiple defector Colonel Hurry (his foe in 1645) having joined him at the Ord of Caithness, but he had too few troops. The main local Royalist landowner, the Earl of Seaforth, who had temporarily joined Montrose in 1645 and 1646, was in exile in Holland and his brother and their Mackenzie clan failed to turn up; the Earl of Sutherland stayed loyal to the regime, and Leslie's troops held out in the local castles. Marching south towards the Gordons' lands beyond the Great Glen, Montrose was caught by surprise by Leslie's deputy Colonel Strachan at Carbisdale in Strath Oykel on 27 April and routed – a repeat of his disaster at Philiphaugh. As on the earlier occasion, his scouting was inadequate. Taking to the hills, he was captured hiding at Ardvreck Castle due to the treachery of Neil MacLeod of Assynt and handed over to the Covenanter leadership for the implementation of his 1644 death sentence. No mercy could be expected from the ruthless Argyll, and it was correctly assumed that Charles II was too desperate for their aid to make difficulties about Montrose being executed. The Royalist commander was duly hanged at the Mercat Cross in Edinburgh as a common criminal, a gratuitous piece of spite to an earl who could have expected a 'proper' execution, after a harangue from the clergy about his past wickedness. His body was cut up for display as usual for those executed for treason, and was still on display as Charles, the man who had asked him to invade, arrived in Scotland. Montrose duly entered Royalist legend as a martyr, and his subsequent admirers have been legion – with Argyll cast as the villain of the story. But in defence of the Covenanters' vitriolic attitude to him it should be noted that his campaigns had been marked by atrocities, especially at Aberdeen in 1644, and that thousands of their Lowlander troops and civilians had been butchered by his Highlanders.

(ii) The Jacobites *versus* William II and the Killiecrankie campaign

James II's flight from London to Catholic France in December 1688 left the throne of England declared vacant, but the authorities in Scotland did not follow their counterparts' deposition of him immediately. The Catholic king had been as controversial for his aggressive policy of promoting his co-religionists in the Scots Lowlands as in England, relying on a narrow clique of ultra-Royalist ministers led by the Drummond brothers and arranging Catholic services in the royal chapel of Holyrood Abbey to the fury of the Protestant citizens of Edinburgh. As a result, when his English regime fell his paralysed and militarily weak regime had been overthrown by a popular rising in the capital and Catholics as well as ministers had fled for their lives as their homes and chapels were ransacked. Even the royal tombs at Holyrood had been vandalised, and an army of extremist rural Covenanter militants from Galloway, the 'Cameronians' (at war with the royal troops for years in a low-level guerrilla campaign), had collected their hidden weapons and marched on Edinburgh to demand a restored, non-episcopal Calvinist Church. In this situation, as of January 1689, the most extreme Presbyterian elements in the Lowlands were in charge – or at least unhindered – in Edinburgh and the rift with the Highlands of the late 1630s and early 1640s was reopened. Technically James was still King of Scots as well as King of Ireland in early 1689, and a Convention of Estates did not meet in Edinburgh to decide on the new government until the new King William sent orders to summon one in March 1689. The third Duke of Hamilton, son-in-law of Charles I's cousin and minister, served as commissioner. By this time the extremist 'Cameronians', as well as more moderate Covenant loyalists, had poured into Edinburgh to join in the Presbyterian triumph, and with their armed militants roaming the streets in alliance with the city's crowds it was no surprise that many elected

Episcopalian representatives to the convention failed to take their seats. Similarly, those extremists who were elected were emboldened to demand the abolition of episcopacy and a return to the pristine Covenanter Church of the 1640s, and other attacks were made on the political 'model' of the 1680s with demands to secure free parliaments by abolishing the controlling committee of 'Lords of the Articles'.

William's appointee General Hugh Mackay of Scorie (related to Clan Mackay of Sutherland, as a descendant of the third Lord Mackay) landed at Leith with around 600 men to assist the council and police the convention. Ironically, both he and the king's loyalist current military leader in Edinburgh, the bold and swashbuckling anti-Presbyterian John Graham of Claverhouse, had been trained as officers in the modernised Catholic army of the era's premier warlord, Louis XIV of France (now the refugee King James's host), against William's Dutchmen in the early to mid-1670s – along with the leading military defector from James to William in England in 1688, the future Duke of Marlborough (John Churchill). Mackay had been trusted by James to command one of his regiments in Dutch service in 1685–87 but, unlike Graham, was so perturbed at James's aggressive Catholic proselytising (which included signing up Catholics for the army) that he refused to come home when summoned and joined William's invasion of England. Mackay was outnumbered by the self-appointed militia of civilian Presbyterian militants who had stolen weapons from the state arsenals and in the case of 'Cameronians' brought their own from hiding. Mackay shrewdly incorporated some of them into his army and so disciplined them and used their fervour for William's cause– but their goodwill was dependant on a Presbyterian religious settlement. William also sent a conciliatory letter to the convention, promising to redress grievances, and disastrously James (in France) would only demand their support without any guarantees for the Protestant religion. The ex-king's supporters, soon to be known as 'Jacobites', were a minority in the Convention and were intimidated by the Presbyterian representatives and militia, and in a few weeks they withdrew to plan a military solution. Their best general, John Graham (now Viscount Dundee), who had led the royal attempt to coerce the Galloway Calvinist militants by armed occupation in 1678–79 from which he was later nicknamed 'Bloody Clavers', had been rallying the loyalists in Edinburgh as commander of a troop of dragoons and holding talks with the first Duke of Gordon, the Catholic son of Montrose's ally Lord Aboyne (d. 1653) and commander of Edinburgh Castle for King James, to persuade him to hold out. Graham retired to his home at Dudhope after failing to persuade his allies to gather a rival convention for King James at Stirling and being accused by the Edinburgh Williamites of meeting 'rebel' Gordon and being threatened with arrest. He attracted little local support and had to flee as the new regime's forces advanced, going to the western Highlands to gather a clan host as Montrose had done in 1644–45. He summoned a clan gathering in Glen Lyon on 18 May, arriving there on the 16th. He relied on a mixture of Catholic and Royalist sentiment from the clan chiefs and alarm at the exiling of the king and fear of a second Presbyterian takeover echoing that of 1637–60. His small but well-armed force around 2,000 men, mostly MacDonalds (of Keppoch and Clanranald) and MacIains of Ardnamurchan, were also motivated by their traditional hatred of the Campbells as the new, tenth Earl of Argyll (his father executed by King James after an invasion of Argyll in 1685) was backing William and seeking the recovery of his family's extensive pre-1681 lands and power from the new king. The 'Jacobites' advanced into Atholl to pre-empt General Mackay's march there from Perth, but Graham failed to find a militarily advantageous position to hold up the larger Williamite army and withdrew to his base in mid-June. Most of his army then dispersed, but the news of Mackay's advance on the fortified home of the 'Williamite' Marquis of Atholl, head of a branch of the Stuarts and a prominent Carolean councillor of the 1670s, at Blair Castle (in the middle Tay valley), seized on Graham's orders by the marquis's loyalist kinsman Patrick Stewart, led Graham to organise an expedition to get there first. (The marquis had retired to England to avoid involvement with either side.) Luckily for Graham, his main body of Lochaber reinforcements under Sir Ewan Cameron reached him just before he intercepted Mackay en route to Blair Atholl, at the pass of Killiecrankie. Colonel Cannon and the Irish reinforcements also arrived in time.

Advancing to the rescue with about 2,400 men, Graham defeated Mackay's larger army of around 4,000 in a bloody clash at the pass of Killiecrankie on 27 July. He had secured the hillside before the enemy arrived, and the 'Williamites' could not easily tackle the attackers up on their ridge so they resorted to musket fire to pick them off. The Jacobites had the sun in their eyes, so they waited for the evening before attacking. Around half the 'Williamite' troops were killed in a ferocious clan charge at sunset that overpowered the latter's more disciplined regiments, and although the defenders had the advantage of modern rifles (the attackers had mostly thrown theirs down to charge with claymores) they were unable to hit anyone while the enemy was crossing land hidden behind an intervening ridge. Once the Highlanders emerged for the final rush down the slope the firing resumed, but this had no time to do more than dent the attack and the unnerved defenders did not calculate accurately how much time they had left to fix bayonets before combat commenced. They could not shoot while they were fixing bayonets, and many could not fix them in time to fight either and were cut to pieces. The survivors fled and the Tay valley was opened, but Graham, 'Bonnie Dundee' of later heroic laments, was killed by a stray bullet in his hour of triumph and the victorious army was left without an effective leader. The veteran clan chief Sir Ewan Cameron of Lochiel had most men, but he was denied the command and left for home. This possibly persuaded fence-sitting local magnates with armed tenants to hand such as John Campbell of Glenorchy, Earl of Breadalbane, not to join the Jacobite cause and the ex-king's army under Colonel Cannon was halted at Dunkeld by an inferior but determined garrison of 'Cameronians' on 21 August. Several hours of fighting saw the defenders holding out until the Highlanders lost heart and retreated, although the defenders' commander and many of their men fell in the bloody struggle for the town. The threat of Jacobites overrunning the Lowlands was ended although the retreating army was not finally cornered and broken up until General Buchan won the Battle of Cromdale near Grantown-on-Spey on 1 May 1690.

(ii) The 'Fifteen' and after

The eviction of James VII and II – the first Catholic monarch of Scotland since Queen Mary Stuart and the first of England since Queen Mary Tudor – from his thrones by the 'Glorious Revolution' was, as seen above, more decisive in England than in Scotland. Revolution in Scotland in late 1688 and early 1689 was a result of the invasion of (and rebellion in) England, not a spontaneous popular or noble uprising, and the results left a Protestant elite in charge of governance in Edinburgh and the extremist, anti-episcopal faction of the Presbyterian movement in charge of the Church. Both were to the detriment of the marginalised Highlands, where most clans except the pro-Williamite Campbells were still Catholic. There was no sense of any loyalty to the new half-Dutch, Calvinist King William (II of Scotland and III of England), who had Continental priorities of fighting Louis XIV of France and saving his Dutch realm from conquest – and who indeed saw England and its Celtic dependants as a useful source of men and money. He notably never set foot in Scotland, even when peace returned in 1697, and he initially relied on a group of anti-James II Scots Presbyterian exiles from the 1680s for advice in dealing with that country. Effective resistance was, however, impossible after James failed to secure all of Ulster as a base for invasion in 1689 (symbolised by the siege of Londonderry) and then lost crucial exiled Scots personnel and control of eastern Ireland after the Battle of the Boyne in July 1690. From then on Ireland, a Catholic-majority country with a viable Catholic political and military elite turned into a redoubt by James and his French troops in 1689–90, was no potential base for a Highlands expedition and the Jacobite/French forces were driven out in 1690–91. Protestant England resumed its dominance of the British Isles, ending the long-term potential (viable since the 1540s) of a Continental Catholic power backing up a Catholic 'autonomist' stronghold in the 'Celtic' lands of northern Scotland and Ireland in which the Catholic Highlands could have had an important role.

Open Highland revolt was impossible without foreign troops or a collapse of the Protestant politico-military 'establishment' in Edinburgh, and a suitable 'example' to deter potential 'traitors' was famously made of the MacIain branch of the MacDonald clan in Glencoe in January 1692. In fact the MacIain chief was not wilfully defying the government orders to turn up at the nearest military base and swear allegiance to William and Mary by New Year 1692, the official excuse for the 'Massacre of Glencoe'; he had done his best to obey and had arrived at the nearby Fort William base on time to be told he would have to go on to Inverness instead. He was unable to complete the journey by 1 January due to snow, not obduracy, and he was not the only chieftain to miss the deadline either but was the only one punished. The likelihood is that the new king's most senior ministers in Edinburgh, John and James Dalrymple, had marked down any clan within easy reach with a 'Jacobite' record for exemplary punishment as an example and so bent the rules to impress the other clans with their ruthlessness and deter future revolt. The fact that it was a MacDonald 'sept' involved while the nearest government commanders and troops were Campbells made the resultant billeting of the latter, and the subsequent treacherous killing of their hosts, another round in the two clans' history of feuds. With the Highlands under military occupation and resistance cowed, from now on those restless or pro-Jacobite Highland lords and their sons who did not want to serve in the British Army would have an outlet (like the dispossessed Catholic Irish) in serving as mercenaries in the Continental Catholic armies, as the famous 'Wild Geese' – some of them gaining experience to use in fighting for their Stuart king when the time came. Other lords would go into exile to join the Stuart court, relying on rents smuggled out of Scotland from their tenants to sustain them, and all such men travelling out of Britain would be under government surveillance concerning their real loyalties; the nimbler or less scrupulous would endeavour to satisfy both sides so as to be safe whatever happened. After William's Queen, James's daughter Mary II, died in December

1694 the link between the Highlands and the Orange/Stuart dynasty was even more remote, with the cost of the king's Continental wars adding to the new regime's unpopularity. William had no direct heir, and the succession of Mary's staunchly Anglican younger sister Anne (who had briefly lived in Edinburgh with her father in the early 1680s) posed new problems. Anne had no surviving children and her exiled father died in September 1701, so the choice for the next ruler lay between her dispossessed Catholic half-brother James VII and II's son Prince James Francis Edward (living in France) and the family of Charles I's late sister Elizabeth of the Palatinate – either her late eldest son's family, who were the nearest but Catholic Stuart relatives (and half-French), or her surviving Protestant youngest daughter the Electress Sophia of Hanover. The latter was chosen by English Parliament by the Act of Succession in 1701, but the possibility arose of the Scots – alienated by the cost of the Dutch king's wars, wartime economic depression and the financial catastrophe of the Darien colonial scheme of 1697 – choosing a Catholic and Francophile ruler for Scotland and breaking up the 1603 Union of Crowns.

The resumption of British/French war in 1701/02 over the Spanish succession made it imperative that a monarch hostile to the British war effort did not succeed the ailing Anne, and accordingly the Scots elite were bought off and where necessary blackmailed into accepting the full union of the two kingdoms in 1707, closing down the independent Scots Parliament. From now on the Scots kingdom was tied to the political will of London and the Catholic Highlands and Islands lords were even more marginal – and quite apart from complete cultural and religious alienation from the London government they were suspected of being Jacobites. The role of the reliable and pro-Union Campbell clan under the new Duke of Argyll, military strongman of the Edinburgh regime, in keeping the Highlands in order became even more crucial, though the financial and political promises made to the Scots elite in exchange for their votes in 1707 were rarely met and so the potential for a political eruption in favour of James 'VIII and III' in France rose. Similarly, the embattled French government of Louis XIV sought to ward off the steady advance of the Duke of Marlborough's allied British/Dutch/German army across the Netherlands by distracting London with a Jacobite rising in Scotland. As in Ireland in 1689–91, the French army was the best hope of the embattled Catholic Celts on the margins of the new Protestant super-state in the British Isles, and in September 1708 James was sent to Scotland on board a French squadron to start a rising. The Duke of Atholl, leading magnate of his eponymous county and in command of a large army of his tenants whom the western

Highlanders would join, had promised to raise revolt and the French ships eluded the British Navy's blockade of Dunkirk in a gale and took James and his troops successfully to the Firth of Forth ahead of pursuit. There was a possible chance to land in strength and spark off revolt, but unfortunately James had contracted measles and was bedridden; then the pursuing ships arrived and the French had to move off, successfully, to Buchan, where James asked to be out ashore to join his allies as the French admiral was too cautious to land his troops. The latter replied that his orders were not to allow James to land either if his life would be at risk, and the exiled Stuart claimant was shipped back to France while the rebellion was called off. After this the collapse of French fortunes on the battlefield led to Louis having to sue for peace, and by the terms of the Treaty of Utrecht in 1713 he had to recognise the Hanoverian succession to Britain and send James packing (just over the eastern French frontier to Bar so he could be recalled if needed).

The accession of the new Elector of Hanover, George, to the British throne in August 1714 provided a new chance of Jacobite revolt in England as well as Scotland as George spoke at most poor English, had little knowledge of England and less of Scotland, and swiftly broke up the uneasy coalition of English 'Whigs' and 'Tories' ruling in London to sideline the latter as possible Jacobites and rely wholly on the Whigs. The ex-Secretary of State Lord Bolingbroke, who had endeavoured to secure James's succession to Anne in 1711–14 but had been frustrated by James's refusal to abandon Catholicism or leave France, and the Irish ex-commander-in-chief the Marquis of Ormonde were among leading Tories who fled to the Continent to help a Jacobite invasion, and more disaffected landowners were expected to stage a revolt in western England that would at least tie down the British Army at home and enable a Scots revolt to succeed. The alienated former Secretary of State for Scotland, the eleventh Earl of Mar (derisively nicknamed 'Bobbing John' for his habitual political wavering), head of a major Protestant dynasty that had long had the honour of safeguarding the heirs to the Scots throne, was lined up to lead the Scots revolt and made contact with many Catholic Highland lords with militarily experienced tenants at hand – including the MacDonalds of Clanranald and Glengarry and the Camerons of Lochiel, plus the Gordons and the normally pro-government Keiths. Money and weapons were smuggled into the Highlands and a cache of arms was set up near Fort William, ready for a rising in late summer 1715. Unfortunately Louis XIV, who was planning to lend unofficial support without breaking his treaty with England and who let James stockpile weapons and hire men for two ships at Dunkirk, died on 1 September just as the rising was about to commence; his infant great-grandson's Anglophile regent the Duke of Orleans nervously cancelled the plan and impounded the ships as Britain requested. The French would not move unless they were confident of a Jacobite victory, which only a major revolt already underway in Britain would provide – and many English Jacobites would not rise without a sign of French troops being en route. Nor would James's choice as commander, his talented and highly experienced half-brother the Duke of Berwick, leave his role as a French officer to lead the rebellion, although Mar had already proclaimed himself as its commander already without waiting for his king's orders. The militarily formidable Swedish king Charles XII was not yet ready to attack Britain, and as the Hanoverian regime flooded southern and western England with troops the only English revolts were occurring in the Catholic areas of Cumbria and Northumberland – led by an illegitimate grandson of Charles II, James's cousin James Radcliffe, third Earl of Derwentwater (b. 1689), who had been brought up with him at St Germain-en-Laye and had courage but no military experience. Ormonde, who was out of favour with King George and had promised James to stay in England ready to use his popularity in raising volunteers when needed, panicked and fled to France, leaving the south-western rising to the little-known Lord Lansdowne. The Scots revolt had to go ahead with minimal external support.

Having been snubbed at court in person by the new king on 2 August, the indignant Mar finally made up his mind to revolt and headed in disguise by sea to his Aberdeenshire estates, where he summoned his allies on pretence of a grand hunting party at Aboyne. This excuse enabled the guests to bring along attendants and horses in large numbers, and among those who turned up to the 28 August 1715 rendezvous were the MacDonald chiefs of Clanranald and Glengarry, Cameron of Lochiel, the Earl Marischal (head of the Keiths), the earls of Erroll and Seaforth, and (useful southern Uplanders) Traquair and Nithsdale, the heirs of the cautious Duke of Atholl (the Marquis of Tullibardine) and of the Marquis of Huntly, and Lord Kenmure, who was to raise the Borders. The rebellion duly began with Mar raising King James's standard on 6 or 18 September at Braemar, though the gold ball on top promptly blew off in the gale – a near repeat of what had happened to Charles I in 1642. Aberdeen, Montrose, Brechin and Dundee all proclaimed James as king and, as Mar and his 5,000-odd troops occupied Perth, the Stuart cause soon controlled most of central, western and north-eastern Scotland – although the Earl of Sutherland, Duncan Forbes of Culloden, and the crafty and unreliable multiple defector Simon Fraser, self-promoting claimant to the Fraser of Lovat peerage, held Inverness, Fort William and the far north for the government. The latter's Scots strongman, Argyll, had only 1,500 troops to hand, though more well-armed regiments (including veterans of the recent war) were called in from England and he had far better cavalry and artillery than the 'rebels'. He could only hold near-impregnable Stirling with the Forth crossing, and on 13 November his northern allies were to be driven out of Inverness. But time was on his side as once the government had dealt with the limited English revolt it could send reinforcements, and unlike Argyll (or Berwick and Ormonde on the Jacobite side) Mar had little military experience, had never fought a battle and had no sense of urgency. Nor had he informed James of his intended timetable, though the exiled king had no ship available anyway as one ordered by Berwick from Spain to take him north was late arriving in Dunkirk. As Sellars and Yeatman were to quip in *1066 and All That*, James was late for his own rebellion – though that was hardly his fault. Meanwhile, the sole serious rebellion in northern England started late as Derwentwater, also totally inexperienced, hesitant and only driven to revolt by news of his impending arrest, dithered at his home near his eponymous lake and only raised the Stuart flag on 6 October, which was little use for the Scots though closer to the planned date of the English risings intended for Plymouth, Bath and Oxford. Marching into Northumberland to link up with local Jacobites plus Lord Kenmure's southern Uplands Scots force but short of arms and doing little useful, the rebels could not decide whether to concentrate on England or Scotland – the English and Scots both preferred to tackle their own country. Mar sent a small force under experienced Brigadier William Mackintosh of Borlum (b. 1658), a former officer of James II's, from Perth to aid them, and they landed unopposed at Leith to Argyll's rear. Having failed to take Edinburgh Castle, they moved on South to join Kenmure and Derwentwater in the Borders. This combined force could easily have threatened Argyll in the rear and put him in serious peril, but despite Derwentwater's wishes they eventually headed into Lancashire to try to raise the local Catholics in a repeat of the failed Royalist tactics of 1648 and 1651. The English Jacobites thus won out over their Scots allies in choosing targets. As in 1651, the Jacobites soon had a better-armed government force (from Newcastle under General Carpenter) pursuing them and were never going to attract the support of any but staunch loyalists and gamblers; about a third (500) of Mackintosh's Highlanders wrote the campaign off as suicidal and went home. The remaining army under local Thomas Forster of Etherstone (chosen as a Protestant), with Derwentwater, Kenmure, Nithsdale and Mackintosh assisting, had 1,700 men – with enough size and momentum to take Penrith unopposed on 2 November and head south to Lancaster (7 November) and Preston (12 November) in search of Ormonde's rumoured army of south-western English rebels. In fact, Ormonde was still in France and by the time he sailed for Cornwall (mid-October) the government were rounding up the south-western rebel leadership and occupying Bath and Oxford. Only a few recruits dribbled in, and at Preston on 12 November General Wills' government advance guard trapped them and tried to storm the town. Mackintosh's Highlanders held one barricade and Lord Charles Murray's Highlanders led the defence of a second as they successfully beat back the attackers with heavy losses, but when General Carpenter with the main government army arrived next day the Jacobites were seriously outnumbered and their commanders considered surrendering to prevent a slaughter. The Highlanders and Scots peers would have preferred to try to fight, but Forster pre-empted them by surrendering without consultation. Seventy-five English nobles and gentry and 400 'other ranks' plus 143 Scots nobles and gentry and around 1,000 'other ranks' were captured, all of whom would have been more use reinforcing Mar by taking Argyll's army at Stirling in the rear. Instead, the southern rising ended in the usual round of exemplary executions, with one memorable exception as Lord Nithsdale's indomitable wife famously changed clothes with him as she was visiting him in the Tower of London so he was able to escape. Mackintosh also escaped, from Newgate Prison, and most of the 'other ranks' were spared but sent as indentured servants to America.

While the southern rebels delayed their rising and then marched away from the direction of the main confrontation in Scotland, taking Kenmure's men with them, the unexpectedly reprieved Argyll had had another success in Lord Drummond's failure to take Edinburgh Castle. This planned surprise attack was equally inept – some of the rebels smuggled into the city boasted about their plans in the city inns before the rendezvous so the garrison were alerted and when the attackers tried to swarm up ropes to the battlements the ropes were too short. Finally Mar made a belated move from Perth to cross the Tay southwards and head for the upper Forth west of Stirling on 10 November, trying to bypass the latter and head on towards Carlisle to meet Forster's army. But Argyll was soon aware of his intentions thanks to efficient scouts and moved forward to intercept him north-east of Dunblane. The result was the Battle of Sheriffmuir on 13 November, where Mar had the advantage of numbers with around 12,000 Jacobites to around 4000 government troops but had poorer artillery and less cavalry. Nor did he adopt any masterful or decisive plan of battle; a textbook 'push and shove' head-on clash saw each side's right wing prevail and chase the enemy left wing off the battlefield. The Jacobite right wing outnumbered and outfought General Whetham's government left wing, who had to withdraw in disorder, but was prevented from a complete victory by Argyll, who was having similar success on his own right wing against the sluggish General George Hamilton, halting his men and leading them to tackle the Jacobite right wing in turn. The government forces suffered more casualties, officially listed at 663 losses (killed, wounded and captured) to 223 Jacobite losses, though the latter included MacDonald of Clanranald and the young fifth Earl of Strathmore, chief of the Lyons of Glamis, and Argyll only lost a few prominent officers. Had Mar pressed ahead with his triumphant wing against Argyll's wing, who were outnumbered by around three to one and had poor defences, at the end of the battle he might well have expected a decisive success. It was Argyll who had to pull back from the battlefield afterwards, a wise precaution, but Mar failed to attack again or to endeavour to march around the enemy position and dare them to challenge him. His subordinates were urging one of these courses, and Mar's failure to act and resultant cautious withdrawal to his base at Perth was seen by some as inexplicable and undermined morale; it led to his small French and Spanish volunteer contingents abandoning the campaign as lost. Argyll claimed victory and was able to hold out until reinforcements arrived from England, while James finally left Dunkirk in disguise on a ship hired by Ormonde in late December and landed at Peterhead on 2 January. By this time Mar's inaction at Perth was causing his men to drift away and Argyll was being reinforced after the government had defeated the northern English rising, so his timing was poor though not his responsibility; he secured enthusiasm and goodwill but had no troops or weapons to offer. The Earl of Seaforth and the Marquis of Huntly excused themselves from marching to Perth with their king on account of their men having dispersed homewards for a rest after Sheriffmuir and the threat of pro-government Sutherland forces to their north – in fact Huntly, as cautious as his ancestor in the 1640s, was already in touch with London about a pardon. Instead James was received by Hamilton, the loser of his part of the Sheriffmuir clash, and sent him off to France to avoid further disaster, while Fraser/Lovat and Duncan Forbes had retaken Inverness. He accompanied his local Jacobite 'strongman', the Earl Marischal, to the latter's home at Fetteresso (in disguise again) amid morale-damaging heavy snow to meet Mar, and after a delay due to illness made his way on to Glamis, a rousing reception at Dundee, and, on 8 January, Perth. His review of his mainly Highland troops at Perth was a public relations flop, with accounts of it speaking of his chilliness and reserve, in stark contrast to his dashing son's persona in 1745–46; James was always a more cautious and dignified personality like his father, and at this point he was probably both worn down by the cold and illness and out of his depth away from the dignified grandeur of the French court and the exiled Stuart court at St Germain-en-Laye. The planned coronation at nearby Scone was abandoned, no troops or money arrived from Bolingbroke in France (a ship full of Spanish ingots sank in a storm off Dundee) and canny Berwick refused to come to his half-brother's aid in a losing cause.

On 29 January Argyll finally left Stirling to advance on Perth as General Cadogan and a large English force headed across the Border despite the snowy roads to aid him, and that day James abandoned a bold plan to use the frozen ground to cross the Tay towards Stirling on a southerly raid and agreed to retreat north via Dundee. His men were increasingly outnumbered and declining in morale, and the retreat added to the impression of a losing cause; he hoped to make a stand in suitable country beyond Aberdeen, but Mar talked him out of it and bundled him away from the army in secret to Aberdeen to find a ship. His 'desertion' of his men without notice was blamed on Mar and reduced morale further. On 4 February 1716 he left Scotland for the last time, and in his wake Argyll moved his troops up to occupy the east coast towns and link up with the loyalists at Inverness but was criticised in London for not tackling those nobles and gentry who got away safely to the western Highlands. (Some negotiated their pardons; others made for France.) The western Highlands remained effectively beyond government control for much of 1716, but any hope of a Jacobite stand there was useless due to the lack of leadership from great nobles mostly keen to save their estates from confiscation by negotiating their pardons or if that was hopeless to arrange their departure for exile with as much money as possible. The stronger latent Jacobite loyalty of the clans was to be shown by a further Continental expedition on James's behalf in 1719 which has tended to be airbrushed out of history as at best a footnote, at a time of war between George I's Great Britain and Philip V's Spain when the Spanish chief minister Cardinal Alberoni resorted to his master's late grandfather King Louis' diversionary tactics of 1708. A Spanish naval force took 300 soldiers and a force of exiled Jacobites from both Spain and France, led by the Earl Marischal and his brother, north to the remote Outer Hebrides in March 1719 while the British fleet was preoccupied elsewhere, and landed them successfully on Lewis. The endemic inter-familial jealousies of the Jacobite nobles hindered their effectiveness as Atholl's heir Lord Tullibardine disputed the command by the Keiths, but they were able to cross the Minch to Loch Alsh and take Eilean Donan castle and were joined by around a thousand Highlanders, mostly from the Mackenzies of Seaforth and the Camerons. The Spanish ships then left for home, and the Jacobites settled down to wait for Spanish military reinforcements (7,000 men), presumed to be accompanied by Ormonde, which in fact had only just left Cadiz and were primarily intended for an attack on western England if the expected revolt occurred there. James himself was in Italy awaiting the arrival of his Polish bride-to-be Clementina Sobieska, granddaughter of the heroic late King Jan Sobieski (d. 1696), and managed to slip across to Catalonia without interception but was far from Scotland.

Once again the weather intervened to the Jacobites' detriment as a storm scattered the Spanish fleet off Finnisterre and it had to limp back to port; without this a major invasion of Lochaber and a possible more effective prequel to the 1745 rising would have been likely, or at least a Spanish landing and land-bound campaign in the direction of Fort William. Instead a British naval squadron sailed unopposed into Loch Alsh (8 May) and bombarded the Jacobite headquarters and arsenal at Eilean Donan Castle, occupied by a Spanish garrison after the main Jacobite force had left for the Mackenzies' Kintail lands en route to Inverness. The castle was stormed and spectacularly blown up to wreck the rebel cause after its garrison surrendered. The clan army of around 1,000 (including the competent veterans the fifth Earl of Seaforth, the Mackenzie clan chief, and Brigadier Mackintosh, and the future 1745 commander Lord George Murray, younger brother of Tullibardine) had already headed east to fend off the advance of General Wightman's troops from Inverness. The Spanish regiments were backed up by 200 or so of Seaforth's clansmen and a further 200-odd Mackenzies, and had been joined by smallish forces of clansmen, mostly Cameron of Lochiel's tenants (*c.* 150 men) and Lord George Murray's clansmen (*c.* 150 men) plus the famous Loch Lomond region cattle rustler 'Rob Roy' MacGregor and around forty of his clan, and set up a strong defensive position on the road from the Kyle of Lochalsh to Inverness near the 'Five Sisters of Kintail' mountains. But the revolt ended with the defeat of the Jacobites and Spanish by Wightman's equally sized force at this spot, the 'Battle of Glenshiel' on 10 June 1719, their king's birthday and the last foreign presence on a British battlefield. Wightman sent his left wing, including Clayton's regiment and the volunteer Highland force raised by loyalist officer Sir George Munro of Foulis (later founder of the 'Black Watch'), westwards to drive back the Jacobite right wing south of the road, and then while his superior cannons kept the professional Spanish soldiers in the centre (plus Mackintosh of Borlum) under cover his right wing drove the Mackenzies back on the Jacobite left. Seaforth was seriously wounded, as was 'Rob Roy', who tried to rescue his wing, and the Jacobites had to pull back; afterwards their leadership escaped to France. The sole Jacobite success was the rescue of James's bride, interned en route to Italy by request of the British government, by his swashbuckling officers; his marriage to Clementina was to provide two sons to continue his cause but end in disaster as a mixture of religious mania and probable anorexia overcame the new Stuart 'queen'.

(iii) The 'Forty-Five': The road to Culloden

The prospect of Continental troops from a 'Great Power' at odds with the Hanoverian government sending troops to aid a Scottish revolt resumed with the Anglo-Spanish war (the so-called 'War of Jenkins' Ear') from 1739. This then expanded into the 'War of Austrian Succession' the following year, bringing the opportunity of French military aid, with James's elder son Charles Edward Stuart now the most active Stuart prince and eager to lead a campaign while his cautious father remained holed up at his small court in Rome. However, the Jacobite leadership in Scotland was divided and riven by feuds and mostly had less influence on Charles than a coterie of exiled Irish officers, the exiled Earl Marischal had resigned his commandership of the Jacobite army in disgust and the only activist Highlands clan chief at all involved in planning was Cameron of Lochiel (who was to be taken by surprise by Charles' arrival in 1745). By now Simon Fraser, Lord Lovat, was supposedly Jacobite and prepared to use his clan for an attack on Inverness, but he was not to be trusted. Nor were the Jacobites in England strong or united enough to provide a viable rising. Drummond of Balhaldy, one of Charles's two senior agents in Scotland, returned home in 1742 promising a French expedition in the autumn but nothing transpired. The French were only prepared to use the Jacobites as a distraction to undermine the British army in the Netherlands when the time was right and did not declare war until early 1744, the Jacobites in England would not rise without visible French help and both King Louis XV in Versailles and 'King' James in Rome were wary about risky gambles. Finally, in early 1744, Louis invited Charles to Paris in secret ready to lead an invasion and prepared a fleet at Dunkirk, though it was unclear if this would be heading for England or Scotland. As with Spain's invasion force in 1719, a disastrous storm battered that part of the French fleet that had just arrived from Brittany at Dunkirk ready to transport Charles and his French troops in March 1744 and the attack was postponed. The French concentrated on their war in the Netherlands, and Charles was left kicking his heels in Paris, where he came under the influence of bolder, mostly Irish officer Jacobites, who urged him to head for disaffected Scotland and spark off a revolt without waiting for the mirage of a

French expedition. The 'Forty-Five' was indeed to be described by one of Charles's new advisers, banker Aeneas MacDonald, as an Irish project, while Murray of Broughton encouraged the prince to sail even without any military assistance and persuaded some Scots magnates to sign letters promising to join him whether he had French troops or not. Charles duly promised to come to Scotland in 1745, with or without military help; whether he bothered to consider the actual amount of men these enthusiasts could raise and their chances of success is questionable, though his lack of local knowledge makes his naivety excusable and Murray's mistakes were far worse. The main organisation of Scots conspirators in Edinburgh (whom Murray had sidelined, presumably as unreliably timid) found out about this and sent Lord Traquair to Paris to tell him they could not rise without French troops and he should not come to Scotland alone, but by the time Traquair arrived Charles had set out. The prince sidelined his more cautious allies, borrowed money to hire weapons and two ships in secret, and without telling his father in Rome until it was too late to stop him left Paris with a small escort of enthusiasts; the recent French victory over the British army in the Netherlands at Fontenoy could be taken as a sign that his allies were in the ascendant and would be able to land troops in England to help him. He duly went aboard the brig *Du Taillay* on 22 June 1745 near the port of St Nazaire and set sail for Scotland; in fact only two of his companions, the famous 'Seven Men of Moidart', were Scots (the Paris banker Aeneas MacDonald and the exiled 1715 and 1719 commander the Marquis of Tullibardine, rightful Duke of Atholl) and four were Irish (one of them Sir John MacDonnell/MacDonald, a former Spanish officer). Two were the prince's tutors, namely the Boyne veteran Sir Thomas Sheridan and the Englishman Francis Strickland, one was an Irish priest (Father George Kelly, a veteran Jacobite courier), and only one – Colonel Francis Sullivan – was a distinguished and competent soldier. He was hampered by his quarrelsome character and ended up spending most of the campaign squabbling with the Scots officers, and was not even given a military role in the campaign but was put in charge of the commissariat. Only Tullibardine had any real knowledge of the Hebridean/Highlands locale they were aiming for. The leadership in Edinburgh sent Murray of Broughton off to the Highlands to tell Charles that the time was not right for a revolt and he should go home.

The prospects for the campaign were not good and the party's immanent arrival was not expected either, though the strain of the Continental war had denuded the usual government garrisons in the Highlands and the recent defeat at Fontenoy meant that the London regime would be concentrating on saving Flanders not on a Highlands rising. It would take time for the government to react to events hundreds of miles away, and in the interim the advantage would lie with a bold, adventurous and charismatic leader with the ability to rally support among a people accustomed to personal leadership and steadfast loyalty to a historic cause – quantities which the young, flamboyant and good-looking Charles famously had in abundance in contrast to his father. But the rising was nearly aborted when Charles was en route as the HMS *Lion* spotted his two ships off Cornwall and attacked them; one ship, the *Elisabeth*, had to act as decoy and hold up the pursuer while the *Du Tellay* sailed on, and some aboard the latter advised Charles to give up and head back to France. Instead he pursued his course to sight land and drop anchor at Eriskay, at the southernmost end of the Outer Hebrides, on 22 July, where the party went ashore to spend the night at a fisherman's hut. In one of the all too frequent descents of potential high drama into farce, the chimney was smoky as a fish supper was prepared and the prince kept on having to go outside for fresh air, to his host's irritation. The island was in MacDonald territory, with South Uist, owned by Clanranald, to the north and beyond that the MacDonalds of Sleat's North Uist; as news of the prince's arrival was spread to summon recruits next morning Clanranald's local uncle Alexander MacDonald of Boisdale arrived on Eriskay to tell the prince that a rising was impractical without French troops and he should 'go home'. As if on cue, Charles replied that this was his home. He did his best to rally local help in the Outer Hebrides while Aeneas MacDonald moved on to the mainland to contact his Clanranald kinsmen and prepare for his master's arrival, and on the 25th the *Du Teillay* sailed on to Loch Nan Uamh in Moidart. MacDonald of Clanranald, Aeneas's brother MacDonald of Kinlochmoidart and other kinsmen, the lairds of Glenaladale, Dalily and Glencoe, and Glengarry's representative MacDonald of Keppoch had assembled there, and when the ship had anchored they came aboard to meet the prince and advised him that the time was not right to revolt as he had no French troops. He persisted and they gave way, loyalty overcoming prudence, and Clanranald agreed to go to Skye for him and try to rouse the MacDonalds of Sleat and MacLeods of Dunvegan while Kinlochmoidart would collect Cameron of Lochiel, the Drummond chief (the Duke of Perth), and Murray of Broughton who had been waiting for the prince's arrival on the coast but had now gone home. But Clanranald was unsuccessful in his mission, and instead MacLeod of Dunvegan wrote to 'Lord Advocate' Duncan Forbes of Culloden in Edinburgh on 3 August to inform him of the prince's arrival and assure him that he and Alexander MacDonald of Sleat, backed by their clans, would use their influence to ensure that nobody of consequence joined the doomed and 'mad' rebellion. Kinlochmoidart and his younger brother reassured Charles of their own backing, which may have proved decisive in holding Clanranald, Keppoch and Glencoe steady, and it was only once the MacDonalds were lined up to back Charles that Cameron of Lochiel's brother Dr Archibald Cameron arrived with his message asking the prince to go home (see section on the Camerons, above). Charles refused to give up and successfully invited Lochiel to come and see him in person; the Cameron chief did and was won over by his chivalric instincts, and after this Charles had enough men and confidence to issue a general appeal for aid and call his planned rally of the clans at Glenfinnan. On the 19th he arrived at Glenfinnan to the initially ominous sight of only a few companies of Clanranald MacDonalds. But in fact his Cameron and Glengarry MacDonell supporters had already had a morale-boosting clash with government troops at Highbridge on the River Spean to stiffen their resolve (see above), and within a few hours firstly MacDonald of Morar and 150 more Clanranald volunteers and then Lochiel and 750 Camerons (with their 'redcoat' prisoners from Highbridge) arrived, the latter with bagpipes playing. The rally was able to go ahead in a suitably triumphant manner, the prince's banner was unfurled, and the campaign was successfully launched.

The roll call of Highland support for the prince as of mid to late August 1745 shows that backing was limited, even without the Campbells whose backing for the government was to be expected. Only a limited number of the MacLeods of Dunvegan and Harris and the MacDonalds of Sleat ignored their loyalist clan chiefs and joined the rebellion, and the loyalties of the Gordons, Grants, Mackenzies, Mackintoshes and Murrays of Atholl were divided too; Lord Lovat, as head of the Frasers, delayed choosing sides and eventually came down for the prince as he seemed to be winning but for once miscalculated. As in the 1640s with Montrose's campaign, the Mackays, Munroes and Sutherlands of the far north backed the regime in Edinburgh and refused to back the Stuarts. The Stewarts of Appin (neighbours and victims of the expansionist Campbells), Macleans, MacKinnons and Macphersons were solidly in favour of the prince, as were most of the mainland MacDonalds, and as usual there were numerous canny figures who delayed a choice to see who was likely to win – with initial momentum on the Jacobites' side as they advanced on Edinburgh. The Jacobite army of around 1,400 men might lack an experienced overall commander (Charles had observed warfare in Italy but never commanded in battle) or adequate and modern weapons and ammunition, but there were only around 4,000 government troops in Scotland (three and a half battalions of infantry and two of cavalry) under General John Cope, a better officer than suggested by the comic song made after his defeat at Prestonpans but commanding often inexperienced and undisciplined men who had rarely fought before. Charles decided on avoiding a time-consuming siege of the two main local garrisons at Fort William and Fort Augustus and did not have the transport to convey his few cannons there anyway; he proceeded to Invergarry Castle as MacDonell of Glengarry's guest for the night of 26/27 August and then went on to Aberchalder while an advance party set up an ambush for Cope's advancing army at the Corrieyairach Pass west of the main Grampian range, on the government troops' expected route west. But Cope was warned of this by a Highbridge prisoner who had been released on parole and after a brief clash there on the 29th did not press on but swerved aside to head north for Inverness instead. This left the road from the Great Glen to the Lowlands open, and although Lovat now came down on the prince's side and wrote inviting him to come and help him tackle Cope at Inverness Charles headed south-east instead. He crossed the central Highlands into Atholl, reaching Blair Atholl Castle on 1 September, whose lord's heir Tullibardine could rally more nobles and gentry backing.

On 3 September he reached Perth. Among his significant recruits were the head of the Drummonds, the French-educated James, Duke of Perth (whose Catholicising family had been the 'strongmen' of James VII and II's regime in the 1680s), socially important and good-natured but militarily inexperienced despite which he was appointed as lieutenant-general of the army along with the older, more talented but arrogant and quarrelsome Lord George Murray (Tullibardine's younger brother, now fifty-one). These two thus represented the adherence of the Drummond and Murray dynasties to the Jacobite cause, but were personally at odds and arguably military liabilities – though the reasons for their appointment were normal for the era in all armies. Murray was popular with the Highlanders and had potentially useful personal contacts with currently loyalist Hanoverians, though this exacerbated the distrust of some of his (mostly Irish) rivals. The incompetence of Sullivan as quartermaster-general and Charles' lackadaisical failure to realise that he was a liability was more serious. But Charles was correct in assessing that the psychological advantages of continuous attack would cause panic among his enemies and win over waverers. On 11 September Charles left Perth as Cope began his advance southwards from Inverness by entering Aberdeen; on the 13th the Jacobites reached the Forth above Stirling at the Fords of Frew. A small force of waiting government dragoons pulled back to let them cross, and the garrison of Stirling Castle did not use their cannons as the prince's men passed within range. Bannockburn and then (14 September) Falkirk were occupied,

Murray pressed on with the advance force towards Edinburgh, and the outnumbered and disheartened government dragoons left around Edinburgh were ordered back to Leith, abandoning the city. They pulled back even further to await Cope and ended up abandoning their camp and retreating to Dunbar on a rumour of imminent Highland attack, leaving piles of equipment littering the roads, inciting public ridicule. The nervous commander of Edinburgh Castle, General Guest, barricaded himself inside and refused to try to defend the city, and the wavering civic authorities had technically more men than Charles did (*c.* 3,500) and initially attempted to hold out until Cope arrived by sea, holding up the prince by negotiating. But panic was spreading at a rumour that 12,000 ferocious Highlanders were en route, and as luck had it a small Jacobite force under Cameron of Lochiel and Sullivan was able to secretly follow the city's delegation as it returned from a negotiating visit to the prince at Corstorphine on 16 September. At dawn next day it rushed the Netherbow Port as the gate was reopened after the delegation had passed through it to let their coach return to its stable outside. The Highlanders entered the city to occupy the civic guardhouse without resistance, and boldness carried the day aided by relief from the citizens that the invaders were behaving properly and not robbing or attacking anyone. The city mob came out in favour of the prince, his foes fled, and thus later on 17 September Charles was able to stage a highly effective and morale-boosting entry to Edinburgh – though in practical terms he had to keep out of range of the strongly defended castle, and was unable to secure it. That day Cope landed by sea at Dunbar to join the troops fleeing from Edinburgh.

With James VIII and III proclaimed at the Mercat Cross in Edinburgh on the 17th, the revolt had already achieved much more than the 'Fifteen', and for the first time since December 1688 the Catholic Stuarts were in control of the capital of Scotland. On the 21st Cope and his army, now landed and based at Prestonpans, were routed in a surprise attack at first light that nearly did not work – the advancing troops (now with Clanranald leading the column) made too much noise and government scouts were alerted. The prince then fell into a ditch while crossing it, but the government troops were too slow to react and let the Jacobites have time to form up their army; Cope was too cautious and orthodox a general to attack. Then their superior numbers and weaponry and disciplined training were nullified by their fear of the Highlanders. As the latter – particularly the Camerons – charged, the government gunners opposite them (on the Hanoverian right wing) abandoned their cannon and ran for it, and Colonel Whitney's cavalry next to them crumpled and galloped off after a brief exchange of fire; in both cases the nervous and undisciplined men deserted their superior officers. With the government right wing crumpled, the Highlanders threw away their heavy muskets and charged at the centre in an unorthodox but psychologically effective move; the government infantry broke and ran, 'like rabbits', as the prince later wrote. Most of the government infantry are said by well-informed compatriots to have been untrained and had little experience in using their supposedly superior muskets, and the small number of veteran soldiers were useless. The panicking deserters then found themselves piling up against the walls of nearby Preston Park house and were slaughtered by the pursuing Highlanders. Possibly 500 government troops and thirty Jacobites (the latter's figures) were killed, though government 'spin' tried to pretend that they had only lost 200 men. The south of Scotland and the road to England were opened. But in practical terms time was not on the prince's side, and vastly superior numbers and better-trained government troops were now brought into play as much of the army in Flanders was recalled and a 'blocking' force under General Wade was sent by sea to Newcastle while troops from Ireland moved to Chester. The question now arose of whether Charles would concentrate on securing his father's rule in Scotland – where he did not hold the far north or even Edinburgh Castle – or attempt to invade England and take the war to the enemy.

The latter decision was taken, and as the Jacobites camped at Dalkeith it was arranged that the prince and around 2,500 Highlanders – including the clan regiments of Glengarry, Clanranald, Keppoch, Cameron, Macpherson and Appin – would take an easterly route to Kelso, as if heading for the English base at Newcastle, and then swerve away south-west to the Liddel Water to join a westerly force of Lowlanders and cross into England near Carlisle. They would then proceed into Lancashire to hopefully raise the local Catholics and exploit pro-Stuart loyalties in the north en route to link up with rebels from western England and Wales, repeating the plans of 1648, 1651 and 1715. The arrival of four French ships, carrying money and Louis XV's ambassadors, and the fall of Aberdeen to the fourth Earl of Stoneywood on 15 September added to morale, and the Highland warriors were ranging around the Borders rounding up horses from the local gentry. (One of the most famous incidents was when MacDonell of Glengarry and his men called on the absent, pro-government Earl of Marchmont's mansion at Redbraes on 9 October and exchanged pleasantries while requisitioning from his womenfolk.) Meanwhile the first main body of regular English troops serving in Flanders, commanded by Lord Albermarle, sailed into the Tyne to Newcastle on 26 October, and three days later the strongest part of the army still in (eastern) England, commanded by Wade, arrived by land to join them and block the eastern route to the south. This army amounted to around 4,500 Dutch and Swiss infantry, 4,950 British infantry, and 1,500 British cavalry, and so was more than a match for the prince's army; a further 8,500 British infantry and 2,200 cavalry were gathering in the East Midlands under General Ligonier while a small force at Chester awaited the Dublin regiments. (Charles's nemesis Duke William Augustus of Cumberland, King George's twenty-four-year-old second son, would take over Ligonier's army on 27 November.)

On 3 November the eastern division of the Jacobite army left Dalkieth, proceeding to Kelso (evening of 4 November to morning of 6 November), Jedburgh and thence the upper Liddel Water (7 November), and the lower Liddel Water, where the prince and an escort of Camerons riding ahead of the main force crossed the River Eden into England (8 November). While they proceeded on to surround the walled but poorly maintained garrison city of Carlisle on 9 November, the western, Lowland division of the army that had been marching on a more westerly course (led by Tullibardine and the Duke of Perth) arrived at Peebles on 3 November and late on the 8th at Ecclefechan, and made haste over the Border to catch up with the Highlanders the following day. The army was by now denuded by desertions from those unwilling to risk the English campaign and to its rear the pro-government civic dignitaries of Edinburgh had recovered their nerve and admitted troops sent by Wade from Newcastle, but the surrender of Carlisle, the city by its officials and the small and panicking garrison by its elderly commander Colonel Durand, on 15 November lured the prince to head on south. While snow held Wade's march to recover the city up at Hexham, Charles pressed on into Lancashire with his army leaving Carlisle in two sections on 20 and 21 November, Lord George leading the first, the cavalry detachment. It was a risk relying on English support and there was no visible sign of enthusiasm until Preston or a rush of recruits en route until around 200 men in Manchester; there was no resistance to Charles's requisitioning and sporadic welcome bonfires and public receptions, but this was probably due to civic prudence and a fear of annoying the 'savage Highlanders', who were much feared. In the absence of any military challenge from Wade, Charles was confident of success and pressed on south, though this achievement owed more to Lord George distracting the blocking, numerically superior army under Cumberland (c. 8,000 infantry and 2,000 cavalry) at Stafford into moving away west to prepare for battle at Stone on 3 December in fear of a Jacobite march into north Wales.

Murray's feint attack on a government force at Congleton alarmed Cumberland and enabled the Jacobite vanguard to reach Derby on

4 December, the prince's section following hours later from their overnight halt at Leek. This news famously caused panic in London on 6 December with rumours that King George had his yacht ready at Greenwich to flee to Hanover. An army was stationed at Hampstead Heath and Finchley ready to fight, but it was mostly militiamen whom pro-Jacobite writers have maintained would have fled if faced with a Highland charge. Cumberland was recalled to the capital and the prince intended to try to race him there, but at a meeting of Charles's council on the morning of 5 December most of the latter agreed that even if they could reach London first they were outnumbered by around 30,000 (in the two English armies, Cumberland's and Wade's) to 5,000, so going on was too dangerous. Lord George's cautious opinion (backed by a spy who was really a government agent) was probably decisive, though only Perth openly dissented from him. Charles was informed of the *fait accompli* afterwards, to his dismay; he lambasted the commanders as cowards but after a second meeting that evening submitted to a retreat. Making it clear that he was furious, and encouraged by the more daring Irish officers, he nevertheless announced the retreat to his men on the 6th and while London was panicking that day the Highlanders were already pulling back towards the Border, via Manchester on the 10th. They were pursued by Cumberland, whose forces fought with Murray's rearguard at Clifton Moor near Shap during the retreat across Cumbria on the 18th. A small force of government dragoons blocked the road to Murray's men at the Shap ridge summit and retired over this out of sight, but eager Jacobites charged uphill to meet them; Murray sent the Glengarry regiment to help, only to find the outnumbered enemy had withdrawn and the road was clear. Later that day a skirmish was fought down at Clifton, with a few casualties on each side as the Glengarry (whose chief was wounded) and Macpherson regiments fought off the 'redcoats'. But Wade was too far to the east to join Cumberland quickly, and Charles and his men reached the Border on 19 December and marched on to Glasgow. Quite apart from the damage to morale of retreat and the constant bickering of the leaders over whose fault it was, Charles's concentration on England had lost him control of Edinburgh and the east of Scotland. He retreated from Glasgow on 3 January 1746 to Bannockburn to prepare for a siege of Stirling Castle, and ironically thanks to local reinforcements had the largest army he had mustered yet – over 5,000 – as generals Cope and Hawley marched out of Edinburgh to tackle him. On 17 January his army fought them off at the Battle of Falkirk, where the Jacobite advance to seize a strategic ridge near the town was spotted by scouts but was negligently written off by Hawley as a feint and the government troops had to hurry up the ridge in disorder

when their officers heard that it was being occupied. A Highland charge by the MacDonald regiments on the right wing led to the government dragoons opposite them fleeing amid heavy casualties, though a ravine prevented similar success on the left wing; the government side estimated their losses at around seventy, but the Jacobites said that the enemy lost around 500 and they lost around fifty.

But with Cumberland soon in Edinburgh and advancing on Stirling the nervous Jacobite leadership induced the unwilling prince to abandon the siege and retreat into the Highlands in a council at Crieff on 2 February, and at Perth another acrimonious council ended with the decision that Charles would take the Highland regiments through the mountains to attack Inverness while Lord George, with whom he was barely on speaking terms, took the Lowland regiments along the coast road. The army set out on the 4th and Lord Loudoun duly abandoned Inverness and retreated into the Black Isle as the Jacobites approached, but reducing Fort William failed while the prince, at Elgin, refused to send adequate troops south to enable Lord George to retake his family home of Blair Castle. Finally Cumberland, who had been lingering in Aberdeenshire awaiting reinforcements during bad weather, advanced on 8 April after his vanguard division under Bland drove John Roy Stewart's men back in Strathbogie. The duke crossed the Spey on 10 April as Lord John Drummond's force there pulled back without using their cannon (a major mistake as a clash would probably have made the opponents more equal at Culloden), and arrived at Nairn on 14 April. Drummond and the Duke of Perth at Elgin were bypassed and hurried back to join the prince. The stage was set for the final confrontation on the moors near Charles's base at Culloden House, occupied home of the government's senior minister Duncan Forbes – with the Jacobites outnumbered by better-armed and better-fed regulars and in poor morale, amid accusations that basic measures to bring bread out from Inverness had been forgotten. The resulting problems as the Jacobite leadership indulged in more squabbles on the eve of battle are well known, and focussed on the mistrust between Charles and Lord George again. The prince compensated for overruling Murray on the choice of site by accepting his request to take the position of honour on the right wing on 15 April, thus denying the MacDonalds their usual honour and infuriating them. The Jacobites stood to arms for hours only to find that Cumberland's men were celebrating his birthday in camp and there would be no battle; O'Sullivan proposed a night-time march round Nairn to take the hopefully drunken enemy by surprise but the chiefs vetoed it until Keppoch arrived to even up the numbers. Murray then changed his mind and agreed to it, and the army marched in two columns across the rough country in the dark, tiring themselves out to little avail as vanguard commander Murray, well ahead of the others, refused orders to attack on his own due to lack of numbers (worsened by ominous desertions). As drums in the distance showed that the enemy was stirring and not to be taken by surprise, Murray turned about and the attack was abandoned, with Charles (at the rear) not informed until he heard that Perth's second column had turned back too, not understanding the reason, and then vainly demanding an attack.

After this debacle Charles planned to rest his men for the day, but Cumberland would not oblige and the late morning of the 16th saw the government army advancing prepared to fight while their exhausted foes had to wake up and scramble into position. Technically the Camerons should have had the post of honour on the right wing that day but Charles allowed Murray's Athollmen to keep it; the Duke of Perth commanded on the left and Lord John Drummond in the centre. The MacDonald regiments were on the extreme left, and the Appin and Cameron regiments on the right next to Murray's men; the low enclosure walls of two 'parks' on the Culloden estate, one near each Jacobite wing, hampered movement and were not adequate defences either. The enclosure beyond the right wing was indeed secured unhindered by a force of government soldiers, posing a threat of a flank attack on Lord George's men. The marshy ground in front of the Jacobite lines, which O'Sullivan had ignored when choosing the site, would hamper a charge, and although Cumberland's intimidatingly disciplined advance was held up as his accompanying cannon met boggy ground, the delay was not exploited by Lord George attacking him (probably as he had not readied all his line of battle yet). More muddle was caused as Lord George unilaterally moved his men down the line of the park wall on the right wing, probably to place themselves more favourably with firmer ground in front for their charge. Perth's left wing stayed put, opening up a large gap which O'Sullivan had to send reserve troops from the rear to (imperfectly) fill. The freezing rain blew in the Jacobites' faces, and as Cumberland's more numerous guns opened fire with greater effect and accuracy at around two o'clock the battle began. The Jacobites' only hope against a cannonade was the usual devastating charge, but further losses were caused during a delay of around half an hour until Lord George's request for an order from Charles was met (one messenger was killed); why did Charles not send an order to charge quickly without prompting? The MacDonald regiments allegedly did not follow Perth's orders to charge, in the absence of any parallel movement on the right wing to cover them; they had around 200 yards further to run to reach the enemy than the right wing anyway. When they did advance, this was not as far as the government troops; after an exchange of gunshot they pulled back. Were they trying to tempt the 'redcoats' to come within sword's reach and failing? The right and centre then attacked piecemeal with Clan Chattan leading, but the latter ran at an angle of forty-five degrees to a line of direct advance (possibly to avoid a bog) and thus the rest of the line had to slow down and bunch up to avoid running into them. They were all met with a hail of devastatingly accurate fire and their crowded position prevented the usual running charge from developing. Still, part of the Jacobite army did reach the enemy and inflicted around forty fatalities on the 4th and 37th regiments of foot, capturing a standard, before being forced back by reinforcements. Amid the visible chaos and losses most of the left wing broke and fled, leaving the MacDonalds exposed until most of them followed. The Keppoch chief bravely charged regardless of any support and was shot down, refusing advice to flee and being killed as he got up to charge again, and Clanranald was severely wounded but was smuggled to safety by his men; Lochiel was also shot (in the legs) and carried off.

The battle was lost in what turned into a virtual turkey shoot for the government regiments, and around 1,500 to 2,000 Jacobites were killed or wounded against officially fifty government soldiers (probably more of the latter's wounded died later). Some 154 Scots/English Jacobite soldiers and 222 'French' soldiers (mostly exiled Irish in French service) were listed as taken prisoner, and Charles got away safely with an escort to reach Fort Augustus next day. Any chance of a stand by those troops who reached a rendezvous at Ruthven was abandoned. All that remained was for those who could save themselves to do so while Cumberland and his officers notoriously exacted savage reprisals to crush the clans, killing men, women and children alike, burning homes and food supplies, and driving the survivors out into the wilderness to starve. The banning of Highland dress and demolition of the traditional structure of clan governance was to follow. In retrospect, the charge at Culloden was to serve as the final stand of the traditional Highland way of life against the eighteenth-century British state.

Bibliography

Primary Sources

Acts of the Lords of the Isles, 1336 to 1493, ed. Jean Munro and R. W. Munro (Edinburgh: Scottish History Society, 1996).

The Annals of Connacht AD 1284–1544, ed. A Freeman (Dublin, 1944).

The Annals of Loch Ce, ed. W. M. Hennessy (London: Rolls Series, 1870).

The Annals of Ulster, ed. W. M. Hennessy and B. MacCarthy (Dublin, 1887–1901).

Barbour, John, *Barbour's Bruce*, eds M. P. MacDiarmaid and J. A. Stevenson, 3 vols (Edinburgh: Scottish Text Society, 1985).

Boece, Hector, *The History and Chronicles of Scotland*, trans. John Bellenden (Edinburgh, 1821).

'The Book of Clanranald', in A. Cameron, *Reliquiae Celticae: Texts, Studies and Papers in Gaelic Literature and Philology*, ed. A McBain and J. Kennedy (Inverness, 1894).

The Book of Lecan, ed. Kathleen Mulchrone (Dublin, 1937).

The Chronicle of Man and the Sudreys, ed. P. A. Munch and Revd Dr Goss (Manx Society, 1874).

Heimskringla: History of the Kings of Norway, trans. L. Hollander (Austin, Texas, 1964).

The Orkneyinga Saga, trans. Hermann Palsson (London: Penguin Classics, 1981).

Snorri Sturlason, 'The Saga of Olaf Tryggvason', in *Heimskringla, ibid.*

Wyntoun, Andrew, *The Original Chronicle of Scotland*, ed. D. Laing (Edinburgh, 1872–79).

Secondary Sources

Anderson, P. O., *The Life and Times of Orkney* (John Donald Publishers, 1999).

Balfour-Melville, E. W. M., *James I, King of Scots 1406–1437* (London, 1936).

Barrow, G. W., *The Kingdom of the Scots* (London, 1973).

Barrow, G. W., *Robert the Bruce and the Community of the Realm of Scotland* (Edinburgh, 1988 edn).

Baynes, J. C. M., *The Jacobite Rising of 1715* (London, 1970).

Boardman, Stephen, *The Early Stewart Kings: Robert II and Robert III* (East Linton: Tuckwell Press, 1996).

Boardman, Stephen and A. Ron, eds, *The Exercise of Power in Medieval Scotland 1200–1500* (Dublin: Four Courts Press, 2003).

Broderick, George, 'Irish and Welsh Strands in the Genealogy of Godred Crovan' in *Journal of the Manx Museum*, vol. viii, no. 38 (1980), pp. 32–38.

Brown, M. H., *James I* (Edinburgh, 1994).

Buchan, John, *Montrose* (London, 1928).

Bulloch, J. M., *The House of Gordon*, 3 vols (Edinburgh: Spalding Club, 1903–12).

Byng, Kevin, *Colcitto* (Colonsay, 1997).

Byrne, F. J., *Irish Kings and High Kings* (London, 1973).

Campbell, Alistair, *The History of the Clan Campbell*, vol. 1 (Edinburgh, 2000).

Campbell, Duncan, *The Clan Campbell* (Edinburgh, 1913–22).

Campbell, M., *Argyll: The Enduring Heartland* (London, 1977).

Cowan, E. J., *Montrose: For Covenant and King* (London, 1977).

Crawford, Barbara, *Scandinavian Scotland* (Leicester UP, 1987).

Cunliffe, Barry, *Facing The Ocean: The Atlantic and Its Peoples 8000 BC–AD 1500* (Oxford UP, 2001).

Duffy, S., ed., *A New History of the Isle of Man, Vol III: The Medieval Period* (Liverpool UP, 2005)

Duncan, A. M. and Brown, A. L., 'Argyll and the Isles in the Early Middle Ages', *Proceedings of the Antiquaries of Scotland*, XC (1956–57).

Fergusson, J., *Alexander the Third* (London, 1937).

Fraser, James, *Chronicle of the Frasers: The Wardlaw Manuscript* (Scottish Historical Society, 1906).

Gibson, J. A., *Lochiel of the '45* (Edinburgh, 1994).

Gordon, Sir Robert, *General History of the Earldom of Sutherland* (1616, repr. 1813).

Grant, I. F., *The Lordship of the Isles* (Edinburgh, 1935).

Grant, I. F., *The MacLeods: History of a Clan* (1959).

Gregory, Donald, *A History of the Western Highlands* (London, 1881).

Grimble, Ian, *Clans and Chiefs* (Edinburgh: Birlinn, 2000).

Hill, J. M., *Fire and Sword: Sorley Boy MacDonell* (London, 1993).

Jones, Gwyn, *A History of the Vikings* (Oxford UP, 1984 edn).

Kinvig, R. H., *A History of the Isle of Man* (3rd edn; Liverpool UP, 1975).

MacDonald, A. and A., *Clan Donald* (Inverness, 1890).

MacDonald, Hugh, 'History of the MacDonalds', *Highland Papers*, 1, ed. J. MacPhail (Scottish History Society, 1914).

MacDonald, Norman, *The Clan Donald of Knoydart and Glengarry* (private publication, 1979).

MacDonald, R. A., 'The Death and Burial of Somerled of Argyll', *West Highland Notes and Queries*, 2nd series, VIII (Nov. 1991).

MacDonald, R. A., *The Kingdom of the Isles: Scotland's Western Seaboard* c. *1100–c. 1336* (Edinburgh: Tuckwell Press, 1997).

MacDonald, R. A. and Maclean, S., 'Somerled of Argyll: a New Look at Old Problems', *Scottish History Review*, LXXI (1992).

MacDougall, Norman, *James III: A Political Study* (Edinburgh, 1982).

MacDougall, Norman, *James IV* (East Linton, Tuckwell Press, 1997).

MacGladdery, C. A., *James II* (Edinburgh, 1990).

Mackay Brown, George, *Magnus* (Edinburgh: Canongate Books, 1998).

Morrison, Alick, *The Chiefs of Clan MacLeod* (1986).

Paterson Maclean, J., *A History of the Clan Maclean from its First Settlement at Duard Castle, in the Isle of Mull, to the Present Period* (Clarke & Co., 1889).

Reid, Stuart, *The Campaigns of Montrose: A Military History of the Civil War in Scotland 1639 to 1646* (Edinburgh: Mercat Press, 1990).

Ritchie, Anne, *Orkney* (Edinburgh: Mercat Press, 1996).

Roberts, John L., *Feuds, Forays and Rebellions: A History of the Highland Clans, 1475–1625* (Edinburgh UP, 1999).

Sellar, W. D., 'The Origins and Ancestry of Somerled', *Scottish Historical Review*, 45 (1966), pp. 123–42.

Shaw, A. M., *The Clan Battle at Perth in 1396* (Wimbledon, 1874).

Sinclair, A. M., *Clan Gillean* (Charlottetown, Canada, 1899).

Skene, W. F., *Chronicles of the Picts, Chronicles of the Scots and Other Early Memorials of Scottish History* (Edinburgh, 1867).

Skene, W. F., *Celtic Scotland*, 3 vols (Edinburgh, 1890).

Stevenson, David, *Alisdair MacColla and the Highland Problem in the Seventeenth Century* (Edinburgh, 1970).

Stevenson, David, *Revolution and Counter-Revolution in Scotland 1644–51* (London, 1977).

Thompson, E., *The New History of Orkney* (Edinburgh: Mercat Press, 2001).

Thomson, Oliver, *The Great Feud: Campbells* versus *MacDonalds* (Sutton, 2001).

Tomasson, C. and Buist, F., *Battles of the Forty-Five* (London: Batsford, 1962).

William, Ronald, *The Lords of the Isles: Clan Donald and the Early Kingdom of the Scots* (House of Lochar, 1997).

Wishart, George, *Memoirs of James, Marquis of Montrose 1639–1650*, ed. Revd G. Murdoch (London, 1950).

Internet

www.st.andrews.ac.uk/history/staff/alexwoolf: copy of article, 'The origins and ancestry of Somerled: Godfriad MacFergusa and the "Annals of the Four Masters"'

www.scotweb.co.uk/info/macdonald-of-clanranald

www.clancameron.org

www.clandonald-heritage.com

www.clan-macleod-scotland.org.uk

www.gutenberg.org/files/598/598-h.htm (*Heimskringla* text)

www.highcouncilofclandonald.org

www.isle-of-man.com/manxnotebook/manxsoc/msvol22 (*Manx Chronicle*).

www.scotclans.com/scottish-clans

www.Maclean.org/clan-Maclean

www.macdonald.com/glengarry

List of Illustrations

All photos reproduced under the Creative Commons licence remain under the copyright of their named original photographers. Details of the licence used can be found at the following address: http://creativecommons.org/licenses/by-sa/2.0/.

Index

Also available from Amberley Publishing

The
KINGS
& QUEENS
of
Wales

Timothy Venning

Available from all good bookshops or to order direct
Please call **01453–847–800**
www.amberley-books.com